Unlawful Carna

Wendy Holden, who lives an senior journalist with the *D* travelled extensively for the paper, across America, the Middle East and Europe. A frequent visitor to Ireland and to Belfast, she was also the longest serving reporter in Baghdad during the Gulf crisis.

Unlawful
Carnal Knowledge

THE TRUE STORY
OF THE IRISH 'X' CASE

Wendy Holden

HarperCollins*Publishers*

HarperCollins*Publishers*
77–85 Fulham Palace Road,
Hammersmith, London W6 8JB

A Paperback Original 1994
1 3 5 7 9 8 6 4 2

A catalogue record for this book
is available from the British Library

ISBN 0 00 638258 4

Set in Linotron Meridien by
Rowland Phototypesetting Ltd
Bury St Edmunds, Suffolk

Printed in Great Britain by
HarperCollinsManufacturing Glasgow

For 'X'

Contents

Acknowledgements

My heartfelt thanks to all those who cannot be named who found the time and courage to talk to me and believed in what I was trying to achieve.

To Val Hudson of HarperCollins and Mark Lucas of Peters Fraser & Dunlop for their infectious optimism and unfailing confidence; Max Hastings, editor of the *Daily Telegraph*, for his encouragement, and to Sue Ryan and David Sapsted for allowing me to test their patience repeatedly.

Dr Mary Henry for her considerable help and inspiration, Senator David Norris for his enthusiasm, Jackie Coogan for her unflinching efficiency and Sunniva McDonagh for her precision.

Especial thanks to Liz Allen of the *Irish Independent*, Sam Smyth of the *Sunday Independent* and his wife Faela, and Tom McPhail of *Ireland International*, for keeping me informed and sane; Michael Kealey and Patrick Swaffer for their expert legal guidance; Graham Noble for his criticism and expertise, Karen Whitlock for her fine-tuning and Janet Plaskow, systems supremo, for helping me with all my glitches.

Also thanks to family and friends for their unceasing interest and support – especially Clare Arron for her much-needed frivolity, Laurel and John for the warm welcomes home, and Neil Darbyshire for the original motivation.

Sincerest gratitude to the world's most helpful librarians Lorraine Curren and Niall at the *Irish Independent*; also to Matt Walsh and the marvellous June for the pictures and Martyn Turner for the use of his cartoon.

Helen Moran and Una deserve special mention for their hospitality and kindness at Raglan Lodge; and last but by no means least, Chris, for forgoing two years' holidays, putting up with the sleepless nights and for lighting the darkest moments with his love, laughter and unquestioning loyalty.

Introduction

It was while sitting in a tiny District Court in the suburbs of Dublin watching the girl in the 'X' case quietly giving her evidence for the first time that I realized that someone should tell her story.

There had been so much international furore about the Irish abortion issue that her personal tragedy had rekindled, and so many politicians and campaigners for both sides jumping on the bandwagon to gain some sort of advantage from her plight. The eyes of the world had been focused on Ireland and the moralizing and the self-interested debating that went on made most of those involved with the girl and her family sick to the stomach.

But on that day, in that courtroom, sitting in the witness box just a few feet away from her attacker, entirely alone and in a soft Irish accent, she made the few people watching her realize that *she* was really all that mattered.

Her parents sat behind her, stiff with tension. Her abuser studied his fingernails casually and looked as if he wished it would all soon be over. But for almost two hours her little voice filled the hushed courtroom. The sun shimmered on a tiny gold crucifix dangling from her collar and the light it reflected danced on the walls and ceiling of what had once been an old schoolhouse.

When it was over, she was gone as suddenly as she had arrived. Back to the anonymity promised her by the legal system, back to the home where her parents were still struggling to come to terms with all that had happened, and back to the fragments of teenage life she was trying so hard to piece together even after her abuse, the pregnancy and its aftermath.

Unlawful Carnal Knowledge is the story of this girl: 'X' as she will always be known. It is the story of an ordinary little girl from an ordinary home, in an ordinary street, but living in an extraordinary country where events that took place long before she was grown were to affect her in a most dramatic and shocking way.

This is a full and frank report of the events that happened, as they happened to the people involved. It is set down for posterity, in the hope that the lessons learned from it will prevent it from ever happening again.

It is also written for 'X' so that she might one day fully understand the enormity of the events which must have baffled and bewildered her as a child. Her courage and that of her parents are the abiding themes. Her eventual recovery is all one can hope for. I dedicate this book to her and to her family with my sincerest best wishes and my immeasurable admiration.

ONE

She watched the countryside racing past as she pressed her face closer to the car window. It was a warm summer's day and she could feel the sun's heat on her arm through the glass. The window was slightly open and the breeze caught her long brown hair and whipped it back off her face.

Twelve years old, thirteen in a few weeks' time, she was looking forward to her forthcoming birthday and to the rest of the summer holiday, relaxing with her friends and enjoying the long, carefree days away from the nuns and school.

Awakening from her reverie, she studied the thick greying hair of the man in front of her, who was driving the car. He was twenty-eight years older than her, the father of her best friend, her own father's golfing partner and the man who lived a few doors down the road from her family house.

He was talking to her, but she hadn't been listening. She could see his eyes watching her in the rear-view mirror. She was holding his baby daughter in her arms and day-dreaming and enjoying the drive back from the north Dublin hills, where they had just dropped her best friend off at her grandfather's house for the weekend. It was her friend's father who had suggested she go along with them, and look after the baby on the journey home. The trip would give his wife a few hours' peace at home, he said.

Suddenly, he stopped talking and pulled the car off the road and into a derelict building site down a bumpy driveway. He switched off the engine. She looked at him quizzically and wondered why he had parked in such an isolated spot. Perhaps he needed to go to the toilet.

Stepping out of the driver's seat, he walked slowly to the rear passenger door. Opening it, he looked in at her in a way she had never seen before. Without knowing why, she was suddenly afraid. Her whole body tensed and butterflies pranced in her stomach. He smiled strangely as he leaned in towards her. She heard a high-pitched voice cry out 'No!' before she realized it was hers.

Taken aback, he hesitated and frowned into her wide, frightened eyes. His baby daughter began to whimper in her arms, sensing her fear, and he knew he had lost his chance. With a heavy sigh, he closed the door and walked back to the driver's seat. Murmuring to himself, he started up the engine and drove off, heading back to their tree-lined south Dublin street. Neither of them said a word.

On the long journey home she stared hard out of the window, wondering what it had all meant. She felt guilty, as if she had somehow done something wrong and disappointed him. Most of all she felt overwhelmingly that her carefree days were over.

It had all started that June afternoon in 1990 in the building site on the way back from the mountains. When she had cried out in protest, she had stopped him in his tracks. But he knew it wouldn't be long before he had her on her own again.

He did not have long to wait. His daughter had to be collected from her grandfather's house a few days later and he arranged once again for the girl to go with him on the forty-mile round trip.

Nothing untoward had happened on the way, she was relieved to note as they pulled the car into the long driveway of the grandfather's house. But when he had switched off the engine after parking by the garage at the bottom of the pathway leading to the house, he suddenly turned round in the driver's seat and, reassuring her that he cared very much for her, started fondling her breasts and between her legs through her clothing.

Shocked and flushed with embarrassment, she knew that

what he was doing must be wrong. But she was too dumb-founded to speak. The man was, after all, her father's best friend and like a second father to her. He kept repeating her name and telling her that everything was all right. Frozen to the seat, she endured his fumbling, despite her pounding heart. Squirming inside, she waited for it all to end. It was only when she could see his daughter, her best friend, running excitedly down the driveway from the house to greet them that she pushed his hands quickly away and fled from the car.

She grabbed the baby and handed it to her friend, who had arrived at the car panting and smiling a welcome. The girl stumbled quickly towards the house, hastily re-arranging her clothes, as her attacker calmly stepped from the car and embraced his own twelve-year-old daughter enthusiastically while watching his quarry escaping.

Making what may have been her biggest mistake, the girl told no one of what had taken place. She was, after all, at the home of strangers, her own family some twenty miles away, and she felt she had no one to turn to.

Too humiliated, confused and distressed to tell anyone when she eventually got home, she was too naive to know that a twelve-year-old girl can tell a grown-up not to do something she doesn't want him to and stop it before it gets out of control.

She went over and over what had happened in her mind. What did it mean? Should she tell someone? Maybe it would never happen again and she had misunderstood him? What would her father say if he knew? She began to dread being left alone with the man, thinking up elaborate excuses not to be on her own. She stuck close to her parents, reassured by their presence and hoping that she wouldn't unwittingly be placed in such a compromising situation again.

Unable to explain to her family why she suddenly no longer felt at ease in his company, she could not find an explanation later that summer as to why she should object to a week-long stay at his family house while her devoutly Catholic parents went on a long-planned pilgrimage to Lourdes. She told them that she did not want to stay behind, and asked if she could go with them, but they laughed and told her not to be silly. She would have a lovely time with her friend, they told her.

At a family gathering later, the man told the girl's parents how very much he was looking forward to having her to stay. Her parents expressed their gratitude for the chance of getting away on their own. The girl sat listening helplessly.

Sent to her room to pack her clothes and a few belongings for the forthcoming visit, she prayed for a miracle to keep her from the attentions of her father's best friend. But none was forthcoming.

Her molester could hardly wait to get her alone. She successfully avoided him for a few days, but he was eager to continue where he had left off, and soon found himself alone with her in the living room of his house. Once again he began his insidious manipulation of the child, the same age as his own daughter.

This time there was no escape. Her parents were hundreds of miles away in France and she was at his mercy. Trapped and bewildered by this uncontrollable turn of events, she felt she had little choice but to let him do what he wanted with her. Perhaps he would just stop it all as unexpectedly as he had started, she hoped.

After a few days spent in his clutches, the girl realized that, sadly, this was unlikely; and within a matter of weeks the man, who was later to display to the police some of the calculated cunning he had used on his young victim, had succeeded in completely paralysing her senses. In a short time he had transformed her from the trembling, reluctant victim to a stiff but compliant witness to her abuse who had cut herself off completely from her own emotions.

Displaying tendencies of shock recognized in child abuse victims, she rejected what was happening to her physically by freezing completely – saying nothing, doing nothing and showing no affection or emotion in return. She hated what he was doing to her, but she could see no way of stopping him. Only when she was away from his influence did she behave relatively normally to those around her, feeling unjustifiably guilty at her own role in her abuse, and desperate not to do anything that would make her parents suspect what was going on. If she occasionally seemed withdrawn or emotional, her parents put it down to the normal growing pains of a teenage daughter. In the solitude of her bedroom she often cried herself to sleep and wondered what she could do.

In this state of strange detachment from her own body – a silent witness to her own abuse – her assailant knew that he could do what he wanted with her, whenever and wherever he liked. And he continued to do so for nearly two years.

She had been a young girl approaching womanhood with all the anticipation that it can bring, who had enjoyed a happy childhood and a close relationship with her loving parents and her younger brother, who was a bright and talented sibling.

The family had always lived in Dublin and had moved to their smart southern suburb more than ten years earlier as her father had climbed the career ladder at a multi-national corporation in the city centre. Often away from home in his role as an international sales executive, her father had not always been around to give the flattery and attention that his daughter sought. Her best friend's father was.

He lived just a few doors away, less than a hundred yards down the hill on the new red-brick estate. His daughter accompanied her every day to the local convent school.

A self-employed businessman, he suffered from intermittent periods of unemployment and claimed the dole. When he did work, it was largely from home and he pleased himself as to his working hours. He was more often than not available to drive his daughter and her best friend to their regular singing lessons, get a film for them from the video shop or take them swimming at the local pool.

His attention to his neighbour's child was regarded fondly by both his own wife and the girl's parents. His wife of twenty years doted on her tall good-looking husband, the father of her three children – the twelve-year-old daughter, the baby girl and a teenage son. She was proud to go to Mass with him and her children each week and take an active part in the local community. She considered his special fondness of their neighbour's girl as nothing more than paternal and benign. The girl, after all, was like another daughter to them.

The girl's Catholic parents, too, never suspected anything but kindness. The man was their amiable, affable friend, with an infectious smile and twinkling eyes, who helped their family cope with what seemed to be the almost constant ferrying around of their daughter and younger son.

With the girl's father so often away from home on business, her mother relied on her friend and neighbour to act as a surrogate father figure to her children. 'She trusted him implicitly,' explained one family friend. 'She used him to chide and scold the children if they acted up. He was the rock of sense.'

The man was also very friendly with the girl's father. They played golf together, drank together in the local pub, and the four adults regularly enjoyed dinner parties and evenings out.

When his business ran into hard times and he needed money in 1990, the girl's father obliged with a large cash loan. A foreign businessman friend of the girl's father, who was also the next-door neighbour of the man and his wife, became a useful source of contacts.

In the confines of their comfortable, middle-class 1980s four-bedroom house, with its festoon blinds and trimmed hedges, the girl's parents believed they had nothing to fear. Their daughter's bedroom, filled with the detritus of teenage infatuation, was a haven as she made her way in the world. Little did they know that further down the road, at the almost identical house of their friend and neighbour, where they so often innocently left her alone, there was to be no such sanctuary.

His initial attempts to molest her in the back of the car that sunny afternoon were to develop into an eighteen-month reign of sexual assault as he repeatedly preyed on her innocence and vulnerability. His calculating manipulation of the girl from his first bungled attempt to his final full sexual act played on her emotional insecurity as she struggled with the bewilderment of early teenage-hood and her own sexuality.

The smiling seducer who had terrified the girl into silent sub-mission after months of progressive abuse cared little where he satisfied his lust – in his sitting room, in the conservatory, the downstairs lavatory, even up against the radiator in his kitchen. He grew bolder as time went on, having sex with her while his teenage son sat watching a favourite television programme in another room. He even forced sex on her downstairs one day while his wife and children were asleep upstairs.

It was his special secret to share with her, he told her. No one must ever know. He could never have imagined that his sordid little secret, whispered behind locked doors, would one day be so utterly exposed that it would shock the country with its political and moral implications, and indirectly lead to a climate of social change which for the first time in Irish history would properly address the issue of abortion.

His audacity knew no bounds. He picked her up in his car outside the local sweet shop, in the middle of their small main street, and had sex with her in a car park a few miles away, oblivious to who might have seen them. He told her again and again never to tell anyone. He said he would be locked away and his family would split up if she did. The family he was referring to included his eldest daughter – her dearest friend and formerly closest confidante – and the idea of the heartache she might cause was unthinkable.

She continued to suffer in silence, sharing her private

thoughts only with her diary. Even that wasn't sacrosanct. His control over her was such that he could also influence her when she was away from his company. Showing a chilling sense of premeditation and to cover the eventuality that he might one day be suspected of child abuse, he told the girl to write the letter 'A' in her diary every time he sexually assaulted her. The letter stood for the first initial of her young friend and neighbour, the teenage son of the foreign businessman who had been so kind and useful to him. If anyone ever asked her about sexual abuse, she was to say that she had been 'fooling around' with 'A', he told her.

He also instructed her to insert a few extra 'A's in the diary to confuse the situation. He said that if ever her mother read her diary she would assume she was in the throes of a childish fling with the young boy and would suspect nothing more. The innocent boy, who knew nothing of this and was openly friendly with the girl and her family, was unwittingly being set up for a statutory rape charge if ever the abuse became public. Detectives believe that the man would have followed his calculated plan of action through to the end and could even have watched the boy face a criminal prosecution in his place, if events had not proved the teenager's innocence later on.

It was a cold and inhospitable night on Saturday 7 December 1991 when the 42-year-old abuser – the genial poor-boy-made-good who grew up in one of Dublin's bleakest inner-city areas – committed the crime that was to prove his eventual downfall.

Forcing himself upon the girl, now fourteen years old, in the front seat of his car, parked in an unlit alleyway behind a swimming pool in south Dublin, he planted the seed for what was to become the most controversial foetus in the whole of Irish history. 'Don't ladder your tights when you pull them up,' he told her afterwards, handing her a box of tissues. In such a healthy young girl, fourteen days into her menstrual cycle and forced early into womanhood by his attentions, the spawn of his crime was to remain and grow inside her to haunt him.

Later that month, the man and his wife attended a party at the girl's house, long-planned, at which both families were present. The girl helped her mother prepare the small eats and serve the drinks to the four adults, who laughed and joked with each other as they always did at their regular gatherings together. The girl avoided all eye contact with the man who, just a short time before, had so callously impregnated her body. He quipped with the parents that the girl seemed to be in a bad mood and they complained about the tribulations of having an emotional teenage daughter.

The girl found solitude in the kitchen, where she grimaced as she listened to them all enjoying themselves. Christmas was fast approaching and with it, a New Year. The talk among the adults was of parties, presents and religious celebrations and festivities. Quietly the girl had her own thoughts and prayers. She wanted some new music cassettes and some jewellery, and hoped her parents would have taken the hint that she needed some fashionable new clothes. But most of all she hoped that 1992 would bring an end to her nightmare and that her abuser would leave her in peace. What she failed to realize was that there was a tiny foetus taking shape within her which would soon come to dominate her life and fire the people of her nation with such passion that huge crowds would be chanting on the streets about its future.

With no real understanding of contraception or the sexual reproductive process, the girl had no idea that she was pregnant, or if she did she denied it to herself. She did not understand why she felt so strange as her body went through the normal hormonal changes of early pregnancy. Naturally pale of complexion, she looked so much paler that her mother thought she might have caught some sort of virus. She complained of feeling nauseous and faint.

Her mother advised rest and nourishment and promised to

take her to a doctor if she did not feel better in a few days. Now nearing the end of January, the girl's period was markedly late. Her mother did not suspect anything sinister at first. After all, the girl didn't even have a boyfriend, she thought. She took her to the local doctor's surgery and told the GP she did not know what was wrong with her sad, silent child. The doctor took a urine sample and conducted an iron test, which was clear, and sent the mother and daughter home.

The girl told her abuser that she was not feeling well and had been to the doctor. He panicked and told her he could get her a 'morning after' contraceptive pill. Not really understanding the consequences of what he meant, the girl told him it was all right, the doctor had given her the 'all clear'. Relieved, he told her: 'Thank goodness. Now I can get a good night's sleep.'

The mother, however, was not so reassured. She kept a close watch on her daughter for several days and saw with dismay that the nausea and symptoms were continuing.

At the end of January, she went to a chemist and bought a do-it-yourself pregnancy testing kit. Returning home and asking her daughter to provide her with a urine sample 'for another iron test', she conducted the test herself and was horrified to see it change colour to give a positive result.

Racked with worry, and waiting for an appropriate moment to tell her husband, she decided to air her concerns with a close friend. Who else should she turn to but her confidante and neighbour, the wife of her daughter's attacker, in whom she previously had confided many of her private thoughts? As the two women sat talking in hushed tones, mulling over the dreadful possibilities, neither could have dreamt who was the father. They speculated about who could be the culprit and when it could have happened. The girl's mother spoke of her anxiety at breaking the news to her husband.

She wondered aloud about the boy 'A', who she thought had recently been spending more time with the girl. She also mentioned the exchange student who had been staying with her family for a short time before Christmas. It is commonplace in Ireland for European students to stay with Irish families as part of a hugely popular educational exchange scheme and they had put up such a boy for a few weeks.

The mother was distraught and talking abstractedly, her friend sitting close by and utterly sympathetic. Their conversation – and the private mention of the two boys' names – was later to be cited by the man as an indication of his innocence and the girl's guilt.

The mother told her husband, who went to see the girl in her room and confronted her with what they knew. The girl refused to say anything at first, but then broke down completely. Two years of suppression spilled out in a confused jumble of confessions and accusations. She told her parents everything: from the first incident eighteen months earlier, to what had happened in the swimming pool alleyway a few weeks before. She said she had been frightened and that she had not known who to turn to. She told her parents that they had not been around when it first started and that her abuser had threatened her if she ever told anybody.

The mother and her child wept openly and clung to each other. The father, stunned enough by the revelation that his daughter was seven weeks pregnant, was then stunned to listen to her telling him over and over that the baby's father was his best friend and neighbour.

The colour drained from his face and he slumped into a chair. From that moment, none of their lives was ever to be the same again.

TWO

The news was almost more than the girl's parents could bear. Their obvious anguish further distressed their now silent daughter, who stopped her own weeping and, for the first time, expressed a heartfelt desire to be dead.

The doctor was called to the house. Immediate family members – relatives of the girl's mother and her grandmother – were called to bolster them through the first few terrible days, and the local priest was summoned.

The girl's father, a quiet, thoughtful man, was too shocked to think of revenge or retribution at this stage. Ever the organized businessman and accustomed to dealing with the minutiae of life, he contacted the man's house and blankly told the family that he and his wife would be unable to attend a dinner dance the two families were planning to go to that month. He said a family problem had come up.

The man's wife, knowing almost the whole story already, suspected that the crisis had come to a head and walked up to their house to offer her support. She was shown in by the girl's grandmother, who was unaware of who she was. She saw the girl lying distressed on the sofa and, in answer to her questions, was told the girl was pregnant 'and worse'. In the absence of any further explanation, she left the house without realizing that the 'and worse' referred to the fact that her husband was the baby's father.

With no more information offered, she went home to tell her husband the news. Appearing calm and unconcerned, he said he wasn't surprised and shrugged off the incident as the foolish actions of a child.

14

The girl's father called a family summit and after several hours of discussion and prayer the girl was taken to the Sexual Assault Unit of Dublin's Rotunda Maternity Hospital. Two days later, on Thursday, 30 January 1992, the police were summoned.

Officers from the Garda Siochana police listened to the accusations made by the girl against the man and scratched their heads. As gently as they could, they explained how the criminal system against child abusers worked and raised concerns about the success of any prosecution against him. The pregnant girl would have to give detailed evidence against her abuser in a courtroom, unless he admitted to his crimes, which was unlikely. Without any proof of a struggle, evidence of bruising or any stained clothing, it would be a case of her word against his.

The experience of a trial – in which she would have to admit that despite being under the age of consent he had never actually physically forced her to have sex with him – could be as harrowing for the victim as the abuse itself. He would probably try to deny that he was the father and slur the girl's character by suggesting that she was the type to sleep around. She would have to prove that she was not.

The girl and her family listened to all of this with horror. Was there to be no end to their anguish? Determined not to let the man get away with his crimes, however, they asked the police to proceed with the case.

Doctors at the hospital confirmed the pregnancy with an ultra-sound scan and asked the police to wait a day or two before interviewing the overcome girl. A woman police officer was sent to her room to remain with her while she was being treated. The girl was withdrawn and hardly spoke a word. When she did speak she was very specific and said she had thought about running away and that that would be the end of the matter. She told the woman officer that she was looking at ways out of the dilemma, and said she sometimes thought about throwing herself downstairs.

Two days later, on 3 February, the girl was taken to the police station with her mother to make a detailed statement. Ann Vaughan, a police officer trained in rape counselling, gently coaxed details of the abuse from her as she told them that she 'wished it were all over'.

Consumed with guilt for bringing her family into disrepute, she told one police officer that when her father had commented that the situation was 'worse than a death in the family', she had replied: 'Not if it was me.'

As the girl's mother sat next to her daughter, listening quietly to the answers she gave to the questions gently asked about what had happened, it seemed almost inconceivable to her that the man she thought she knew so well could be the same man who had systematically abused her daughter under her very nose.

The girl herself said, during her statement, that she feared she would not be believed, as her attacker was a grown-up and much older than her.

One of the officers connected with the case said later: 'She wanted to corroborate what she was saying was true. She felt everyone was sceptical of what she was saying, that she wasn't being believed because of all our questions.'

The girl's mother sat listening to her daughter's evidence, piecing together all the incidents, and suddenly realized that it all fell into place. She was horrified that she had been so trusting of the man and that on at least one occasion she had insisted that her daughter go to his house alone, despite her inexplicable reluctance at the time. Not only had she been unable to protect her little girl, she believed, she had accidentally despatched her into the arms of a child abuser. She resolved never to let her daughter out of her sight again.

For the fourteen-year-old, now caught up in the bewildering machinery of a police investigation, life would never be the same again. From that day on she was to be known as Miss 'X' throughout Ireland and all the world, to protect her from ever being identified by anyone but those immediately around her.

Hardly able to contemplate the prospect of a criminal trial or consider what might happen to her attacker, her overriding emotion was one of rejection for the foetus growing within her and terror at having to give birth to it. She begged her parents not to let her go through with the pregnancy, which would be such a visible and harrowing reminder of her abuse. She told them she wanted to get rid of it, that she could not envisage ever keeping it, and pleaded with them for their help.

Abortion, specifically illegal in predominantly Catholic Ireland for more than 130 years (except in extreme medical circumstances), strictly taboo and only generally possible via a trip to a private clinic in Britain, was something her parents had hoped never to have to contemplate.

Practising Catholics, they had voted against abortion in a 1983 national referendum on the issue – little knowing that it would prove to be a legal time bomb which would directly affect their daughter most profoundly nine years later. Faced now with the prospect of sanctioning something they were vehemently opposed to in principle, was a further shock in a worsening scenario. The mother and the girl slept side by side in the same bed, holding each other close night after night.

The family talked the matter over and over and the girl repeated her express wish for the pregnancy to be terminated. After so much heart-searching they decided between them that an abortion was the only answer, if they were to consider what was to be best for the girl.

The mother was later to tell a court: 'We discussed the possibility of termination of her pregnancy and [she] was totally in agreement with the suggestion. I say and truly believe that both myself and my husband felt that in the circumstances of the case it was the best option, and the option that would serve our daughter's welfare to the greatest extent.'

She said her daughter had been very clear in her own mind about the abortion and had repeated her wishes to them over and over. She and her husband were, she said, 'extremely fearful' that she would suffer 'a complete nervous breakdown' if the abortion did not go ahead.

Like the thousands of pregnant women and girls annually forced by Irish law to fly or sail to Britain to undergo abortions – often by themselves and without the knowledge of their families – the girl and her family planned to go to Britain immediately and get it over with. Counsellors at the Sexual Assault Unit put them in touch with those who had details of an abortion clinic in London and the father made his daughter an appointment. Too numb to take it all in, the girl was told to pack a few belongings and prepare herself for the next stage of her ordeal.

Her parents then had another equally difficult decision to make. The police had been informed of their daughter's pregnancy and its exact circumstances. They would undoubtedly find out that the girl had had an abortion if she were suddenly not pregnant. Although it was not illegal in Ireland to travel to another country for an abortion – or so they thought – the parents wanted to know if the absence of a foetus would jeopardize the prosecution case.

Acutely law-abiding and well aware of the possible legal implications, her father informed the police exactly what he and his family planned to do and sought their advice on this point. His attitude to the law, Prime Minister Albert Reynolds was later to say, was 'most upright' and he 'appeared to be motivated by the highest ideals'.

Well-informed on such matters, even though they were rarely spoken of in polite Irish society, the parents specifically asked if blood tests for DNA, also known as genetic fingerprinting, could be taken from an aborted foetus to prove the paternity of the culprit.

Jarring at the very principle of the Catholic pro-life thinking behind the original outlawing of abortions, performing an invasive technique on a God-given life (however newly-formed) was considered sacrilegious and anathema to the Republic and had never before been tested in the courts.

Recognized in the UK, America and across Europe as the most conclusive method for deciding parentage, DNA fingerprinting from whatever source is believed to prove familial relationships beyond all reasonable doubt. A sample of blood, tissue or other fluid is taken from the suspected father and from the child or foetus and, using the most advanced scientific technology of its kind available, blood relationships are identified through genetic similarities.

It is used in at least thirty countries worldwide for paternity disputes, immigration cases and rape and murder trials, as well as for animal breeding. But, although used in a handful of straightforward criminal cases in Ireland, it was unknown by experience in a foetal case. Detectives at the grey-brick Tallaght police station, more used to dealing with domestic disturbances, burglaries and drunkenness, did not know the answer to such a sensitive question, but said they would make enquiries.

On Wednesday 5 February officers called the forensic department who contacted the Director of Public Prosecutions and State Solicitor's office – who in turn contacted the Attorney General's office for advice. They later telephoned the girl's parents and told her that they thought such evidence would be unconstitutional and inadmissible in an Irish court. Disappointed, but determined to go ahead with the abortion, the family decided not to prolong the agony any longer.

They packed their bags and, leaving their son in the care of his grandmother, drove the ten miles north of Dublin to the city's international airport.

It was a trip the girl's father regularly made alone, from Dublin Airport to the arrivals lounge at Heathrow Airport in London.

But on the morning of Thursday 6 February his wife and daughter were with him – pale, inseparable and mute throughout the 55-minute flight.

He had booked his daughter into a London abortion clinic the following day, but for that night they travelled by Underground train to an anonymous hotel, counting off the hours until the morning.

Their friends and relatives had been wonderfully supportive, filling their home with calm, rational advice. They were there now, helping to look after the couple's teenage son while they were away.

The father decided to call home that afternoon. He wanted to speak to his son, who was utterly bewildered by the strange turn of events, and reassure him that they had arrived safely. The news he heard down the telephone line was unexpected. His son told him that the Gardai had been to the house. They had asked the boy to tell his father to telephone them immediately if he called home.

The father believed that the police must have had some news for him about the admissibility of DNA testing. This could be vital to the prosecution, he thought, as he dialled the number. What he heard when he finally got through made his blood run cold.

A police officer on the other end of the line told him that interim injunctions had been hurriedly applied for by the Attorney General Harry Whelehan the previous evening to stop the girl from going ahead with the abortion. Having been officially informed that the abortion was about to take place (via the request about the admissibility of DNA evidence), Mr Whelehan had decided that it was his constitutional duty to prevent the Irish foetus from being aborted in a British clinic.

Hearing the application in camera, Mr Justice Declan Costello, a senior High Court judge, had agreed. He had granted the injunctions and effectively placed the family under a restraining court order to return to Ireland immediately. The police officer read out the full text of the injunctions and the judge's decision on the case.

A senior officer connected with the case later said: 'Strictly, we had to tell them. The whole thing had blown up. Someone in the DPP's office had found out what was afoot and alarm bells and warning bells started going off. The Attorney General's office was contacted and all hell broke loose.

'When they found out what was going on, they said we would have been compounding the crime. They said, "Stop those people, stop them," but they had already left for England. Then it was into the judge's chamber to seek an injunction.

'The crazy thing was that if the father hadn't made that call and the girl had had the abortion, that would have been the end of it. Nobody would have taken it any further.'

Standing with the telephone receiver in his hand, 300 miles from the Irish Four Courts on the banks of Dublin's River Liffey, the girl's father did not realize that and asked the officer on the other end of the line what it all meant. 'You have to come home, Sir,' the policeman told him simply.

The father wondered what he should do. Should he contravene the court order and let his daughter go ahead with the abortion? What would be the consequences for the family for being held in contempt of court? Or should he bundle up his anguished wife and child and take them back on the plane to Dublin to face the legal, moral and political furore? It was a decision he could not make alone. He sought his wife's advice, their half-whispered voices quivering with trepidation.

They telephoned a senior legal adviser back home and were told that they could, in theory, be jailed or heavily fined for contempt of court if they did not immediately return. The father decided that they had no choice. They would go back.

A family friend said: 'A long time afterwards I felt I just had to ask the father what everyone else must have wanted to ask him: "Why on earth did you come back?" He just looked at me as if he was rather surprised at my asking and said, "I am a law-abiding citizen." It was said with such simplicity and conviction that I felt ashamed for even asking.

'He was just the type that would never dream of doing anything remotely against the wishes of the police or the law. It was against his character and it was as simple as that. He is a fine man.'

The girl was too numb to respond when her parents told her that they had to go back to Ireland and would not be having the abortion the next day after all. Her nightmare was worsening and she could see no way out of it. She wondered about throwing herself down the stairs of the hotel to get rid of the baby. She watched her mother re-pack her things while her father went to pay the hotel bill.

As he signed his credit card slip, he noticed that the telephone call he had so eagerly made to the police in Ireland – unaware of the fact that he would be told such shattering news – had cost him in excess of £60.00 (sterling).

The family managed to book a flight home that night and made their way wearily back to the airport. Everything would be all right, they assured the girl. They would just sort out this little legal problem and then they would come straight back to the clinic and end her misery once and for all. The girl was not convinced. *En route* to the airport, she considered throwing herself under a Tube train. She was very distressed in the plane on the way home and could hardly speak. Withdrawn and subdued, she arrived back home shortly before 11.00 p.m.

The following day, 7 February, the family approached the small but reputable Dublin law firm of O'Higgins in Ballsbridge, after they were told by the police that they were specialists in domestic law, who could handle their case. Mr James O'Higgins, the firm's benevolent senior partner, took the case on in his Georgian offices late on a busy Friday afternoon, little realizing that an international drama was about to unfold before him.

He took down all the details and promised to consider the case over the weekend. He had a heavy workload already, but there was something about this particular case and this particular family, who were so terribly distressed, that seemed to demand his attention.

Like so many people originally involved on the periphery in this case, he was to become a key player and a close friend of the family. From that first brief encounter with their extraordinary story, through the tortuous route to the final episode, he personally attended each court hearing and followed each development with the fastidiousness of a private detective. With his soft blue eyes and kindly smile, he was to become a welcome visitor at the family house. His friendship with the girl and her parents was to strengthen over the years.

The girl's parents told Mr O'Higgins that earlier that day they had also contacted a psychologist who worked for the Eastern Health Board, whose name they were given by the police. An acknowledged British expert in the field of child sex abuse and suicide who had been working in Ireland since 1979, he agreed to see the girl at his clinic that afternoon as an emergency case.

He was immediately struck by her severe distress and sense of shock. 'She seemed almost in a trance and she herself stated that she could not believe this was happening to her,' he said.

'She had been crying on her own and was hiding her feelings deliberately from her parents in order to protect them from further distress. Her vacant, expressionless manner suggested she was coping with this appalling crisis in her life by a denial of her emotions.

'For this reason she did not seem depressed, but I feared that when her feelings surfaced she would face a psychological crisis.'

She repeatedly told him that she had let her parents down and was afraid that they would not stand by her. She loathed the foetus growing within her and said she wanted to get rid of it. She had not eaten for four days and was vomiting due to morning sickness. She was in pain, weak and dehydrated and needed urgent medical treatment.

In a newspaper article in the *Irish Press* a few months later, the psychologist described her appearance:

There are six questions we normally put to our seriously suicidal patients. I asked: 'How do you see the future?' and she just said: 'I don't see any future.'

She saw this really as something that left her hopeless. She said in answer to the second question – Has life seemed quite hopeless? – that yes, indeed, that is what she was saying.

I asked her did she ever think of ending it all and she specifically said that she thought the best thing was to end it all. Her mother confirmed that she had been talking quite specifically about suicide.

She hadn't actually tried anything then, but when people are trapped or put in prison, in an inescapable situation, that's when young people are most likely to do something desperate.

The psychologist interviewed the girl, both in the presence of her parents and alone, for a total of nearly three hours. He judged that the parents' upset was so great that they could not give their daughter the 24-hour supervision she needed. He also judged that the girl was so at risk that she could not be left alone even for a minute in a waiting room. Instead, he had her sit on a chair behind her parents in his consulting room while he spoke to them about her.

He told them that he was to arrange for her to be admitted to a private room in the maternity wing at Dublin's Rotunda Hospital immediately because she was in need of medical treatment for the pregnancy and also because he was fearful that she might try to take her own life.

Her parents drove her there straight away and settled her into her room. Nursing staff said she was distracted and seemed hardly to know where she was or why.

Placed on fluids and medication, her physical condition quickly stabilized and she was considered to be out of immediate tangible danger. Psychologically, however, she was still irrational and confused and considered to be a long way from safety. Her parents and doctors tried to talk to her about the future, and about what she wanted, but she was largely negative and non-responsive. When the suggestion was put to her that she might have to go through with the pregnancy and then put the baby up for adoption, she was adamant that she didn't want that either.

Adopted herself as a baby, she developed rambling theories about what would happen to the baby. Her mother said: 'She emphatically stated that she felt no love for the child.'

In the words of a later court judgement: 'The daughter expressed the view that were she to have the baby she would not be able to look at its face when it was born. At the same time she felt that she could not give up the child for adoption lest it should suffer the same fate as she had at the hands of the man who had abused her.'

In her highly anxious state she was somehow implying that any adoptive parents of her baby might not be able to prevent the same thing happening to the child.

She had also formed the view somehow that the foetus within her was female. Bonded to her mother through her ordeal, and largely surrounded by women as nurses, police officers or counsellors at this stage, she was rejecting the concept of a male child as the product of the man's abuse.

Nobody was in any doubt that the girl required urgent psychological help. And by now it was recognized that her mother, too, was in a state of extreme anxiety and would need all the help she could get. Her husband, the girl's father, felt more and more isolated as events slipped further and further from his control. The cracks in his relationship with his family were beginning to show and he felt increasingly powerless to cement them together.

THREE

When Detective Inspector Anthony Sourke, recently promoted, was first informed of the girl's accusations against her family friend, he regarded it as nothing more than another sad case of child abuse.

After more than twenty years in the Garda, he was only too well aware of the unfortunate frequency with which these cases arose. This was really no more unusual than any other he had dealt with. In many ways it was simpler. The question of incest, so often seen in such instances, was not an issue and perhaps the only additional complication to the charges was that the girl was now pregnant and needed to be handled with more sensitivity.

He assigned a team of three of his officers to the initial investigation, and turned his attention to his other more pressing cases. The busy senior detective, who was later to find himself suddenly in the midst of the most controversial case in Ireland, had no idea at this stage how important his team's investigations would become.

His officers, Detective Gardai Pat Treacy, Aubrey Steadman and Ann Vaughan, put into action a well-formulated plan of action, tried and tested in dozens of similar cases. Detective Vaughan would have most of the direct, personal contact with the girl and her parents, and would be with her at all times during police interviews and any court hearings. Her male colleagues, working with Detective Bill O'Brien, would deal with the accused and the legal and forensic side of things.

None of the officers, who were also to become deeply involved with the family, could ever have predicted all that was to happen in those early days of the case. Nor could they have realized how important they would become to the family. Detective Steadman, particularly, was to become a close personal friend of the girl and came to be relied upon heavily by her mother in later years. Detectives Vaughan and Treacy were also to become regarded with considerable fondness, as the family became more and more isolated from the outside world.

The officers began the investigation by examining the law relating to child abuse, and relating it to the facts of the case as they had been told them. Under Irish law, the girl was a legal minor and could not be considered to be capable of either giving or withholding her consent to sexual intercourse until she was seventeen years old. In the light of the evidence they had, that the abuse had taken place with a certain degree of passivity on the girl's part and had not been forced upon her with violence, the accused man could not be charged with rape. If he were ever to come to court, he would have to be charged under the Criminal Law (Rape) Act of 1981, with the crime of statutory rape, known in Ireland as unlawful carnal knowledge.

With, at this stage, no inkling of the huge controversy that was about to envelop this particular case, DI Sourke told his officers that his chief concern was the close proximity of the two main parties, and the fear of any interference of witnesses. Whatever the case's eventual outcome, he knew instinctively that this was a difficult situation and one that had to be handled with extreme care. In such close-knit communities, with their staunchly loyal extended families nearby, it is quite common for aggrieved parties or their relatives to try to take the law into their own hands. DI Sourke did not want a blood-bath spilling on to the streets, so he advised the girl and her family to move away for a while.

This suggestion, which the family asked for some time to consider, was to become all the more important later when their 'routine' case took on the significance that it did, with the intervention of the highest courts in the land.

* * *

For all of those involved, this case was to become one of the most formidable they had ever come across. Forced to put their own feelings to one side, the police, barristers, clerks and the judiciary had to deal dispassionately with the anguish faced by the girl and her family as they fought to clarify the law.

Attorney General Harry Whelehan, the man on whose shoulders much of the responsibility would lie, was first alerted to the situation by a member of his staff in the State Solicitor's office who told him there was a problem. One of the first appointments of the recently elected Fianna Fail government, and billed as 'a safe pair of hands', he had been in his job for just one week. Some have since wondered if the reaction to the case would have been different if it had come at the end of an Attorney General's tenure rather than at the beginning. An Attorney General who was fully acclimatized to his role and perhaps less anxious to be seen to be doing the right thing from the outset might have reacted with less fastidiousness.

Nobody was in any doubt that Mr Whelehan was in an uncomfortable situation. One observer said he was 'caught between the devil and the deep blue sea – one option being to do what he saw as legally imperative but harsh and the alternative being to lay himself open to damning criticism that he had failed to uphold the law.'

For more than nine years since the 1983 referendum on abortion, Mr Whelehan's predecessors had all managed to escape the unwelcome test case that they knew might one day directly challenge the Constitution. But just a few working days into his term of office, this former part-time counsellor with the Catholic Marriage Advisory Bureau was now faced with that very case and knew that he would come in for some strong criticism whichever way he handled it.

A member of both the British and Irish bars, he served on a legal panel backing the defeated Fianna Fail candidate in the 1990 presidential election. He was said to hold outspoken views on moral issues and to be strongly opposed to any form of legalized abortion in Ireland.

Determined to act very precisely within the constraints of the law as it stood, he and his staff braced themselves for the possible consequences and looked up the exact wording of the Constitution relating to abortion. They found it in Article 40, Section 3, Sub-section 3, as inserted by the Eighth Amendment to the Constitution voted in by the people in a referendum in 1983, which said:

> The State acknowledges the right to life of the unborn and, with due regard to the equal right to life of the mother, guarantees in its laws to respect, and, as far as practicable, by its laws to defend and vindicate that right.

There were also case-law references to the constitutional 'sacred trust' of the right to life of the unborn 'to which all the organs of government must lend their support'.

Under those strictures he knew that he had no choice, having been alerted to the intention to terminate the girl's pregnancy, but to obtain interim injunctions in the High Court.

He was later to say that he felt an 'emotional empathy' with the plight of the girl and that he had very much regretted having to take such action. Speaking in Brussels a month after the final Supreme Court decision in the case, he said: 'The Supreme Court and the High Court all said I had no option but to do what I did.

'In so far as I was doing my duty and had no option, I can have no regrets. As to the trauma it caused to individuals and generally, it is a matter of great regret to me.'

He added some months later: 'The case was one of the saddest and most difficult . . . that anybody could envisage being confronted with.' He was never to comment further.

John Rogers, Senior Counsel, was first instructed to take the case when the family returned from England in early February 1992.

Mr O'Higgins, who had already been engaged by the family, passed their case on to senior advisers. Mr Rogers was specifically chosen for the unique expertise and experience he could bring to the case. A 42-year-old father of two, born in Clontarf, Dublin, the son of a carpenter, and a former Attorney General in the early 1980s, he had been known as 'the Boy Attorney General' for being the youngest ever, at thirty-four, to take up the post.

Great friends with the Irish Labour leader Dick Spring, with whom he had attended Trinity College, he had formerly been a legal adviser to the Labour Party when he was keen on introducing social legislation. He had helped Mr Spring formulate the opposition to the Fianna Fail party's wording to the 1983 pro-life constitutional amendment. He had also advocated divorce in circumstances of irretrievable marriage breakdown.

At the time of the 'X' case his own daughter Kitty was twelve years old – the same age as 'X' was when she was first abused.

Within a very short time of being assigned to the case, Mr Rogers and his legal team were thrown in at the deep end. They had to become experts on the law relating to abortion, European Community regulations and the Irish Constitution all in a matter of days. They issued an immediate challenge to the injunctions on the grounds that the family had a right to travel from the jurisdiction to do what was lawful elsewhere; that the girl's right to life itself was in peril and that such injunctions were unprecedented and ought not to have been granted.

They would never forget those first few weeks of the case, which were to become perhaps one of the most exciting and gruelling episodes in their careers.

While the wheels of law turned slowly in the High Court's chambers and junior counsel in the Law Library pored over tomes searching for precedents to challenge the Constitution, the atmosphere in the street where the two families lived was electric. The girl's abuser, who had been told nothing officially, but who had seen strangers coming and going from his neighbour's home for days, feared the worst. Telling his wife to stay well away from their neighbour's house, he waited for the knock on the door.

It came on the morning of Saturday 7 February – the day after the girl and her family were forced to return to Ireland. The man was just about to leave the house to take his children out when the three officers from the Criminal Detection Unit arrived on his doorstep. His wife was upstairs when he was arrested and cautioned. He rushed upstairs to alert her. 'Get me a solicitor!' he shouted, as he was led from the house.

He was taken to the local police station and interviewed for twelve hours by a team of detectives. They told him of the pregnancy and the abortion attempt and of the injunctions to stop the girl going through with it. They also said that the girl was reportedly suicidal.

One of the officers connected with the case said afterwards: 'He strenuously denied the accusations. He was most indignant. He said to us: "Who's been telling lies?"

'He confirmed that he had been alone with the girl on each of the occasions she said she had been abused, but he emphatically denied any bodily contact. He never admitted anything and ridiculed the suggestion. He said: "I suppose I raped my own daughter, did I?"

'He seemed to be very co-operative and answered our questions fully and frankly. We were rather dubious about whether the girl was telling the truth at that time.'

His solicitor arrived at the police station after a call from the man's wife and spoke at length to his client. Hoping to throw police off the scent before the situation got out of hand and fully believing – after his conversation with her about getting 'the all clear' – that he was safe, the accused immediately offered to provide blood samples to prove parentage.

Two samples, one from each arm, were taken by Dr James

Maloney, a registered medical practitioner who often undertook police work. After the sample-taking, the accused was taken home and asked to let police know if he planned to leave the area. He was not charged and no constraints were put upon him not to disappear. The police were not to call at his house again for another four months.

Back home, the man explained the situation to his stunned wife. He convinced her that the girl was nothing more than a foolish teenager with a schoolgirl crush who was now trying to explain her pregnancy at the hands of some local boy. 'She believed him blindly,' said someone who was in contact with them at the time. 'He convinced them all that he was totally innocent. Furthermore, he had certain influential people putting it about that he was an innocent victim.'

His wife offered her husband her complete support and tried to contain her growing resentment of the girl who, as she saw it, was trying to destroy everything that was precious to her. She told her friends that she had loved the girl and viewed her as a daughter, but claimed she was 'very unlikely' to have threatened to commit suicide.

The man falsely claimed that the girl's father had a drink problem and tried to portray the girl's parents as emotionally unstable. He made repeated mention of the girl's diary, which, he said, would establish her disturbed emotional state and prove that she had been less than honest with police. The name of 'A', the son of the man's next-door neighbour, was repeatedly mentioned by him as the probable father of the child.

The accused took the vendetta against the respectable foreign family further. Taking an expensive silk scarf he had once been given by 'A's father as a traditional token of friendship, he went next door to the businessman's house. He tied the scarf around a tree in the front garden and left it there. When 'A's father saw the scarf and realized the significance of what his neighbour was trying to suggest, he was furious. He left the scarf tied to the tree for months to show people what malice the man was capable of.

'He refused to be intimidated,' said one of those connected with the case. 'He was a tough man. He said that in his country a man accused of sex crimes against a child would have been buried up to the neck in the ground and stoned to death.'

The foreign father ignored his neighbour's threats and tried to concentrate on offering support for his son, a gifted pupil of a local college and a keen rugby player. When the college eventually informed the father that the boy would have to leave because he had fallen so far behind with his work, the family believed the real reason to be the slur campaign mounted against him. They tried to fight the decision, but to no avail. They were furious and felt grievously personally wronged by the circumstances. As one officer in the case said: 'This boy had done nothing wrong, but became as much a victim of the accused as the girl. Here were two young lives this man was ruining in an attempt to save his own neck.'

Those who had dealings with the accused man at this time found it extremely difficult to assess his mental state. He appeared to be so ebullient and confident that his name would be cleared, it was hard to believe that he could be guilty. So sure was he that he had dominated his young victim to such an extent that she would never proceed with the charges against him, he may have even believed at this stage that when the pregnancy was over, the two families could go back to the way they had been before.

Mr Tony Black, chief psychologist at Broadmoor mental hospital in Britain for over twenty-five years and an expert on the mental processes of sexual abusers, said the man displayed the typical characteristics of 'the bull of the herd'. He added: 'He seemed to have regarded himself as the gregarious head of the neighbourhood, who could take an opportunity for sex with this girl when it first presented itself to him, and could then portray an astonishing amount of callousness in turning all sorts of later situations to his own advantage.'

Mr Black said the man did not comply with the usual characteristics of sexual abusers. 'They are usually much younger, single, and have difficulties forming relationships with women of their own age. Hence they go for younger girls – who are uncomplicated and uncritical – or for much older women who are regarded as grateful for what they can get.

'This man seems to have been in an apparently normal marital relationship, with three children of his own, and just gave in to an overwhelming sexual desire for this young girl.

'Towards the end of his dealings with her, he seemed to have regarded her as his "bit on the side". He seemed to have seen their relationship as being a completely normal extra-marital affair, with snatched moments whenever the possibility arose, and which gave him total satisfaction and fulfilment, without thinking too much about what he was doing.

'It never seemed to enter his head that he was likely to be in very serious trouble if he had been caught having sex with her in his car in a public place, or caught by his wife or children in their home.

'It may have been that the risks he was taking aroused him even further, in which case he was actually quite a dangerous person to be with.'

Mr Black said the man was 'very clearly aware' of the unlawfulness and social unacceptability of his crimes, as he repeatedly told the girl he would go to prison if she told anyone. 'But that seems to have been completely overwhelmed by his sexual urges for this girl, who presented herself almost as a sitting victim bearing in mind the closeness of the two families involved.

'Her endearing immaturity and tendency to regard him as a sort of father or uncle figure would have brought out in him emotions of wanting to protect her, to keep her to himself, to teach her things, as he perceived it, in the right way.

'Despite what seems to have been his very clever manipulation of her and others, he may have actually been extremely tender and caring towards her in their private moments, aroused by her sexual inexperience and wanting to show her what he could do.

'That doesn't make it any the less damaging, distressing or humiliating for the girl – in fact it may even make it worse in the long run – and this chap seems to have been guilty most of all of a terrible abuse of her trust.'

Dazzled by her abuser's cunning, Mr Black believed the girl may never have told anyone of her private torment unless her pregnancy had forced it out into the open. 'His control of her seemed to be that complete,' he said.

One of the detectives connected with the case agreed. 'He was able to persuade her not to say anything. Once you do that and get away with it the first time, it can go on,' he said.

'He told her she would get into terrible trouble with her mother, that she would be responsible for breaking up his family and that his daughter wouldn't talk to her.

'But there is no suggestion that she ever actively sought her participation. She just went along with it because she didn't know anything else.'

Ms Caroline Ainscough, a consultant clinical psychologist and co-author of a book called *Breaking Free: Help for Survivors of Child Abuse*, concurred. 'She would have been very confused and shocked by what happened at first. Children, especially those from strict Catholic homes, are often too embarrassed to talk about sex at all, so they certainly feel unable to talk about sexual abuse.

'They worry that they might have done something to encourage it and just try to hope that it won't happen again. When it does, and they didn't say anything the first time, they feel that they cannot say anything this time or their parents will ask why they didn't tell them before or accuse them of telling stories.'

Ms Ainscough said that child abusers are also extremely clever at exploiting their victims. 'In this instance, it seems that he waited until she was a long way from home and unable to run to her parents for help before he started his abuse.

'He persisted with her when she was once again out of the reach of help, and continued with it when her parents were far away. By the time they had come back, she would have felt unable to say anything and would have been well and truly hooked by this man.'

At the girl's house, the legal morass and its full implications for them had taken over almost every waking moment. They sought the advice of professionals and were told in no uncertain terms that theirs could become a mould-breaking test case for Irish abortion law.

'We don't want to change the law, we just want what is best for our daughter,' the despairing parents told one adviser. 'The longer this drags on the longer she has to live with being pregnant. Just do what you have to do and let's get this over with.'

Reassured that they would never be named, they were none the less told to brace themselves for expected massive publicity about their case as the details of the legal proceedings were about to reach the debating house of the government and the newspapers. Already emotionally battered, this was an added anxiety that they had not previously considered, but which now became an almost overriding obsession. From that moment on, they insisted on absolute privacy, vowing never to give an interview or further expose their daughter in any way to the media spotlight which was about to be so brightly shone on her.

They drew their curtains and were careful to whom they opened the door. Telephone calls were monitored and they urged their son as he left for school each morning not to say anything about what had happened to anyone.

Within weeks everyone in their street would know who they

were and their personal situation would be discussed by the whole neighbourhood. Their local high street, with its coffee shop, hairdresser and newsagents would be buzzing with gossip, which would abruptly stop as soon as any member of their family or the man's walked into earshot. As one local resident who had recently moved into the area said: 'This was the most shocking thing to have happened round here in living memory and people just couldn't stop talking about it. It was like Chinese whispers, and the stories became more and more wild.

'Children in the area all went to the street where they lived and pointed out the girl's house to anyone who asked. The area became the most popular place for skate-boarding, football and general hanging out, as the children waited for the film crews to arrive, or for the girl to show her face.

'Word got out at the girl's little brother's school and everyone kept asking him about it. In the end he had to move schools too, because of all the questions.

'People didn't know how to behave to the accused or to his family. They seemed to be able to come and go as they chose and he appeared not to be affected by it at all. He would walk down the main street like he owned it and stop and say "Hiya!" to anyone he met. People who knew him said he was a nice outgoing man with a nice family and a nice job. The rumours split the local community, with one half insisting he was innocent and other half saying he was guilty.

'The trouble was he just didn't look like a child molester. He was a good-looking man and always so smartly dressed and well turned out. And here he was, walking down the street as bold as brass, not cowering at home guiltily.

'When we didn't see much of the girl and her family, but we saw him every day, it was hard not to think that here was a man with nothing to hide.'

Those who were in the same line of work as the man were not so generous of spirit. His business suffered from cancelled orders as people expressed a wish not to be associated with him.

He continued to claim unemployment assistance throughout this time and worked intermittently from home, but those in his industry began to spurn him one by one as his connection with the 'X' case became known.

Much to the chagrin of his victim's family, he took to collecting money for charities at their church every Sunday. He would either sell items for charity or pass a collecting box. The girl's mother complained to the police about it, but there was nothing they could do.

His wife, meanwhile, continued to go to work – in a Dublin store – to make ends meet. Still shattered by what was happening to her husband, she struggled to keep life as normal as possible for his sake and for the sake of their children. The couple were bolstered by their large extended family, who rallied round and offered their support and whatever help they could. But the high emotions of the case led to a loss of reason from some quarters, and a mood of intimidation and ostracism for *both* families – who all received threatening phone calls – pervaded the neighbourhood.

Even some of the police officers in the case fell victim to the mood of harassment and concern, and felt threatened by some quarters. Genuine feelings of grievance for the parties involved turned to malice and even threats of violence in some instances. Pressure groups and special interest organizations contacted some of the officers involved both at work and at their homes. Anonymous telephone calls were to become a regular annoyance for almost all of those connected with the case. Some even had to have their numbers changed. 'It was an extremely difficult time for everyone involved,' recalled one officer. 'It completely took over all our lives for a long time.'

Quite apart from the pressures of the case itself, there were their careers to think of. Few Garda officers could have had their investigation so closely scrutinized by the authorities, or questioned at every turn by senior officers.

'The strain was enormous,' said one close to the case. 'We just wanted to get this particular chapter of our lives closed and get back to normal. Little did we know how long that was going to take.'

FOUR

A brief front page story in *The Irish Times* on Wednesday 12 February 1992 gave the first limited details of the case that was to confront Prime Minister Albert Reynolds with a political crisis just six days after taking office as the new Taoiseach.

Under a colour photograph of himself receiving his scroll of office from President Mary Robinson, he saw with dismay that news had leaked that Attorney General Whelehan had taken legal action to prevent the 14-year-old abuse victim from seeking an abortion.

Mr Whelehan had not officially sought the approval or advice of the government. He insisted (and others later agreed) that his hands were tied and that he was entitled to act independently in accordance with the law as it stood.

Mr Reynolds, a father of seven – including five daughters – a veteran campaigner and ardent pro-Europe supporter, was confronted with an issue that would haunt him for years to come on the day of his government's first cabinet meeting. Like the majority of the people of his nation he was against abortion in principle, but, an astute politician, he could feel the spirit of liberalization sweeping through the streets and the mood for change. If the girl was not allowed to travel abroad, the public uproar at her being stopped could undermine his fledgling government.

Keen to be at the forefront of legislation to alter the law if it was necessary, it was he who later encouraged the girl's family to challenge the High Court decision and to go to the Supreme Court. He also offered to waive the predicted IR £50,000 costs of their legal battle. He would have liked to have met the family and to have offered his personal support, but never did because they had requested absolute privacy from the start and he respected that request.

Asked what he would do if he were the girl's father, Mr Reynolds replied: 'I would obey the law of the land.'

In the face of calls for the resignation of the Attorney General as public sympathy for the girl and her family gathered momentum, Mr Reynolds defended Mr Whelehan publicly: 'The Attorney General told me that, irrespective of his sympathy for the girl and her parents, his constitutional duty was to take whatever steps were necessary to protect the life which it was proposed to terminate,' he said.

He rejected suggestions that the Attorney General should have 'turned a blind eye' to the legal requirements. 'I do not believe that the people of this country want, or deserve, a situation of nods and winks in the application of the law,' he added. 'If the principal law officer of the State were to engage in such conduct in the present case, how could he ever again be trusted to observe the Constitution or the law in any future situation where there might be an obvious temptation ... for him to take the easy way out?'

For Mrs Mary Robinson, the first woman President of Ireland – elected in 1990 to much surprise after a controversial campaign – the case presented uneasy issues at a time when she had just achieved the highest office.

A Catholic mother of three, married to a Protestant solicitor who is also an architectural conservationist and political cartoonist, she had made her name as a feminist barrister and leading campaigner against the 1983 anti-abortion amendment. Educated at Harvard at a time when America was in the grips of the Vietnam War and the civil rights movement and at the time of President Kennedy's assassination, her Irish political career had been forged on the back of her passionate objection to the proposed amendment to the Constitution on abortion.

Her campaign for the right of Irish people to contraceptives came to a head when she became the architect of the failed Family Planning Bill in the 1970s – during which she was sent used condoms through the post from ill-wishers.

Her campaign slogan to the women of Ireland had been 'You have a voice. I will make it heard,' but she found herself politically muted during the one case on which everyone expected to hear her voice. 'The hand that rocks the cradle can rock the system,' she had once promised, but found herself forced into prudent circumspection when the Irish Constitution was being rocked to its very foundations.

At a long-planned lecture she was to give at Trinity College, Dublin – which fell in the middle of the crisis in February 1992 – hundreds of people turned up, expecting to hear her speak on a subject which they knew was so close to her heart. After all, wasn't it was she who, during the 1983 referendum debate that had set the scene for the current crisis, had warned that one day there would be such a case that would challenge the proposed amendment? Yet on that night, in the vast lecture hall of Trinity College, there was nothing but disappointment for those who had gathered, even though they knew she would be running an unenviable gauntlet if she had spoken out. Before giving a general lecture on women's role in society, Mrs Robinson told the audience that it would be 'neither appropriate nor possible' for her to get involved in 'the tragic court case' on everybody's mind.

Her decision not to say anything may have been influenced by the widespread criticism of her a few days earlier when she spoke to a gathering of women's groups in Waterford and briefly commented that the case presented a 'deep crisis in ourselves' that the country had to resolve.

In what the Irish press described as an 'unprecedented' speech for a President on a live issue, she said she was in touch with people all over the country and had found them deeply troubled, hurt, bewildered and feeling 'a sense of frustration and helplessness'. Reminding her audience that she had no role or function in the issue, she added, 'I hope we have the courage, which we have not always had in the past, to face up to and look squarely at this issue and say: This is a problem which we have got to resolve.'

She urged the nation, in an era of 'increasing self-development of women and confidence', to 'move on to a more compassionate society . . . we must pull together and make progress in this very difficult area.'

Her message seemed clear, but her delivery of it stopped there. Bound by the chains of her office, she has been unable to speak publicly on the matter since, although many believe that her role behind the scenes may have been crucial.

In an interview two years after the 'X' crisis, she spoke cryptically of the power of influence in a job in which politics were taboo. 'I have learned a lot about what is power, what is leadership and what is influence,' she said. Asked what made her accept the post of President, she said: 'I became more and more convinced that this was one of those rare opportunities, first to listen very carefully and then to represent and encourage and energize and, I suppose, inspire.'

As arguably the most widely respected politician in the Republic in several decades, she continued to command ninety per cent approval ratings from an adoring public. On her fiftieth birthday in 1994, the astute commentator Fintan O'Toole of *The Irish Times* wrote:

What is so extraordinary is that she has done so not from a background of balmy graciousness but of furious ideological struggle . . . By any normal criteria, a political figure so centrally involved with one side of such a passionate debate should not be able to command the almost universal approval that she does.

The news of the 'X' case shocked and appalled Senator David Norris. Someone who was well used to the vagaries of Irish law, he had challenged the courts himself a few years earlier when he became the first Irish politician to confess to being homosexual and challenged the Oireachtas or Irish Parliament to legalize homosexuality amongst consenting adults, in line with European policy.

Under a rarely invoked nineteenth-century Irish law, people engaging in homosexual acts previously faced life imprisonment in Ireland. Senator Norris, forty-eight, was determined to challenge that and in June 1993, in the wake of a landmark judgement against Dublin in the European Court of Human Rights, the Irish Parliament decided to legalize homosexuality, by passing unopposed the second reading of his bill to allow homosexuality over the age of seventeen. It was a victory that placed him in the firing line and made him many enemies. It was also a battle that taught him that it was not a simple matter to change the nature of Irish law overnight.

'When I first heard about the girl, my heart went out to her,' he said, in his elegant Dublin townhouse. 'I was the first to raise the matter in the Senate, and the shock and emotion expressed at that first discussion of the case was both touching and genuine.'

Senator Norris offered his services to the family and became a trustee of the Child Victim Support Appeal, which started to raise funds for their forthcoming legal battle. At one point during the campaign, he received an anonymous letter telling him that the girl's family were embarrassed and mortified that he, as a homosexual, should have been the one to take up their cause, and had expressed a wish that he would desist. Considered to be a witty academic and a world authority on James Joyce, Senator Norris said: 'I realize that I am not the most palatable of characters to some people, but I was very upset to think that I may have in some way added to the family's distress. I contacted them immediately and asked them outright if they were embarrassed. The answer I got gladdened my heart. They invited me to their home for dinner and made me feel as welcome as the flowers in spring. They were a warm, loving family and they were very keen not to alienate anyone who had gone out of their way to help them.'

Another member of the appeal fund for the girl, Dr Mary Henry, a respected physician attached to the Rotunda and Adelaide Hospitals and later a popular senator, held a press conference to convey the family's appreciation of growing public support. 'The family have expressed tremendous gratitude and are very moved that they are getting such support. They would like to convey their thanks and appreciation for what's been done, especially by the media,' she said.

The trustees said that any donations would provide a 'cushion' for the family, who had by that time been forced to move house and who were suffering financial hardship as the father took extended leave of absence from work. They should not be viewed as in any way 'taking sides' in the debate, the trustees reassured the Irish people. In the end, their words went largely unheeded. Despite the public outcry about their plight, a little over IR £6,000 was raised, and a great many of those donations came from Britain, America, Holland and Germany.

Dr Henry said later: 'I think it was a combination of factors. Partly people felt that if they gave money to the family then they might be construed as supporting abortion, but mainly I think it was because the government publicly waived the legal costs soon afterwards and people just didn't think there was a need for any money.

'In any event, the family were very grateful for what they got. They were in no sense on the make, and would never have accepted charity over and above their legitimate costs.'

Senator Henry, who has spent a lifetime devoted to women's rights, said the impact of the case was 'devastating' to the opponents of those rights. 'People were just appalled and horrified that this poor girl had been so badly treated by the State that they came out fighting on her side, before they even realized that what that meant was that, perhaps for the first time, they were agreeing with abortion in limited circumstances.

'I can remember hardly believing it when Mary Robinson became the first woman President of Ireland and I think I felt the same way about this case. Tragic and disastrous as it was, it was to be the most important breakthrough in more than a decade of hot air and rhetoric.'

The tidal wave of emotion that swept through the Republic showed no sign of abating as the girl and the nation anxiously waited for the next round in the legal battle for her rights.

Effectively hoist by their own petard, the population engaged in increasing public keening and wailing over the dilemma which had been inadvertently caused by a referendum in which the vast majority had voted for an anti-abortion amendment.

It was in the climate of the bitterest emotions that the pro-life anti-abortion faction had achieved in 1983 the Eighth Amendment to the Constitution guaranteeing the rights to life of the unborn. Those who remember the campaign say it bore all the hallmarks of a civil war. Full of verbal violence, it was aptly described by *The Irish Times* (and then adopted as the title for one scholarly study) as 'the second partitioning of Ireland'.

At the beginning of 1981 the two major political parties at the time, Fianna Fail led by Charles Haughey and the opposition Fine Gael headed by Garret FitzGerald, were approached by the founder members of the Pro-Life Amendment Campaign who had recently set themselves up as self-appointed moral guardians of the right to life of the unborn.

Legal in Britain (although not in Northern Ireland) since 1967 and in the USA since 1974, abortion was gradually seeping into the Irish consciousness and the right-wingers wanted to plug the legal loophole which might have allowed it in. Afraid that the Irish Supreme Court (which operates on a basis far more like that in America than the British system) might follow the US example and rule that the choice for abortion was a

fundamental right to privacy, the PLAC decided that the existing constitutional protection for the unborn was simply not
good enough. They were also concerned that Ireland's membership of Europe might somehow allow EC law to overrule any
constitutional provisions.

Ireland was in an unprecedented period of political instability
in 1981. The key issue on the agenda was the IRA hunger
strikers in the Maze prison, culminating in the death of the
'political prisoner' Bobby Sands. Charles Haughey, who had
taken over as Prime Minister mid-term and was having to confront the hunger strike issue head-on, wanted a general election
to give him a mandate for the course of action he wanted to
take. PLAC saw their opportunity to get their foot in the door
and quickly devised an amendment to the Constitution which,
they thought, would permanently ban abortion in Ireland.

A general election was called and with just a few weeks to
go senior PLAC figures met privately with the political leaders
and pressed them for a commitment to introduce it by way of
a referendum if they came to power.

Comprising five senior university professors, twelve senior
consultants in obstetrics and gynaecology and other leading
members of the Dublin community, the campaigners were not
people to be ignored.

'Garret FitzGerald agreed and Charles Haughey said he would
consider it and get his legal department to look at it,' said a
senior member of the campaign, who attended both meetings
in the Dáil. 'There has been a suggestion latterly that both men
were somehow secretly blackmailed into agreeing to our position and that we threatened them with failure in the general
election if they did not agree, but that is all nonsense.

'At that time, we were not seen to be asking for anything too
contentious or earth-shattering. There was a general consensus
that abortion would never be allowed in Ireland anyway and
we were just seen to be reflecting the majority position. The
negotiations weren't high-pressure cloak-and-dagger meetings,

they were far more skin-of-the-teeth, seat-of-the-pants stuff.

'We were extremely lucky that there followed three general elections, in which Haughey and FitzGerald alternated in power, so each time they came to the brink, so to speak, we were able to remind them of their commitment once again.'

After three general elections in less than a year, out of which staggered a minority government, the duty to follow through on what had been a politically expedient if undemocratically-made promise lay on the two parties' shoulders.

The politicians agreed to the wording of an amendment to Article 40 of the 1937 Constitution, which, under the heading 'Fundamental Rights', already stated:

All citizens shall, as human persons, be held equal before the law. The State, shall, in particular, by its laws protect as best it may from unjust attack and, in the case of injustice done, vindicate the life, person, good name and property rights of every citizen.

Bowing to demands to state expressly that the right to life of the unborn was equal, not inferior, to that of the mother, the amendment added:

The State acknowledges the right to life of the unborn and, with due regard to the equal right to life of the mother, guarantees in its laws to respect and, as far as practicable, by its laws to defend and vindicate that right.

It would, it was thought, effectively permanently rule out any abortions in the State, regardless of the European or American rulings.

A referendum was promised the following year and the slow process of the amendment passing as a Bill through Parliament began. American anti-abortionists, disappointed at not being able to stem the increasing flow of terminations in the US, arrived in Ireland to support the campaign. They gave rousing lectures and showed the graphic anti-abortion film *The Silent Scream* in schools and at roadshows throughout the Republic. One of the most famous American speakers, Father Paul Marx, toured the country with an aborted foetus preserved in a glass jar, railing against the 'slaughter of the innocents'. (Nine years later he toured Ireland again, this time with a live specimen – an 'abortion holocaust survivor' – a 15-year-old Californian girl with cerebral palsy who claimed her physical disablement followed an attempt by her mother to have her aborted.)

Their arrival heralded alarmist warnings of an American-style campaign in Ireland, which might lead to violence or worse, but that never happened. Those opposed to the pro-life camp claimed the Americans were funding them, but as one senior member of PLAC said ruefully: 'The reason the American pro-life campaigns have so much money is because they are so reluctant to part with it. We would have welcomed some funding, but apart from a few individual donations, none, sadly, was forthcoming. By and large, the Americans who rushed over here went home disappointed. We had no abortion clinics to picket outside and we did not support a campaign that criticized the individuals involved.'

Other Irish pro-life groups took to the campaign trail instead. They included Family Solidarity and the Society for the Protection of the Unborn Child (SPUC), founded in Ireland in 1980, which demonstrated their whole-hearted support for the anti-abortion movement and organized some of the more intellectualist campaigns.

The Church widely supported the message behind the campaigns and supplied hellfire and damnation sermons from the pulpit to drum the message home to the Catholic population. The influential Archbishop of Dublin, Dr Dermot Ryan, personally urged the masses to vote 'Yes' to the amendment. Other church leaders called the wording 'just and adequate'.

The government changed hands again, this time forming a Labour/Fine Gael coalition ten months before the referendum.

The debate increased in viciousness as TDs (members of Parliament) from all sides formed ranks and fuelled the animosity with political rhetoric.

Those in the newly formed pro-choice Anti-Amendment Campaign (set up a year after their rivals) warned against 'a step back into the Dark Ages' in Ireland. They raised the possibility of a case like 'X', or of cases where a woman would die through illness if she did not have an abortion. Politicians, lawyers, doctors and devout Catholics countered that it would never happen. One founder member of the PLAC, the then chairman of the Institute of Obstetricians and Gynaecologists, said: 'I wish to state categorically that the skilled treatment available to every pregnant woman in Ireland will not be altered in any way whatsoever, whether there is an Amendment or not. I should also like to reassure all my colleagues that there is not the slightest added risk of any legal proceedings being taken against any of them should the present wording be written into the Constitution.'

As the debate increased in intensity, the media rounded on the pro-life groups and, in editorials with headlines like 'In Christ's Name, Stop', implied that they were 'Ayatollahs' and conspiratorial fundamentalists.

The political opposition to the amendment gained momentum, inspired by the astonishing statement of the then Attorney General Peter Sutherland, who looked at the legal implications and called the proposed wording (drawn up by the previous government) 'flabby, imprecise and potentially dangerous'.

Charles Haughey's Fianna Fail supported the amendment, but Fine Gael did not. There was a revolt by members of Fine Gael, who abstained from voting as the wording of the amendment was passed through Parliament – the first time that had ever happened in relation to a constitutional amendment. Despite his initial enthusiasm, Garret FitzGerald went on national television to publicly denounce the amendment and warn the population against voting for it in the forthcoming referendum. He said he had been advised that the wording was defective and contained certain dangers. But his voice was not heard.

On the eve of the referendum one commentator in *The Irish Times* asked: 'What will we find to talk about when the referendum is over?' He concluded: 'Nothing. By the time it is over most of us won't be talking to each other.'

After months of raw emotionalism pitting family against family, woman against woman and politician against politician, one and a quarter million people went to the polling booths on 7 September 1983 and registered their votes. When the ballot papers were counted, 841,233 voted 'Yes' to the amendment and 416,136 voted 'No'. On an election day turn-out of 54 per cent, the motion was carried by a 66.9 per cent majority. 35.79 per cent of the electorate had voted for the Amendment, 17.6 had voted against it and 46.61 per cent had not voted at all.

Feminist groups said, with dismay, that they felt many women had fallen back on what they called 'an Irish solution to an Irish problem' – voting against abortion in Ireland, knowing full well that they could still legally obtain one in England.

According to Dr Michael Solomons, one of Dublin's leading gynaecologists and an active member of the Anti-Amendment Campaign, the country had been duped by the Pro-Life Campaign into believing that the referendum would change nothing. He wrote:

> Nevertheless, it has [since] been used as a campaigning tool to shut down women's counselling services, to censor women's magazines, to get women's health books removed from public libraries and to ensure that newspapers containing abortion information are seized at airports and destroyed.
>
> We drift through uncharted waters. As a nation we find ourselves looking to our legislators and lawyers for a solution. The flabby, imprecise and dangerous wording of the Eighth Amendment had proven to be precisely that.

The *Irish Independent* newspaper, in an editorial during the 'X' controversy, reflected back on what happened after the 1983 referendum:

> Widespread misgivings about the possibility of this kind of outcome were in the end ignored by the people in a ratio of two-to-one.
>
> The politicians themselves, coerced by pressure groups and fearful of the electoral outcome if they resisted such pressures, were then further handicapped by inter-party rivalry which pre-empted an agreed wording and led to the inflexibility of the amendment as we now have it.
>
> Nor was this all. Having behaved fearfully and having muddled the details of constitutional change, the three subsequent administrations, involving both sides of the political divide and all significant political views, failed to give any legislative framework to the wording of the change.
>
> This has left us governed by an amendment and the views on it of the Attorney General and the judiciary. This is a shameful outcome to an extremist view of when life begins, how it should be protected, and who should suffer in the process.

Those in the disbanded PLAC (later to re-emerge in 1992 as the Pro-Life Campaign) disagreed. One senior member said: 'The Irish are a very political people – we actually revel in it – and this issue took precedence over everything else for a while. This was as it should be and entirely justified, because there is hardly another subject more eminently worth debating. People were forced to address the issue and look into their own hearts on the abortion question for the first time.

'If the arguments were divisive that was simply a reflection of the fundamental character of the issues that it raised. It was not an episode that any of us in the campaign would feel other than extremely proud about.'

FIVE

To feminists and those supporting women's rights, the passing of the Eighth Amendment had simply served to reinforce the historically inferior position of women in Irish society.

Long before the 1937 Constitution (in which the index's listing for 'Women' says 'See Family; Sex') spoke of women's role as 'a life within the home ... [where] mothers shall not be obliged by economic necessity to engage in labour to the neglect of their duties in the home', the concept of woman as mother and servant had fully established itself in the Irish male psyche.

The Roman Catholic Church forbade the use of contraception which, it said, killed love and was an insult to God. It suggested instead the rhythm method (where sex was only permitted within roughly defined periods when, it was hoped, the woman was not ovulating) or two other methods involving monitoring body temperature or measuring cervical mucus. In practice this meant that families often had twelve or more children and the partially contraceptive side-effects of breast-feeding offered the only respite for women between pregnancies until menopause or death.

In July 1966 the President of the Irish Medical Association, a consultant gynaecologist, wrote of 'the horrifying numbers of young married women being driven into nervous exhaustion and insanity by continual pregnancies'.

Ireland's birth rate was, and remained in the early 1990s, the highest in Europe. It still had 15 births per 1,000 citizens, amounting to 52,000 annual births, nearly 17 per cent of which are outside marriage. Some seven hundred babies were each year offered up for adoption and an estimated 8 per cent of all

Irish pregnancies ended in abortion (compared with 19 per cent of British ones), although this figure in Ireland was notoriously hard to calculate.

Approximately 30 per cent of its 3.5 million citizens were under the age of fourteen, compared to the UK's 19 per cent, and almost half were under twenty-five. In this climate, unwanted pregnancies had long been a fact of life, and a variety of noxious herbal remedies and inter-uterine devices were regularly used with often disastrous results.

Not only did generations of women throw themselves down stairs, drink gin and soak in boiling hot baths, they used iron hooks, coat hangers and took drugs and other poisons in an attempt to abort their babies. Back-street abortions were rife, often undertaken by inexperienced midwives for a few coins and resulting in the death or disablement of the mother. Those who could not face that prospect bore their children and then smothered them or disposed of them by some other means, claiming that they had died in childbirth.

As far back as the seventh century, in the Irish Penitential of St Finnian, the punishments for such actions were strict: 'If a woman by her magic destroys the child she has conceived of somebody, she shall do penance for half a year with an allowance of bread and water, and abstain for two years from wine and meat and fast for the six forty-day periods with bread and water.'

In 1929, according to an article in the *Cork Examiner*, a presiding judge in the district was quoted as saying: 'The number of newly-born infants in this country who were murdered by their mother at present surpassed belief. Only one out of fifty came up in the courts, but there was a wholesale slaughter of these innocents going on through the country.'

With the twentieth-century advent of women's liberation, the Church warned against 'the contraceptive morality' sweeping the world and reiterated its vehement stance against diminishing the status of the legitimate family. Contraception and abortion were viewed with loathing and suspicion as tools of the feminist lobby to undermine the male-dominated Church and State. Pope Paul VI set up a special commission to examine the widespread use of the contraceptive pill in the 1960s and Ireland waited anxiously for its report.

When it finally came out, in July 1968, it caused universal disappointment and anger. Called 'Humanae Vitae', the 36-page document said: 'The Church, calling men back to the observance of the norms of the natural law . . . teaches that every marriage act must remain open to the transmission of life.'

The commission had actually taken the view that the ban on contraception should be relaxed, but the Pope had disagreed and, believing they were mistaken, exerted his supreme authority as the Vicar of Christ and overruled its findings.

'Humanae Vitae' also absolutely condemned direct abortion, even in therapeutic cases, and sterilization, even temporary. 'Similarly excluded is any action which either before, at the moment of or after sexual intercourse, is specifically intended to prevent procreation, whether as an end or as a means,' it added.

The Irish bishops embraced the teachings as the inheritance of the Church's moral teachings and treated the rising world tide of contraception, abortion, divorce, and homosexuality as 'evils' to be banned from Ireland's shores.

With these strictures, women were forced to look at personal alternatives, regardless of the religious consequences. Few men chose to be sterilized (and few in Ireland still do). A vasectomy was regarded as akin to castration and a diminishing of masculinity in this staunchly male-dominated society. A thriving trade in contraceptive pills and diaphragms began secretly across the border from Northern Ireland or from Britain. Any sympathetic traveller was urged to fill his or her suitcase with condoms, caps and spermicidal jellies.

Former Prime Minister Garret FitzGerald commented several years later: 'The people of Ireland embraced contraception with all the fervour of the newly converted, disregarding as irrelevant to their lives the exhortations the Catholic Church authorities were required by Rome to address to them on this issue.'

As the national birth rate plummeted, the influences of television and then international cable television became an accepted part of Irish life, along with a trend for foreign travel. Open to these outside influences, the nation began to realize for the first time just how conservative and backward it was regarded as elsewhere in the world.

Partly out of fear of this gradual awakening of Ireland, the emotional backlash behind the campaign for the Eighth Amendment began. The anti-abortion lobby believed that the law needed to be fortified against this flood of immorality and free-thinking. It was further panicked into action by the setting up in Dublin of the Fertility Guidance Clinic, the first private organization in the history of Ireland to offer advice and help on contraception. Doctors who supported contraception were, it was seen, able to skirt around the laws by adopting non-controversial language to disguise the real reason for contraception. The pill, for instance, was widely prescribed for women with so-called 'period problems' who needed their 'cycles regulated'. By the 1970s there were an astonishing 50,000 Irish women with 'irregular cycles'.

Then in 1973, the case of *McGee* vs *Attorney General* set further historic precedents that rang alarm bells in the anti-abortion camp. A mother of four with a history of strokes, Mrs Mary McGee, a fisherman's wife from Skerries, Co. Dublin, had – with the blessing of her doctor – arranged for contraceptive items to be sent from England to avoid having further children. They were intercepted by customs and confiscated. She appealed to the High Court to get them back and lost. On appeal to the Supreme Court, the judges found in her favour and ruled that the State ban on the importation of contraceptives for personal use was unconstitutional, partly on the grounds that it breached the right to privacy.

As one commentator at the time put it: 'It chipped the first chunk of mortar out of the legal wall against contraception in Ireland.'

Further warnings were sounded later that year by the 1973 *Roe* vs *Wade* ruling in America which effectively legalized abortion on demand. A Texan woman who claimed to have been gang raped (but later admitted she got pregnant through consensual sex) wanted an abortion which was illegal in her state. She had no money to travel to another state and was forced to have her baby. Challenging the law in the Supreme Court anyway, she successfully claimed that as part of her constitutional fundamental right to privacy, a woman has the right to terminate her pregnancy.

The Washington DC court declared, by seven votes to two, that the Texan abortion ban (save when it was necessary to spare the mother's life) was unconstitutional. It further stated that any law which banned abortion to protect the foetus within the first seven months of pregnancy was unconstitutional. The ruling radically changed the laws of almost every American state and was hailed as a victory for women. Those opposed to abortion could hardly believe that the court had allowed what they regarded as the wholesale slaughter of innocents up to seven months old. They vowed then to wage a war against abortion, which has not enjoyed a cease-fire since.

The woman involved in the case – known only as Jane Roe in court – later had her child and gave it up for adoption. In 1980 she went public and revealed her identity as Ms Norma McCorvey, a bisexual cleaning lady.

The mood of liberalization engendered by the *Roe* vs *Wade* decision was slowly seeping into Ireland. Five years later, in 1979, a small group of feminist women formed the Women's Right to Choose movement, set on de-criminalizing abortion in Ireland once and for all. Setting up the first Irish Pregnancy Counselling Service in Dublin the following year, the group held a series of public meetings which attracted much attention.

At one of these gatherings, in 1981, a woman on the rostrum, Mary Holland, was treated with great hostility when she admitted to having had an abortion. Incensed by the heckling, a woman at the back of the hall, Ruth Riddick, jumped up and said she had never known an Irish man take responsibility for contraception. She became the second Irishwoman to admit publicly to having had an abortion. There have been very few since.

Miss Riddick, a journalist on women's issues, was never able to return to the back row. From that moment on, she remained at the centre of the Irish pro-choice movement, founding Open Line Counselling and becoming a leading light within the Irish Family Planning Association and the Well Woman Centre.

Open Line (later Open Door) was eventually banned from operation by both a High Court and Supreme Court judgement (1986 and 1988), which claimed that even to provide information about abortion in Ireland was unlawful and contrary to the unborn's right to life. (That decision was eventually overturned by the European Court of Human Rights in October 1992, although the service remained closed because it had never been legally approved in Ireland.)

Miss Riddick, aged thirty-eight, an international lecturer in women's studies based at Trinity College, Dublin, saw the 'X' case as a calamity for those involved, but realized that it could become the test case that was needed to break the deadlock. 'It was the first time that a human face had been put on abortion in this country, something which we had been actively trying to do prior to that. When I first stepped forward people just said: "Oh well, she's not typical, because she went public." I was considered immoral and was trapped in a vicious circle.

'But this little girl "X" was someone who everybody identified and sympathized with. People on the streets, in the buses, in the taxis were all saying: "If she was my daughter I would have had her on the first plane to England," or "I would never have brought her back in the first place." It was the first time ever in this country that people were openly saying that there might be circumstances in which abortion would be proper. It was a huge breakthrough.

'When the history of the abortion rights struggle in Ireland comes to be written, 1992 will emerge as a year of unprecedented change,' she added. 'Activists hardly expected so much progress in such a short time.'

Miss Riddick had realized the need for such progress twelve years earlier. Aged twenty-five and in a London nursing home overnight before having her abortion, she found herself reading from a feminist book to a small gathering of Irish women there – including a distraught mother who had accompanied her young daughter.

'I was quite calm about what I had to do and I suddenly found myself as an unofficial counsellor to these poor souls who had hardly spoken to anyone about what was happening to them,' she said.

The need for counselling has not in any way diminished, she believes, although because of the social taboo placed on abortion in Ireland, few women actively seek to discuss it. 'We need to lift the stigma attached to the whole issue of unwanted pregnancy, whether by rape or not. "X" started to very slowly lift that terrible burden.'

Another woman who came to the feminist fore as a result of the Irish abortion issue was Maxine Brady, a single mother from Northern Ireland and former President of the Union of Students in Ireland. Asked to speak to students in England about the Irish experience as a result of the Amendment, she was appalled to learn how widespread the problem was and took up what turned out to be an extended career in the front line of the Irish abortion debate.

She discovered that the amendment had led to a massive increase in the long-standing 'abortion tourism' to Britain, with hundreds of panic-stricken women crossing the Irish Sea by ferry to Liverpool (or flying to London) to get rid of their unwanted babies. Known uncontroversially among Irish women as 'taking the boat', the journey across the choppy waters of the Irish Sea was the only possible answer for thousands of women.

By 1992 their number was an estimated thirteen a day. Of the 1,162 women who had abortions in the first three months of that year, 206 were teenagers, 807 were aged between twenty and thirty-four and the remainder in the thirty-five-plus age bracket.

It was not a new phenomenon historically. Women all over the world had travelled extensively to circumvent abortion restrictions in their own society. British women used to travel to France, French and Spanish women later went to Britain, German and Belgian women went to Holland, and even American women travelled to Britain for abortions.

In 1981 (when abortion was still illegal in Portugal and Belgium as well as Ireland) the problem had become so widespread that the European Parliament had debated it. It noted:

The relevant legislation in member states varies so widely that women in distress frequently have to seek help in other countries. The Parliament requests the Commission to press the Council for decisions at national level such as to obviate the need for journeys of this type which make any form of social aid impossible and lead to unacceptable commercialisation, and to ensure that every woman who finds herself in this difficulty can obtain the necessary assistance in her own country.

('The Position of Women in the European Community', European Parliamentary Debate, Luxembourg, June 1981)

An estimated one hundred Irish women a week travelled by boat or plane to England to have abortions. Some estimates put it as high as 7,000 a year – more than 130 a week – but exact figures are difficult to pin down because few of the women registered their true details or reasons for travelling.

Business had been brisk in Liverpool for many years. It was the first-choice city for Irish women seeking abortions in Britain. Crewmen on the Sealink ferry from Dun Laoghaire, the bustling port seven miles south of Dublin, had long come to accept the dozens of pale, nauseous young women who caught the dawn crossings across the Irish Sea to be in Liverpool in time for their 9.00 a.m. appointments. They cynically referred to those on their way back to Ireland as 'empties', but said they were happier to see their relieved expressions and the colour returned to their cheeks.

'When they were on their way to the clinics, they usually sat alone looking pathetic and scared,' said one senior crew woman. 'But you saw the same girls on the way back and they had generally latched on to a mate, someone they met at the clinic going through the same thing, and with whom to share their relief that it was all over.'

Sympathetic proprietors of Merseyside hotels and guest houses operated a cheap taxi service from the ferry port to the hotel, to the clinics and back again. Their rooms were simply furnished and cheap. Few details were taken and no questions asked. Evening meals (rarely wanted) were taken at nearby cafés. Breakfast was offered but rarely accepted by those told not to eat anything on the morning before they were given the anaesthetic. Plastic buckets were provided for those suffering from morning sickness or for shredded literature relating to their clinic appointment or their hotel stay.

The proprietors understood that most of the women had to lie to their friends and family about why they had gone away for two to three days. They helpfully provided basic tourist information about the city the women would not have the time or inclination to see, so that if questioned back home by family members about their 'holiday' they would not slip up. Some even offered souvenirs to take home as gifts from their purported 'shopping trips'. The women accepted their help gratefully and retired to their rooms to count the cash they had generally borrowed from a friend or relative to pay for the operation and which had to be paid in advance at the door.

At the clinics, like that run by the British Pregnancy Advisory Service in an inconspicuous Victorian town house in the centre of Liverpool, hundreds of Irish women passed through the door, ranging in age from eleven to fifty-eight. Some were not even pregnant, but had convinced themselves that they were. Living in rural communities with only a single chemist and everyone knowing everyone's business, they were often too afraid to ask for a pregnancy tester kit or to approach their GP.

After an initial chat with a counsellor about what they wanted to happen and why, those women who were pregnant were registered, paid their fee (about £500 sterling) and were shown to a ward where they put on their nightwear, slippers and a dressing gown. A nurse would check their details and explain to them the 'treatment' they would be receiving. The foetus would be referred to unambiguously as 'tissue' or 'the contents of the womb', which would be removed vaginally. The women would be told that they would be having a light anaesthetic and should not feel any pain.

If they were further advanced in pregnancy the operation would be more complicated and involve a form of induced labour under sedation, which could last for some twelve hours. They would then have to stay at the clinic for two to three days and undergo a further examination under general anaesthetic to 'make sure that the abortion was complete'.

The literature on the procedure offered by the British Pregnancy Advisory Service added: 'Many women feel tearful and upset after abortion: this is a natural hormonal and emotional response to the stress of unplanned pregnancy and rarely lasts long.' It warned of cramps and heavy bleeding after the operation and of the risk of infection if antibiotics given at the clinic were not taken. Patients would be advised to see a doctor immediately there were any problems, an instruction which many Irish women would have felt almost impossible to carry out because of the secrecy of their visit.

Post-operative checks would be advised six weeks after the operation, which could be carried out by medical staff at the Irish Family Planning Association, or by a list of some one hundred 'sympathetic' GPs throughout Ireland.

Women would be advised that in some instances there was a slight chance that the surgeon could 'miss the pregnancy at operation' and they could require a repeat abortion – an unpleasant prospect for any woman, particularly those coming from another country. The leaflet added: 'This will be carried out free of charge.'

The added burden of the silence and secrecy surrounding an abortion for an Irish woman was rarely considered. Those who had already had to borrow money secretly, lie about their absence from home for three days, and then cope with their roller-coaster emotions over the abortion itself, were then often unable to air their feelings with anyone.

'The effect of the silence for many women is anger,' said Ruth Fletcher, who did an MA in Women's Studies and wrote a thesis on the issue. 'What happened to them was part of their life experience, a major event, and they resented having to be silent about it. There is a great need to protect yourself in Irish society. The image of abortion is such that individuals associated with it would be perceived very negatively. There is also potential material and emotional rejection. There are fears that you might lose your job, that you would be condemned at every level.'

One woman called Sue who gave Ms Fletcher an interview for her thesis, said: 'I couldn't tell my family, so trying to act normal at home was an extra burden and very stressful.'

Another woman, Eilis, a mother of six, was told by the abortion clinic that whilst performing the termination, they had discovered a growth in her womb and they urged her to see her own doctor about it. 'I was too frightened to go to an Irish doctor and say I had had an abortion, and it was only when I could actually feel the growth that I went. I was in hospital and had a hysterectomy the next day.'

Those who worked at the clinics were also under considerable duress. They frequently had to run the gauntlet of anti-abortion venom and some feared for their lives. Slogans were often daubed on the walls and doors, and one Merseyside clinic had to employ security guards after several members of staff had their car tyres slashed and engines interfered with.

The staff argued that they were only fulfilling a vital need and were happy to be able to assist thousands of Irish women in crisis pregnancies. Their critics accused them of being baby murderers and the word 'genocide' was the most commonly used in the painted slogans.

One leading pro-life campaigner in Dublin said that although the movement had initially rejected 'graphic' descriptions of abortion being used in campaign literature and on posters, by 1992 it was beginning to change its mind. 'Most people don't even like to think about what actually happens to the foetus, they just call for choice and close their minds to the reality. If we haven't changed their minds by talking about the philosophical rights to life, then perhaps we should start showing them pictures of abortion aftermaths, and see what they think then.'

Whether people opposed or defended the abortion issue, the seeming hypocrisy of the Irish abortion traffic attracted particular criticism as the last of its kind within the EC in the 1990s. Irish feminist Ailbhe Smyth said at the time: 'Britain has become a vast laundry for the human dirty linen that Irish morality refuses to handle . . . to conserve the moral "purity" of Ireland, bastion of conservative Catholicism in the Western world.'

It was in this climate that Maxine Brady believed that if she and her fellow students could not persuade Ireland to have its own abortion clinics then it should at least help set up a service providing information about abortions in England. The students also raised funds to help poorer women who could not raise the money needed to pay for the abortion and incumbent costs.

Under a separate scheme called Escort, volunteer students in Liverpool arranged to meet women at the airport, station or ferry terminus and stay with them until the abortion was over. The service continued to operate, even after the closing down of the main ferry link between Dublin and Liverpool, and because of it many Irish women continued to go to Liverpool (taking the boat to Holyhead and going on by train) because they felt welcomed there. For those who went to London, the Irish Women's Abortion Support Group offered much the same service.

When Miss Brady got pregnant at the age of twenty and decided to keep her child, those who had accused her of being an arch advocate of baby murder no longer had a leg to stand on. At this time she and her organization were being pursued in the courts by the Society for the Protection of the Unborn Child and the then Attorney General for unlawfully providing information on abortions. 'I was not entirely happy about my pregnancy and it was not something I wanted to publicize, so until it started to show I kept it very quiet,' she said. 'But when I was eight months pregnant touring the country and telling students a few years younger than me that it could happen to them and that if it did they should be allowed to choose what was best for them, it made for a pretty strong impact. I was effectively saying that I didn't approve of abortion personally, and I had chosen not to have one myself, but that everyone should have the fundamental right of freedom of choice. I like to think it did a great deal of harm to the anti-abortion movement.'

She eventually won the right to give out abortion information, although British magazines and newspapers offering abortion clinic information continued to arrive in the Republic with blank spaces where the adverts should have been.

Undeterred, Miss Brady toured the country's colleges and universities, offering advice and information to young women and speaking about choice. She first read about the 'X' case at a railway station in Galway as she was on her way back from a rally. 'I just couldn't believe what I was reading. It was a real shock,' she recalled. 'But to be honest, we could not have asked for a better case, which is partly why we have been accused of setting it up. This case was watertight – she was fourteen, she had been abused, she came from a good Catholic family and she had done everything legally.

'I would love to shake that girl's hand and give her a big hug and tell her that if it wasn't for her we wouldn't be where we are today, but that is an awful sacrifice for a 14-year-old girl to have had to make.'

After retiring from the union, Miss Brady sought work as a freelance writer on feminist issues, but discovered that to many she was regarded as unemployable. 'I think some people just thought: "She is that Chief Abortionist, we don't want her." That was grossly unfair and very soul-destroying because apart from anything else I never actually had an abortion, I chose not to. But that is what I have always been up against in this country.

'I refused to drop out of the struggle for women's rights, but it completely took over my life for many years and I decided I wanted some more time to spend with my child and lead a relatively normal life for a while.'

Spat at by a woman on a bus at the end of 1992, she regularly ran into public demonstrations of disgust about her activities and opinions. Tempted occasionally to alter her distinctive platinum blonde looks and give up the fight, she said she changes her mind each time she looks at her own five-year-old daughter and imagines her life in Ireland or her dilemma as a possible future Miss 'X'.

'I look at her and I think of what she might come up against in similar circumstances and that is when I know I shall have to keep fighting, whatever the cost.'

SIX

As 'X' continued to be treated in hospital for morning sickness, dehydration and trauma, the much-awaited full High Court hearing marking the next stage in the legal conflict began.

Behind closed doors, Mr Justice Declan Costello – who had granted the initial injunction which forced the girl and her family to return from London – began hearing evidence in full on Monday, 17 February from those representing the family and the State.

Described by some as the 'shy man of the bench', Mr Justice Costello was born in Dublin in 1926, the son of John A. Costello, twice Prime Minister of the country. He followed in his father's footsteps and entered politics early, becoming a member of the Fine Gael party in 1951 and being largely responsible for the publication of a party discussion document 'Towards a Just Society'. It was criticized by some as being 'social democratic Catholicism', but it none the less attracted new blood to the party with its talk of better treatment for the under-privileged. But it is thought it may have also played a part in preventing Mr Costello from becoming party leader and he later turned his back on live politics and entered the world of law, becoming Attorney General in the Fine Gael/Labour coalition.

He set up the Law Reform Commission and appointed the first independent Director of Public Prosecutions. In 1976 he resigned and took a seat on the High Court bench, much to the dismay of many who considered him a great loss to politics. In 1979 he headed an official enquiry into a tanker disaster in Bantry Bay which had killed fifty people. His report was seen as an indication of his personal certainty and attracted widespread admiration as a model of thorough research. President of the Irish Legal History Society, he once commented that the law of the Constitution should not be an arcane subject fit only for discussion amongst those who initiated it.

A 66-year-old father of five, he was considered to be very much a traditional, conservative Catholic, renowned for his honesty and integrity.

The application by counsel for the Attorney General was that he should restrain 'X' and her parents from interfering with the right to life of the unborn; restrain her from leaving Ireland for the duration of her pregnancy; and restrain them from procuring or arranging an abortion in or out of Ireland. The judge listened carefully to the arguments on the girl's right to travel as a free citizen, and then asked to hear oral evidence from the psychologist who had interviewed her.

This move seemed to be somewhat unexpected by counsel for the Attorney General, who had expected to win the argument on the travel issue alone. They had not prepared any counter-claim by any other psychologist and, indeed, had not even arranged for the girl to be seen by any other doctor.

Neither the girl's family doctor, who had attended to her from the outset, her obstetrician at the Rotunda, nor any number of other doctors or counsellors at the hospital who had seen her, had been asked to give evidence in court about her mental state. It never became public knowledge whether they had been interviewed at any stage by the legal team representing the girl and her parents in preparation for such an eventuality, or whether the same team had simply decided not to call them or inform the judge of the nature of the evidence they could give.

Because the travel issue alone was thought to be the key issue, the unexpected request by the judge appeared to have caught all those present by surprise, although Mr Rogers was in the best placed position with a witness advocating his case ready and willing to give evidence.

The fact that the judge was going to hear one statement from one psychologist who, on his own admission, had spent a matter of only a few hours with the girl was to become a matter of some contention later.

Some wondered whether counsel for the Attorney General had foreseen this possibility or prepared any counter evidence. In any event, he did not seek an adjournment at this point to enable another doctor to see the girl in hospital and give his assessment. The psychologist for the family had been sitting outside the court and was summoned into the witness box. As the girl's parents sat listening at the back of the court, he restated his concern for their child. He said that by ending her life the girl believed that she would end the problems through which she was putting her parents, 'with whom she had a very strong and loving relationship'.

In the course of replies to questions during the High Court hearing, he stated: 'I was asked to see her with one specific question to be answered – what was her emotional state given the recent events? My assessment was on that alone.'

He said that he found the child strangely distanced from her emotions. She did not seem depressed, but almost 'calculatingly rational' about her condition. 'This is what disturbed me most of all, that she was able to talk about not wishing to put her parents through more of this. She was in crisis, but I don't think she realized the full emotional impact of that. Currently the pregnancy for her is "a pain". A pain is all she is aware of. If she was aware of more she might become panicky about the situation she was in.

'She did not state an intention of how she would do it [suicide]. Simply I concluded it. That is why I used the term "clearly to me ending her life might end her parents' problems".' He said that throwing herself down the stairs would be 'one of the kinds of behaviour' he could have seen as a risk with this girl.

In the final sentence of his report on her, he wrote: 'There is no doubt in my mind the damage of this pregnancy to her mental health is going to be devastating.' Asked to elaborate in court, he said: 'It is all hypothetical at present. I am willing to stand over my statement. This girl is going through a traumatic episode and the pregnancy will involve further trauma which will do permanent damage to her state. For example, there is a high level of guilt and confusion within the child. That wonderment . . . that confusion is going to persist and this is going to go on and on and, even after, there is no real end to the concern . . . this kind of concern is something we must bear in mind in the case of this girl.'

He said her state, as he saw it, suggested that she was going to go through this kind of distress for years to come. When asked if the girl had a good relationship with her parents, he replied: 'Yes, and one of the things she said, perhaps three times, was, "I don't know why I kept it to myself so long. I should have told them more." In the same context, she said, "I should not be putting them through this, I cannot be putting them through this . . . I cannot put them through more. I have put them through enough."'

He was asked what effect he thought not having the abortion would have on her. 'I believe we are in a dilemma whatever happens to this child now. It is a question of minimizing the damage. It was my belief minimizing it would be best achieved by minimizing the episode, by putting some certainty into her life.'

Asked what effect that uncertainty had to the girl's mental stability, he replied: 'She seems to be a bright child – I did not do any testing to confirm this – but she seemed also to be under-achieving. I felt she has potential and that is going to suffer. She herself is only too aware she is going to miss a year, be kept down in school and be harmed socially as a result, as well as academically.'

Asked about his experience of such cases, the psychologist said that in the past two years he had come across seven girls under seventeen who were pregnant. Two of the pregnancies were as a result of incest, one as the result of rape by an uncle and three through under-age sex with boyfriends. Of those, two had the babies and put them up for adoption, two had abortions and he did not know what happened to the other three.

He had never before come across an under-age girl who said she would destroy herself because she had become pregnant in this way. Asked how he would describe the girl's physical and psychological well-being, he said: 'I saw her probably at her weakest. She had been vomiting for four days and had not kept food down. She was in pain. I was concerned about her physical state and was relieved when told by her parents that she had been admitted to the hospital and placed in a situation where she could be fed. She was pale, wan and weak-looking.'

Asked if it was his professional view that she would destroy herself if matters continued as they were, he replied: 'I would not have taken it upon myself to leave that girl alone in the state I saw her in . . . I did feel she would pose a risk if I left her on her own.'

'How would she be at risk?' asked the counsel for the girl and her family.

'It depends how long we protract this trauma for her.'

'Do I take it therefore that she in effect would commit suicide if there was not a termination or abortion?'

'I feel she might commit suicide or decide to terminate it herself by throwing herself down the stairs or something like that. That is the kind of thing which happened in previous cases I dealt with where girls attempt to gain abortion.'

'Is that more prevalent when pregnancy is just confirmed, or might it lessen if the matter is not ended?'

'It often increases because you can feel the kicking of the child inside you and you perhaps become more aware of the pregnancy. At present there are no physical symptoms. The child just feels pain.'

Under cross-examination from Mr James O'Reilly, counsel for the Attorney General, however, the psychologist admitted that he could not say for certain that the girl was planning suicide, no matter how distressed she seemed. Mr O'Reilly sought to distinguish between the certainty of suicide and the possibility of suicide. The psychologist answered that one could never say for certain that someone will definitely commit suicide no matter how distressed they seemed. The only proof is the attempt itself, or death.

On the strength of this evidence, which he said was not proof of 'certainty', Mr Justice Costello ruled that the girl's life was not sufficiently in danger to allow the abortion. The risk to her life was, he said, 'of a lesser magnitude' than the certainty of the death of the foetus.

He said that once the Attorney General had been informed of the family's intention to seek an abortion, he had been constitutionally bound to protect the right to life of the foetus, regardless of the fact that successive governments since the 1983 amendment had failed to do any more to clarify the law as it stood. He also said the girl's right to travel as a free citizen was lawfully halted because of what she and her family had told police they intended to do. And he ruled that European law did not have any jurisdiction on the matter because it had accepted that differences in moral attitudes between member states could occur.

In many ways his decision was indeed an entirely logical consequence of the process which had started nine years before with the Eighth Amendment. That Amendment had been challenged unsuccessfully by pro-choicers who had been offering information and counselling services to women seeking abortions.

Despite later suggestions from the EC that the implications of the Amendment might be in direct breach of Community law, the pattern had been set for the Irish judiciary's interpretation of what the Constitution now meant. And Mr Justice Costello saw no legal reason to alter that pattern.

The judge could have been in no doubt of the sad history of the case and the impact it had on the girl and her family. He spelled it out in grim detail in his seventeen-page judgement, which took over forty-five minutes to deliver and which was later made public because of its national importance.

In it, he said the events which gave rise to the court hearing were 'painful and distressing and have resulted in tragedy and a great measure of human suffering'. He said the girl was now fourteen and a half years old and had a schoolfriend whom she visited regularly. Her friend's parents and her parents were also on friendly terms. 'Her parents had no idea that in letting their daughter visit her friend's house she was being placed in physical and in moral danger,' he said. Adding a sentence which was later to be used by the accused to try to avoid his criminal trial, the judge said: 'Her statement disclosed that her friend's father is a depraved and evil man . . . who began sexually molesting her when she was less than thirteen years old.'

He went on: 'Over the months in which it occurred, this molestation was continuous and took different forms. In June 1990 abuse of a serious nature took place and this occurred again in the early part of 1991. In December 1991 . . . he had full sexual intercourse with her to which she did not consent. As a result she became pregnant. She did not tell anyone of the abuse to which she was being subjected on her visits to her friend's home, but on the 27 January last she told her parents everything that had happened. On that day, following mounting worry and concern by her mother, she and her parents learned from their local doctor that she was pregnant.

'Faced with a most difficult and harrowing decision and after discussing the tragic situation amongst themselves, both the parents and their daughter came to the conclusion that the best course to adopt was to go to England for the abortion.'

He described the application made by the girl's parents to the police to find out whether or not DNA testing on the foetus would be admissible as evidence of the identity of the father. He said the parents were distressed to hear that it was not thought to be legally admissible.

The family went to England for the abortion, he said, but returned when they discovered that an injunction against them had been granted. 'When the [girl] learned that she was pregnant, she naturally was greatly distraught and upset. Later she confided in her mother that when she learned she was pregnant she had wanted to kill herself. On the journey back from London she told her mother that she had wanted to throw herself under a train when in London and that, as she had put her parents through so much trouble, she would rather be dead than continue as she was.

'On the 31 January 1992, in the course of a long discussion with a member of the Garda Siochana she said: "I wish it were all over. Sometimes I feel like throwing myself downstairs." On the day of her return from London the [girl's] parents brought her to a very experienced clinical psychologist. He explained in his report that he had been asked to assess her emotional state; that whilst she was co-operative she was emotionally withdrawn, that he had concluded that she was in a state of shock and had lost touch with her feelings.

'She did not seem depressed, but he said that she "coldly expressed a desire to solve matters by ending her life". In his opinion, in her withdrawn state, "she was capable of such an act, not so much because she is depressed but because she could calculatingly reach the conclusion that death is the best solution".

'He explained that in the course of his consultation with the girl, she had said to him: "It is hard at fourteen to go through the nine months . . . It is better to end it now than in nine months' time." The psychologist understood this to mean that by ending her life she would end the problems through which she was putting her parents, with whom she has a very strong and loving relationship.'

Reviewing the legal involvement in the case, the judge said that acting as required by Irish law and the Chief Justice, the Attorney General had carried out his duty in seeking a High

Court injunction to 'vindicate and defend the right to life of the unborn'. He said the application came before him properly and he had granted an injunction on 6 February, the Thursday the girl and her family left Ireland for London.

The temporary order was granted until Monday, 10 February, when he agreed to hear the trial of the action and was requested to hear it behind closed doors, or in camera.

'As the [girl] was a minor and the distress from which she was suffering would have been immeasurably increased had her name become known and the facts of the case given publicity, I concluded that in her interests I should accede to the request,' he said. He was aware of the 'need to dispose of the case at the earliest possible time' and gave the applicants permission to treat the motion as the trial of the action, with leave to call oral evidence.

The judge said that four key legal issues had to be addressed. The first was the application by the girl's family that the Oireachtas or Irish Parliament – although acknowledging the right to life of the unborn in the Eighth Amendment to the Constitution Act 1983, approved by the people in a referendum – had not enacted any law which reconciled the right to life of the unborn with the right to life of the mother.

On this basis, counsel for the girl argued that the court could not make an order in a case in which an issue of reconciliation arose. The judge disagreed that this submission was well founded and said there had been hundreds of cases in which the courts had carried out their constitutional duty, even though no law had been enacted regulating the manner in which it is to be done. 'The right acknowledged in the Eighth Amendment is clear and unambiguous and the court's duty to protect it is imperative,' he said, in a statement which was later to prove patently unclear.

He added that it was explained by the Chief Justice in the case of the Attorney General (acting for the *Society for the Protection of the Unborn Child* vs *Open Door Counselling* [1988]), in which he had said: 'If it is established to the satisfaction of the court that the admitted activities of the defendants constitute an assistance to pregnant women within the jurisdiction to go out of the jurisdiction for the purpose of having an abortion, then that is an activity which directly threatens the right to life of the unborn, not only in a single case but in all cases of women who are assisted by those activities to have an abortion.'

The judge said that if a court learns of a situation in which the life of the unborn is threatened then it would be failing in its constitutional duty to protect it merely because Parliament had failed to legislate on how it was to have regard to the equal right to life of the mother.

'Complicated and difficult issues of fact may, of course, arise in individual cases, but that does not inhibit the court from applying the clear rule of law laid down in the amendment,' he said.

The second key issue arose from the mother's right to life acknowledged by the Eighth Amendment. The defendants claimed that there was a 'very real danger' that the girl would take her own life if the order were made and she was unable to procure an abortion.

The judge said: 'This is a case in which the risk to the mother's life comes from herself. What the court is asked to do is not to make an order, because if it did the mother may take her own life. I think that in a case such as this, involving a young girl in a highly distressing and deeply disturbing situation, the court has a duty to protect her life, not just from the actions of others but from actions she may herself perform.'

He said the court had to assess the dangers to the life of the unborn and to that of the mother. There was 'a real and immi-nent' danger to the unborn, whose life would be terminated, but a 'risk' only that the girl would take her own life. 'The risk . . . is much less and is of a different order of magnitude than the certainty that the life of the unborn will be terminated if the order is not made,' he said. 'I am strengthened in this view by the knowledge that the young girl has the benefit of the love and care and support of devoted parents who will help her through the difficult months ahead.' In those circumstances, he said, the court's duty was to make the order sought.

The third legal issue, he said, related to the girl's right to liberty, contained in Article 40, section 4 of the Constitution which provides that no citizen shall be deprived of his personal liberty save in accordance with the law. The judge said: 'If a constitutional right is being abused by exercising it to commit a wrong . . . then the court may restrain the wrongful act even though this may involve the curtailment of the exercise of a constitutional right.'

The fourth and final issue Judge Costello felt that he had to address related to European Community law. He said: 'Our courts must enforce Community law; and if that law conflicts with Irish law, including Irish constitutional law, then Community law will prevail.

'It is submitted on the defendant's behalf that a right to travel abroad to obtain an abortion is conferred on the defendant by Community law and if this is so then notwithstanding the provisions of the Constitution and the Eighth Amendment, the court cannot grant an injunction to stop her.'

He added: 'I can find no provision or principle of Community law which would prohibit the exercise of the discretionary power to derogate in the manner contained in the Eighth Amendment. On the contrary, Community law already recognizes that within the Community wide cultural differences exist and has permitted derogations to flow from such differences. I can see no reason why it should refuse to do so when the derogation by a member state arises because of deeply held convictions on moral issues.

'Indeed, I think the attainment of the fundamental objectives of the Treaty [of Rome] is enhanced by laws which assist in the development of a Community in which legitimate differences on moral issues are recognized and which does not seek to impose a spurious and divisive uniformity on its members on such issues.'

Judge Costello concluded: 'The aim of the Eighth Amendment was to ensure that the right to life of the unborn is adequately protected. I do not think that a measure which empowers a court to stop a woman going abroad to terminate the life of the unborn is disproportionate to . . . that aim.'

Granting the orders sought by the Attorney General, he said that unless he did so the protection offered by the Irish Constitution to a foetus would be worthless.

The girl's parents left the court bewildered. The mother broke down in the corridor outside and wept openly when she was told that the ruling meant her daughter could not have an abortion after all. Their lawyers took them into a side room and explained that it might not be the end of the matter, if they were prepared to take the case to the Supreme Court. But they would have to move quickly, before the girl's pregnancy became so advanced that an abortion would be difficult, and before her mental state deteriorated so far that she would never recover.

Already dazed by the formidable legal system stacked against them, the parents asked if they could go home and talk to their daughter and see what she would like them to do.

They wandered through the Round Hall of Dublin's Four Courts building and walked out into the cold February afternoon, the River Liffey winding its way through the city before them. None of the people scurrying past them had any idea who they were or what they had just had to endure at the hands of their great legal system. With heavy hearts, they headed for home.

SEVEN

The decision of the High Court was published later that day and the public furore erupted. People took to the streets in their droves. There were demonstrations by campaigners for both sides. Old women, young men, children, mothers and fathers chanted, sang, clapped and stamped their indignation. Dublin's traffic police had to escort march after march down O'Connell Street, into St Stephen's Green and past Trinity College, their loud-hailers bellowing their views.

Thousands took part in a silent, candlelit march to Leinster House, the Parliament buildings, and festooned the railings with white ribbons on behalf of the girl and her family.

A group of several hundred stood outside the gates of the parliamentary debating chamber, the Dáil, chanting the telephone number of an abortion information line in between cries of 'Not the Church. Not the State. Women Must Decide their Fate.'

In a leaflet handed out to shoppers in O'Connell Street, Dublin's city centre, a message to the Attorney General said: 'Roman Catholic morality has no place in a Constitution.' Others said the crisis proved that Ireland was 'Rome-ruled'. One of the biggest banners read: 'Take Your Rosaries Off Her Ovaries.'

In Waterford in the south, thirty-seven teenage girls at the Sacred Heart of Mary Convent walked out of class to join fellow pupils from the city's Mercy Convent in a demonstration. They said they had 'made their stand for freedom of choice' because of their 'profound sympathy' for the girl. Their disobedience led to mass suspensions.

Newspapers published huge pull-out sections on the crisis. Television shows and radio programmes could talk of little else and there was world-wide discussion and input on the ruling. Ailbhe Smyth, a leading Irish feminist writer, described the mood at the time as 'Ireland riveted by its own barbarism'. Pro-abortionists and family planning associations condemned the ruling as 'a rapist's charter' in 'a moral police state' and claimed it represented a severe infringement of women's rights.

The Irish Family Planning Association said the State appeared more interested in 'protecting the procreative rights of rapists than with protecting the lives of their victims'. A spokesman added: 'Victims of rape now face a double ordeal which puts the credibility of Irish justice in doubt.' It was pointed out that as the accused man had not even been charged with any offence yet, although he was known to the police, he could effectively leave the country when his victim could not.

Senator Nuala Fennell, a former journalist, was in her eleventh year as a respected politician when the 'X' case first appeared in the press. A mother of three and a grandmother, Mrs Fennell, aged fifty-seven, was Minister of State for Women's Affairs from 1982–7, when she had witnessed at first hand the corrosive battle over abortion during the 1983 referendum. She had hoped that there would never be such bitterness of feeling amongst the people of Ireland again.

'As soon as I read about the "X" case in the papers, I went to the Dáil [Houses of Parliament] and tried to get the matter debated in the order of business. I went to see John Bruton, the then leader of my party, Fine Gael, and said, "This is a most serious case and one we should discuss," but his approach initially was "Forget it. We just don't touch the abortion issue."

'He was right, of course. Abortion was just about the most untouchable subject in Ireland and had a ripple effect throughout the country. Politician after politician had decided that they didn't want to grapple with it, but this case just wasn't going to go away and I think everyone was rather slow in realizing that.'

Mrs Fennell wrote a series of newspaper articles about the case, which was already beginning to generate enormous public debate, and was astonished by the strength of people's reaction. 'Anyone who thought this was just going to be one of those cases that would blow over quickly realized that they were quite mistaken. The plight of this girl had really captured the imagination in a most incredible way. People took to the streets and there was an overwhelming feeling that the case had to be resolved.

'Every woman who had previously thought they had individual liberty felt under threat and even the men were stopped in their tracks, when they related it to their own daughters, sisters, nieces or mothers. We were witnessing a revolution and nobody could quite believe it was happening in Ireland.'

In the Dáil, Deputy Monica Barnes requested a one-minute silence 'on behalf of the women of Ireland'. Her request was ruled out of order and one woman journalist present at the time, Mary Holland of *The Irish Times*, wrote: 'If ever there was a metaphor for society in which men control the structures of power and are determined to keep it that way, it was the Dáil . . . [where] there were nine women deputies in the chamber and row upon row of middle-aged men in suits.'

The Green Party said the court judgement erected 'a Berlin Wall around every Irishwoman of child bearing age'. John Bruton, leader of Fine Gael, said the ruling 'had created an atmosphere of trauma, fear and uncertainty and may lead both to a failure to report [rape] and a significantly greater incidence of abortion than would otherwise occur.'

The Teachers Union of Ireland urged its members to encourage pupils to speak immediately if they were abused, so that the 'morning after' contraceptive pill could be made available to them to save them from the same legal quagmire.

One woman, who identified herself only as Joanna, phoned in to a Dublin radio show and claimed she had been raped as 'a small skinny child' at the age of twelve and had an abortion in Liverpool. Offering to travel with Miss 'X' and her family if they went to England for the operation, the woman said it had been 'a huge relief' to be able to go away and get rid of the baby, rather than face a nine-month pregnancy.

'I did not want to have the baby,' she told presenter Marian Finucane. 'I was still going to school and my mother explained to me about abortion . . . so we got the boat over. I think a lot of people forget that young girl, as I was, is at school and has to carry the baby to full term for nine months. I was only a child. I had no idea what to do. I was making myself sick worrying about it. When I first discussed it [abortion] with my mother I realized there was a way out and it was an immense relief.'

Elsewhere, the strength of feeling was overwhelming. People who had voted against abortion in 1983 and who were still against it in principle, called for the girl to be allowed an abortion so that she could take her 'first faltering steps back towards sanity'. Commentators said she had been made a prisoner in her own country and should be freed from her suffering.

One cartoon by Martyn Turner in *The Irish Times* depicted a little girl holding a teddy bear standing in the middle of Ireland surrounded by a barbed-wire fence. The caption read: 'The introduction of internment in Ireland . . . for 14-year-old girls' (see picture section).

Mr Turner, a celebrated Dublin cartoonist, was later contacted by the family and told that his cartoon had been instrumental in their decision to keep on fighting. 'They said it made them realize that the whole country was behind them,' he said. The girl and her mother visited him at his home and the girl asked him to draw a caricature of her mother, which he willingly did. He also gave the girl the original of the internment cartoon to keep and thereafter asked for donations to the Rape Crisis Centre from anyone who wished to reproduce it.

'I was very touched by her visit and I felt it was the least I could do,' he said afterwards. 'I refused to make any money out of the cartoon, but I knew the Rape Crisis Centre could use the donations.'

Elsewhere in the press there was considerable confusion as to why the Attorney General had chosen to intervene in a manner which subjected this particular family to such distress and trauma, when thousands of other women had travelled unhindered to English abortion clinics in the past. Indeed, the numbers of Irish women travelling to England for abortions reached their highest levels ever in the first three months of 1992 as the legal furore continued. As many as 1,162 Irish women took the abortion trail to Britain. More than 17 per cent were aged under nineteen.

The Dublin Rape Crisis Centre said it had been approached by more than fifty women pregnant as a result of rape in 1990. Eight had abortions. What it described as the 'appalling implications' for these women caused widespread public concern.

The Workers Party called for the resignation of the Attorney General and several politicians strongly attacked his decision. Many groups expressed concern that the judgement would deter rape victims from reporting the attacks to police, because if they became pregnant, the authorities would have been alerted to their situation similarly and might prevent them from travelling to England too.

The case was what they called 'the nightmare scenario', warned about during the 1983 referendum on abortion, which had now come back to haunt those who voted for the pro-life amendment to the Constitution.

An editorial in the *Irish Independent* newspaper, headlined 'Tragedy of our times' said: 'The State created the rigid prison in which the family of the 14-year-old victim of alleged rape, together with the girl herself, have to suffer for being entirely innocent victims of sexual violence of the worst kind. And that prison is the Constitution, as amended by the people almost ten years ago.'

Foreign Affairs Minister and former barrister David Andrews expressed the views of many when he publicly questioned the

High Court's decision to restrict the movement of a citizen who had not committed an unlawful act in Ireland.

Opinion polls suggested a two-to-one majority in favour of a change in the abortion laws. The controversy was fuelled further by EC legal experts who said that if the next stage in the legal process – a hearing by the Supreme Court – failed to reach a decision and referred it to the European Court, a hearing could take up to four months, which would be too late for the girl to have an abortion. 'The specific case of this little girl must be sorted out in Ireland by the Irish courts,' said one EC lawyer. 'The only role the EC Court could have would be to prevent – or otherwise – such a situation occurring again.'

Demonstrations of support for the girl and her family were not confined to Ireland. At Irish embassies around the world, groups of people gathered outside to spontaneously express their abhorrence at the family's plight.

The European Parliament's Women's Committee in Brussels wrote to Albert Reynolds complaining about the case. It said the Irish law impeded 'one of the fundamental freedoms enshrined in the EC Treaty, that of the freedom of movement of persons in order to receive services in another member state.' The committee referred the case to the Parliament's lawyers and called for European condemnation of the case.

Reaction elsewhere depended largely on the views on abortion held by each country. In Belgium, Denmark, France, Greece, Italy, Luxembourg and the Netherlands, abortion was available on request or on broad medical and social grounds. This varied from region to region, with some Italian doctors refusing to carry out the operation. The Spanish and Portuguese governments allowed abortion in severe circumstances – which would have included the case of 'X' – and the newly unified Germany was considering whether to permit unrestricted abortion across its nation in its first three months. The Dutch Parliament was urged by some of its people to take diplomatic procedures against Ireland for allegedly contravening human rights as a member of the EC.

A leading German newspaper claimed that the Church, the State and the man accused of abusing the girl had all been 'accomplices in wronging the child'. There were calls in Sweden for the cancellation of a planned state visit to Ireland by King Carl Gustaf and Queen Silvia. In Australia the ruling was said to have dragged Ireland 'back into the Dark Ages'. In France there were claims that the issue had put a question mark over Ireland's status as an EC member.

Ireland was accused in all sections of the international media as being draconian, anti-European and medieval. The Belgian media (in a country where abortion was comparatively recently legalized) compared the Irish situation to that in Ceausescu's Romania, where women aged between twelve and fifty-five could be forcibly examined and confined if they were suspected of being pregnant and planning an abortion.

Other more extreme critics compared Ireland to the Iran of Ayatollah Khomeini – cruel, repressive and despotic. It was a charge which understandably upset the gentle Irish people and led to a flurry of defensive comment on behalf of a bruised and battered nation.

Mr Tony O'Brien of the Irish Family Planning Association, an Irishman who had lived in England for most of his life, had just returned to Ireland to take over as Chief Executive of the IFPA, when the 'X' case splintered on to the streets. 'The IFPA had no personal involvement in the "X" case at all, but because of what we do, we were suddenly inundated with people asking for information about contraception and abortion.

'I suppose I had previously had the holiday-maker's view of Ireland and I was horrified at the degree of oppression around moral issues here. It proved to me that there was something rotten about a government which seeks to legislate on personal morality and meddle in people's private affairs.'

Mr O'Brien, aged thirty, a former student union activist and opponent of the Alton Bill which had tried to reduce the time limit on abortions in the UK in the 1980s, said he had never seen anything like the spontaneous eruption of feeling on abortion as he saw in Dublin in 1992. 'It was such a drastic example of everything I had come to believe was wrong. It had a significant effect on the people of Ireland and proved to them that the abortion issue was not an abstract concept, it was about real people with real problems.

'The pro-life lobby had reduced it to such a simple debate: effectively that if you were in favour of the right to abortion, then you were in favour of killing babies. This case provided a potent symbol that it just wasn't that simple.'

Mr O'Brien believed that the advent of cable television, beaming news reports on the issue from the BBC, Sky, CNN, Super Channel and European stations, had a devastating impact on the viewing public. 'If they watched the Irish national channel RTE, they got a very sanitized view of the case and its muted analysis. But if they pressed the remote control button to look at any of the other stations which they were very familiar with, it was wall-to-wall coverage and highly critical. It was all presented as looking pretty bad for Ireland and the people were ashamed. They wanted to get back in tune with the world as they saw it through their television screens.'

Anne Taylor, chairwoman of the Council for the Status of Women, agreed. 'I think the thing that struck me most was that even the men were expressing their outrage. We would have expected to hear it from women, but the male population – who had always seemed to regard us as another species – were just as angry too. It was such a powerful case and it made people realize that abortion is not a question of black or white – there is a lot of very grey middle ground. For the first time people actually realized that and I think they were hugely relieved.'

Mrs Taylor, who lives primarily in County Tipperary and is well in tune with feeling 'down the country', said the rural community was just as bewildered. 'You are quite often more likely to find the extremists and the zealots in the country, but we didn't hear them crying out then. It was as if the whole case winded them completely and knocked them off their feet. Not long afterwards they picked themselves up again, and we have not heard the last of them by any means, but for a little while there wasn't a sound to be heard.'

Many in Ireland still believe that the majority of country folk would vote against abortion in a straight 'Yes' or 'No' referendum, but if asked about 'X' would say, 'Let the poor girl go and have her abortion' – perhaps with the traditional addendum: 'Not that I've said anything, mind.'

After the High Court ruling, those in the anti-abortion camp, pleased that the first true test of their precious Eighth Amendment had withstood the pressure even in such an emotive case, kept a deliberately low profile. 'We were astonished that so many people were hyped up into such a frenzy about this girl when they had overwhelmingly voted for the amendment nine years earlier,' said one veteran campaigner. 'But we felt confident that the ruling was just and sound and, however unfortunate the girl's circumstances, would prevent abortion on demand in Ireland which is something no one, including the girl's parents, I suspect, would have wanted.'

Officially they stood firm, fearing a slip into what they viewed as a mood of immorality and murderous intent. The Society for the Protection of the Unborn Child publicly welcomed the High Court decision and offered to help the girl prepare herself for the birth. Its President, Dr Mary Lucey, said: 'No matter what the circumstances, once a life has started that life must be respected. This is taking into account the right to life of the unborn, which is paramount.'

She said that SPUC was 'acutely aware' of the suffering caused to the girl and her family, but added: 'I don't think that killing the baby will solve the problem. What abortion would bring to her is death to her unborn child and I think there is ample evidence in our country that killing solves nothing.' She also said that the abortion would just be a further violation of the girl's body. Showing 'heroic courage – dare I say virtue', she said the girl should carry the baby to full term, have it adopted and 'salvage something from those dark days'.

But privately, even some of the staunchest pro-lifers felt uncomfortable having to balance the reality of their moral stance with the plight of a victim who was little more than a child herself. Continuing to wear the symbols of the pro-life movement (gold-plated badges of tiny foetal feet) on their lapels, many anti-abortionists were, however, forced to examine their own consciences. 'For the first time I realized exactly what it could mean for my own daughter,' said one previously out-spoken campaigner. 'And I was sickened to the stomach. This girl's parents had apparently shared my views on abortion until they were faced with this horrible dilemma in their own family and I realized that I, too, might have had to bear that personal anguish.

'I was horrified at how naive I had been to campaign for abortion blindly without considering people like that. I will always be vehemently opposed to abortion, but I now know there are times when it must be allowed.'

A senior member of the pro-life movement, and founder member of the PLAC in 1983, said: 'I don't think any of us did not feel that our heart went out to the people involved, for the personal intrusion, the violence and the anguish, and the exposure after that. None of us had conceived that the amend-ment we campaigned for would ever be interpreted as physically preventing people from travelling for an abortion if that is what they wanted. For us it was an absolute bombshell.'

He countered the charge, often levelled at his group, that it was hypocritical of the campaign to agree to people travelling elsewhere for an abortion while not allowing it in Ireland. 'If that were true then people would say that to avoid hypocrisy we should render our laws equivalent. But that would be for most of us far too high a price to pay in order not to be called hypocritical. It is a juvenile analysis.

'We had seen the issue of the legal position as being one tiny facet of the whole awful problem of crisis pregnancies. We simply wanted to plug the gap in our legal system in light of international trends.

'We have always been susceptible to the charge that we are coldly indifferent to the plight of individuals, and that simply is not true. But we have to divorce ourselves from the awfulness of the situation and consider the rather dry, boring legal questions of whether the right to life of the unborn in Ireland is sustained in law.'

Bridget Anne Ryan, the first woman editor of the 106-year-old *Irish Catholic* weekly newspaper, and a young exponent of modern Catholicism in Ireland, now regards the 'X' case as a welcome catalyst for change. 'In a strange way it was the most important time for the Irish Catholics. It shook people to the core,' she said. 'It forced them to realize that Catholic was a bit of a dirty word in the world at that time, that we have a bit of a credibility problem, and to think about things such as abortion – subjects which are difficult to talk about in any society – but particularly here.

'Of course there was the usual diatribe and people firing angry sentences at each other, which I don't think helped people deepen their understanding of the issues involved, but for many of us it meant that we were forced to look at all our values, perhaps for the first time, and realize that there should be some flexibility.'

Miss Ryan, aged twenty-seven, whose publication sells nearly 40,000 copies across Ireland each week, added: 'I am not surprised that people don't take some Catholics seriously. We are aware of the chasm that exists between our attitudes on life and death and I think the Catholic Church needs to look at that. We have been muddled up about it since the fourth century and, however much we all state our abhorrence at abortion, we have to remember that we live in the real world. Having said that, I don't think having abortion on demand is something people should be clapping themselves on the back about, and the fact that we have resisted it is something we should be proud of.'

Since her arrival as editor at the *Irish Catholic* in 1993 Miss Ryan has slowly tried to introduce more open debate on the important issues facing the Church, even when she has been criticized for doing so. She told the photographers to take more pictures of women for the news pages, and started a column called 'Thinking Out Loud', in which lay people could openly express their ideas about the Church. 'In one column we commissioned by a priest in the islands, he said the Church should get real and warned that people were voting against its teaching with their feet. We got dozens of letters of protest and people calling to say they would cancel their subscriptions, although we also got some letters of support.

'We felt we had to publish about ten prayers in the next edition to make up for what we had done. But at least we had started a debate and got people talking and that is the only real way to change.'

Miss Ryan, who is one of seven children from a farming community, believes that the Irish Catholics are 'creeping forward' and says that one of the best aspects of commitment to the Church is the ability to grow with it. 'There may never be an answer to the abortion question, but we have to keep trying to find one. Being a Catholic is about constantly choosing and working with it and adapting it to your own life.

'I think we should all be looking at a way of living and a way of working with the Church in our society, rather than relying on some half-baked remedy. It is time the hierarchy realized that it is not just about theories and principles, it is about people.

'The "X" case made many of us realize that there are certain circumstances when you cannot just refuse to budge on your viewpoint. Religion cannot be a stagnant thing, an immovable position. It is ever-changing – it has to to survive – and I think we are currently in the middle of one of those necessary and important transitions.'

EIGHT

The family was no less shattered by the High Court decision even after a few days' reflection, and they wondered how much longer their misery would be prolonged. Their daughter had taken a turn for the worse when told the news and was now barely speaking to anyone as she lay in her sick bed.

'God only knows what was going on in that head of hers at that time,' a family friend said. 'She wouldn't eat or speak and hardly slept. She obviously wanted the whole experience just to end and her parents were increasingly concerned that she would try to do herself some harm, or could simply fade away and starve herself to death.'

Their lawyers reassured them as best they could and closely studied the full text of Judge Costello's judgement while monitoring the strength of public and political reaction.

After the Prime Minister publicly agreed to waive all the family's legal costs in the case, the lawyers contacted his office and told them they had 'picked up the signal' that the government would like a Supreme Court adjudication. It was another uncomfortable decision for the family. Although the only possible option if they were to proceed with the abortion, it would mean keeping their very personal tragedy in the public domain, which was something they detested almost above all else.

In the end, it was their continuing concerns for the mental welfare of their daughter that led them to agree, a decision they conveyed to their legal advisers on Thursday, 20 February. The priority had to be her well-being, not their continuing embarrassment, they said, and the decision to proceed was sanctioned.

Albert Reynolds immediately expressed his satisfaction that the matter was to be dealt with by the highest court in the land. Well aware of the urgency of the case, he asked the Supreme Court for the earliest possible hearing of the appeal. He promised that the State would 'cogently' argue that the High Court had correctly interpreted the Constitution, but said that it would not be 'putting extra effort' into the case – reassuring the family that he did not want them to feel that the machinery of the State was ranged against them.

Sent home from hospital to wait for the Supreme Court appeal, the girl continued to receive mild sedation and slept with her mother every night. She had not been to school since the day she broke the news of her abuse to her parents. Too unwell to cope with any private tuition, she had now missed weeks of vital education which was to have prepared her for her junior leaving certificate.

She still could not envisage any future or contemplate having the baby, and her parents also totally rejected the concept of welcoming it into their lives. Despite her initial reluctance to do so, it was decided that if born, the baby would probably be given away for adoption, so that it would not serve as a permanent reminder of their pain. The psychologist, who continued to see the family, said that the girl's rejection of the baby was 'total' and he dismissed arguments that she could have grown to accept and love it.

'Who knows what is possible, but my estimation of the strength of feeling of that girl and her family is that that was not a feasible way of dealing with her,' he said later.

The girl's morning sickness continued, her mother did what she could, and her father tried to concentrate on his job, despite quietly seething at the fact that the man who had caused all this upset was still living in his home and going about his normal business.

The family had accepted an offer of refuge in another house, but it was not their home, they were not surrounded by their belongings and their discomfort only served to put further strain on their relationships.

Friends of the family described them as 'utterly destroyed' at this time, but desperately trying to lead as normal a life as possible as world attention continued to focus on their plight. The girl's father was said to be travelling to work almost every day with only one or two of his senior colleagues aware of his private torment. He and his wife were said to be living 'in fear and dread' of being identified and confronted with the media at any time – an unfounded concern because the Irish press had been well aware of exactly who they were for several weeks and the vast majority had respectfully stayed away.

Deprived of their normal, anonymous lifestyle, the family sat tight and waited. In the privacy of their own company they tried to form an even closer bond as the parents did their best to protect their daughter from the international controversy.

With the help of professional counselling and the friendship of Ann Vaughan, the woman police officer trained in rape procedures, the girl was constantly reassured and told that everything would be over soon. Private tuition was suggested at home, to take her mind off her problems and help her continue her schoolwork, but she was too distracted to take anything in.

The smear campaign against the family continued. The girl's parents were horrified to learn that some anti-abortion campaigners were suggesting that the family had been part of some sort of wider conspiracy to deliberately challenge the laws on abortion, or had been hi-jacked by the pro-choice lobby once their daughter's situation became known.

Trying to rely on prayer and contemplation, they did their best to come to terms with a predicament which seemed to have no resolution and brought no respite. Almost imperceptibly the pressure began very gently to pull them apart.

Quite apart from the legal issues on abortion in Ireland, the girl's case renewed debate on the ethical dilemma presented by the legal and moral stranglehold, particularly facing those in the medical profession.

Doctors in the provinces especially had expressed their concern at the numbers of women travelling to London for abortions without feeling able to tell their GPs first, who were then not in a position to advise the clinic of any specific health problems which might lead to complications. Further, when the women returned home and later needed medical treatment, their doctors would be unaware of the abortion and its possible side-effects.

For those who decided to keep their babies, and who were against abortion in principle, there were other, ethical issues to be considered if they ran into health problems. Under Roman Catholic instruction there was very specific provision for two exceptions to the ban on abortion – ectopic pregnancies and cancer of the womb – based on the principle of 'double effect', where abortion could be allowed in extreme medical circumstances if the death of the foetus were incidental to saving the life of the mother. It was not known how many of these operations were done quietly and without reference to law or ethical code – some put it as high as more than 150 a year – but the principle was not always put into practice and did not cater for other complications.

The Irish Medical Council often referred to the country's low maternal death rates with praise, hailing the numbers as an example of how far its doctors have advanced – to have been able to save both mother and child when, had they lived anywhere else in the world, the child might have been automatically aborted. But their statistics did not take into account later deaths or disabilities caused by childbirth, such as in the common complication of pulmonary embolism for women with circulatory problems on their third or more child. In such cases pregnancy can later result in dangerous blood clotting, which can lead to strokes or death, but an abortion to prevent the pregnancy putting the mother at risk in this way was never considered as an option.

Neither was abortion a lawful option for women who discovered from ultra-sound scans (the only 'non-invasive' test possible on pregnant Irish women who were denied the more sophisticated amniocentesis tests) that their unborn child was severely mentally or physically disabled. This was even so in cases of anencephalic gestations, where the child is effectively formed in the womb without a brain and will either be stillborn or survive for just a few hours after birth. Estimated figures for between 1988 and 1992 claimed that 250 anencephalic births would have been brought to full term in Ireland, to be recorded as still-births or neo-natal deaths – the majority of mothers knowing from as early as the twelfth week of pregnancy that their babies were doomed to die.

In the National Maternity Hospital's Clinical Report of 1985 the question of anencephaly was raised. It said: 'The policy is to await spontaneous labour when anencephaly is diagnosed. Every method of induction carries some risk for the mother. With compassionate counselling and sympathetic support parents accept this approach even in those cases where . . . there is a prolonged pregnancy.'

The Department of Health did not collate figures for the numbers of deaths or disablements of Irish women through complications of pregnancy. Such figures might have caused some disquiet, particularly when, under both the Constitution and the Catholic Code of Ethics, such cases could, officially, have been lawfully treated in a way which necessarily resulted in the death of the foetus.

The Church code stated: 'Operations and treatments necessary for the cure of serious organic pathological conditions of the mother, which cannot be postponed until the foetus is viable, are permitted even though the death of the foetus results. This principle applies to extra-uterine pregnancies.' In an ectopic pregnancy, for example, where the fertilized egg lodges itself in the fallopian tube rather than the womb – threatening death to it and the mother as it enlarges – doctors may remove the tube as 'a diseased organ' without theologically performing an abortion.

Many hospitals carried out a small number of these operations annually without widely publicizing the fact, but some refused to under their ethical code or Bishop's Charter. The constitution of the Irish Medical Council, approved in 1988, stated in its 'Guide to Ethical Conduct and Behaviour': 'Abortion is illegal in Ireland and is professional misconduct. Doctors are reminded of the legal position in Ireland concerning requests for, and advice on, termination of pregnancy.' It added: 'It is ethical for a doctor, by reason of his own beliefs, to refuse to intervene in the process of reproduction or termination of pregnancy or abortion by suggesting to the patients concerned that they consult other doctors.' (The Medical Council was later to compound this statement by declaring that there were no clear medical grounds for performing an abortion.)

No case brought the matter into focus more than that of Sheila Hodgers, who died on 19 March 1983, two days after giving birth to a dead baby girl.

Although her death occurred a full six months before the people were asked to go to the polls in the first constitutional referendum in 1983, it was only brought to the press (and therefore public) attention the week voting was due to take place. By then most people had made up their own minds, and – tired of the endless debating of the issues – had switched off mentally to further emotive news. Mrs Hodgers's death was destined not to be the catalyst that it could have been for change. Few people in Ireland even know who she was.

Sheila Hodgers and her husband Brendan lived in Dundalk, County Louth, fifty miles north of Dublin. Mr Hodgers worked at the Ecco electronics factory in Dundalk and the couple had two daughters aged eight and seven. They were considering trying for a third child when Mrs Hodgers discovered a lump in her breast.

A devout Catholic, Mrs Hodgers was taken to Our Lady of

Lourdes Hospital in Drogheda – administered by the Medical Missionaries of Mary – and had what doctors initially thought was a cyst removed. Further tests showed that it was a deep tumour and a mastectomy was necessary. Mr Hodgers was privately told that without the operation his wife only had a few months to live, and there was still a strong possibility that she could develop secondary tumours later.

Following the operation, however, his wife flourished and all the scans showed that she was clear of cancer. She was prescribed long-term medication and told to stop using the contraceptive pill, which could interfere with her treatment.

'She really was one hundred per cent and believed everything was all right,' her husband later told Padraig Yeates of *The Irish Times*. She enquired of the doctors about having another baby and was told she had a clean bill of health. A year later she fell pregnant and was taken off her cytotoxic drugs. A month later, she developed severe back pains and doctors told her that they suspected a reactive tumour on her back.

Because the hospital was under the highest religious authority in the country, known as the Archbishop's Contract – being in the diocese of the Archbishop of Armagh and Primate of All Ireland – the doctors felt unable to do anything which might harm Mrs Hodgers's unborn child.

Consultants employed by many Catholic hospitals, although paid by the State after signing their Common Contract, effectively sign a second contract with the hospital in which they agreed to abide by that establishment's ethical policy, as set down by an ethics committee on the hospital board. This was the case even if the ethics code took a stricter moral stance than the law of the land.

Mr Hodgers believed his wife would probably have refused an abortion on religious grounds anyway, but said she was never given the opportunity to choose. He said the doctors would not even take an X-ray of her spine to diagnose the size and type of the tumour, in case it damaged the foetus.

The doctors also allegedly resisted requests by Mr Hodgers to induce the birth or perform a Caesarean section prematurely, so that his wife could return to her anti-cancer treatment immediately.

She was admitted to hospital in severe pain. 'I went to see Sheila one night and she was in absolute agony,' he said. 'She was literally screaming at this stage. I could hear her from the front door of the hospital and she was in a ward on the fourth floor.'

Mrs Hodgers was eventually moved to the maternity ward and her husband took to sleeping in a chair next to her bed. On 16 March she went into labour two months prematurely and was delivered of a baby girl on St Patrick's Day. The child was perfectly formed, but stopped breathing almost immediately and could not be resuscitated.

Mrs Hodgers died two days later. She had tumours on her spine, neck and legs. Her husband said: 'They had run rampant from lack of treatment.'

A senior obstetrician dealing with her case said afterwards: 'It was the worst case I have seen like it in a pregnant woman for twenty years. I doubt if any treatment could have saved her.'

Mr Hodgers buried his wife and child and tried to get on with his life, for the sake of his other two children. On the advice of lawyers, he chose not to pursue any legal action against the hospital and said that he hoped publicity about the case would prevent such a death from happening again. 'This country has changed a lot since then,' he said, more than ten years after his wife's death. 'But there are a lot of things that have got to change in this country still.'

Dr Fiona Bradley, of Doctors for Freedom of Information, believed that Sheila Hodgers's death and others like it could have been entirely preventable. 'These sort of cases are not openly talked about, although they should be, but we do hear of them through the grapevine. There was one other I knew about of a pregnant woman who had leukaemia whose treatment was stopped and she died. They generally only have ethics committees in maternity hospitals and this seems to me to be particularly prejudiced and unfair.'

Doctors for Freedom of Information, a 100-member lobbying group, was set up in the aftermath of the 'X' case to campaign for better availability of information for women in crisis pregnancies. 'After X, Irish GPs just were not sure of where they stood in relation to exchange of information and abortion and we felt the situation had to be clarified,' said Dr Bradley.

'Some of our members are pro-choice and some are pro-life, but we felt that, whatever our personal views, the patient had to be given the best information available in a non-directive, non-judgemental way so that she could decide what is best for her. There is far too much judgement and criticism of women in such circumstances, who may wish to consider abortion as an option but who are afraid to even discuss it. We wanted to try to change that.'

A year after Sheila Hodgers's death, two other Irish cases made international headlines and forced Ireland once again to examine its high moral position on unwanted pregnancies.

Ann Lovett, a 15-year-old pregnant schoolgirl from Granard, West Meath, walked through her small town in central Ireland one bitterly cold January day, past the church and the graveyard, and climbed up a steep hill to the secluded granite Grotto to the Blessed Virgin.

Alone at the sacred spot where pilgrims knelt to pray, she gave birth to a seven-pound baby boy on a moss-covered stone beneath a statue of the Virgin Mary. Haemorrhaging and suffering from exposure after a protracted labour during which she seriously bruised her own arms with her fingertips as she clutched herself in pain, she was discovered dying several hours later by three schoolboys who noticed her red satchel lying outside the cave.

She was semi-conscious with her baby dead at her feet and

a pair of scissors at her side to cut the umbilical cord. The priest was called to baptize the child and to perform the last rites on the girl.

Her father and townspeople arrived to comfort her – comfort they had apparently not been able to give before, when she had concealed her pregnancy from all but her best friend for fear of the shame and retribution she and her family would face. She was carried to her home where, 'ice cold', she was laid on a couch next to an oil fire. Her father laid hot water bottles at the feet and head of his tiny grandchild in the vain hope of reviving its lifeless form.

An ambulance arrived and took mother and baby to hospital. They were both pronounced dead a short time afterwards. An inquest found that Ann Lovett, one of nine children from a respected village family, had died of irreversible shock due to haemorrhaging and exposure at childbirth.

Her baby son, probably conceived in a reckless moment with a village boy, died of asphyxia 'more than likely during childbirth'. They were buried together in a hillside cemetery.

Six months later Ann's 14-year-old sister Patricia killed herself with a drugs overdose in her bedroom. She was buried next to her sister. The girls' father suffered a heart attack shortly afterwards and became an invalid.

Government ministers called Ann Lovett's death 'a national tragedy' and demanded an immediate inquiry. Her best friend at school admitted that she had told her she was pregnant on 27 December, as she was in the final stages, but swore her to secrecy. The 1983 Eighth Amendment abortion debate had been raging throughout the country for the previous six months. The friend said she thought Ann would seek help and know what to do.

A local obstetrician, who had given evidence at the inquest, said concealment of pregnancy was still not uncommon in parts of Ireland. She said that she knew of at least five such cases.

The then Minister of State for Women's Affairs, Nuala

Fennell, said: 'This girl must have been living in the most appalling fear. Ann was only a baby herself and it is my deepest wish that we can change attitudes so that other girls who find themselves pregnant can say "I need help" and know where to go for it.'

One Irish commentator reflected: 'The case of Ann Lovett made for shocking headlines. The message was flashed around the world that this retarded little Catholic country with its hypocritical morality had allowed an innocent girl and her child to die in a bleak cave, rather than face up to the reality that she was pregnant and deal with it.

'Had abortion information been available to her, or had the social climate been such that the town could have nurtured and supported her instead of forcing her into a secret birth, she need not have lost her life. It was an accusation that had a great deal of justification and made a lot of people start to wonder if the old conservative ways were always right.'

A few months after Ann Lovett's death, the violent deaths of two babies in County Kerry became an even more internationally infamous case.

The first of 'the Kerry babies' was found by a farmer on some rocks at White Strand beach, Cahirciveen, on 14 April 1984. The naked infant had been beaten, stabbed four times in the heart, had its neck broken and had been thrown into the sea.

Police investigated and discovered that a 24-year-old single woman called Joanne Hayes of Abbeydorney, several miles away near Tralee, had been visibly pregnant but did not seem to have a baby to show for it. She was arrested and interviewed and eventually charged with the baby's murder. Other members of her family who – it emerged later – confessed to helping her dispose of the child's body only under extreme duress, were charged with complicity in the crime.

After a few weeks and much publicity about the case, all the charges were dropped when the baby's blood group was found to be incompatible with that of Miss Hayes. Shortly afterwards, her own dead baby – whom she admitted to accidentally choking at birth – was discovered buried in a field behind the farm where she lived.

Police found out that Miss Hayes had been having a long-standing affair with a local married man, and already had a two-year-old daughter by him. She had lost one baby through miscarriage previously and became pregnant by him again, giving birth to it in the field alone on the night of 12 April.

Distressed and unwell, she said she tried to stop it crying by holding it by the throat. A few minutes later she realized she had killed it and she left it in the field overnight, before returning the next morning to bury it.

A government-ordered tribunal into the case, said to have cost one and a half million Irish punts in legal fees, later ruled that Miss Hayes did not kill the Cahirciveen baby, but had caused the death of her own. She never faced criminal proceedings and was allowed to bury her baby in a local cemetery and return to her family farm.

The Kerry babies case staggered the already battered Irish sense of morality. Was there to be no end to the stories emerging from Ireland about dead babies and their frightened young mothers, forced to give birth alone, in pain or in secret because of the nature of their repressive society? Was this young woman's shame so complete that she and her family were nearly coerced into admitting a murder they did not commit?

No fewer than four books on the case, including Joanne Hayes's own story, were published afterwards and the world's media flew into Kerry in force to report every gruesome detail.

'Before the "X" case, I think the Kerry babies fiasco was the one most significant single event in Ireland relating to women's rights,' said one feminist campaigner years later. 'Although people were initially horrified at the macabre deaths of the two infants, as the evidence emerged it became clear that this unfortunate young woman was as much of a victim as the dead babies. She had suffered at the hands of many people, not least the police conducting the enquiry, and her lover who manipulated her and refused to leave his wife and children while continuing to have regular sex with her.'

The police never discovered the identity of the other dead baby or its mother, but after the harrowing details of Joanne Hayes's pregnancy and the sad, short life of Ann Lovett had been publicized, it and its mother became a poignant symbol for the hundreds of tragic young women of Ireland and their unwanted babies.

The infant was buried in a remote churchyard near to where it was found. Its tombstone said simply: 'In memory of me, the Kerry baby.' For years afterwards its grave was regularly tended by an unknown person or persons who trimmed the grass around it and adorned it with fragrant bunches of fresh flowers.

NINE

World attention continued to focus on the 'X' family's plight, which was still being discussed on every street corner, in every bar and on every current affairs show in Ireland. Abortion, the forbidden 'A' word, so long out of the Irish vocabulary, was back at the top of the agenda.

Political groupies on both sides of the argument jumped on the bandwagon, which they could see would become a test case for abortion in Ireland.

It was not that sexual abuse by a neighbour of his neighbour's child was by any means new in Ireland – untold numbers of teenage rape victims fell pregnant every year. It was just something that was not widely talked about.

Dozens of one- or two-paragraph stories in local newspapers had long told of under-age girls being raped by adult men. In one case in Donegal the same year as 'X', six men who raped a 13-year-old girl and got her pregnant were given suspended sentences by a judge after two of them offered to pay the girl IR £1,000 each to help bring up the child.

At the Irish National Teachers' Organization in 1992, it was claimed that at least 3–4 per cent of the country's children (population over one million aged under sixteen) would suffer from severe or prolonged abuse before they were eighteen. They spoke of confused victims, never given the advantage of a proper sex education, who did not know what it was their abusers were doing to them. When they whispered about it to their priest in confession, he told them it was not a sin for them and advised them to keep out of the way of the abuser.

The only foetuses these girls knew about were those they had seen on what became known as 'the pickled foetus road-show' – anti-abortionist tours of Catholic schools with an assortment of aborted babies peering out from jars of formaldehyde.

Raised in this culture, the 'disgusting practices' of child abuse and unwanted pregnancy were swept under the carpet. A pregnant girl quite often carried the baby to full term and her mother took it in as her own or gave it up for adoption.

In such cases, the abuser was often beaten senseless in a side street by the pregnant girl's father and uncles and the men would never speak of it again. Nobody liked to point a finger at another member of their society or make a show of their own family. But 'X' and her family had not just allowed the pregnancy to go ahead or slipped quietly away to England to arrange the operation. They had sought help, contacted the police, and done everything by the book. As one commentator at the time put it: 'They broke the unwritten rule of the Irish hypocrisy game by acting in an open and honourable manner.' It was their adherence to the law which led to the legal action and the publicity which brought a human focus to an otherwise submerged world of sexual abuse.

There was talk of an appeal to the European Court of Human Rights if the Supreme Court went against them, and widespread speculation about how late the girl's ever-growing foetus could be aborted.

The less scrupulous in the pro-life movement were not idle as the nation waited for the Supreme Court hearing. The rumours that the case had been a set-up continued to abound. The suggestion was that the whole thing had been somehow orchestrated by the pro-choice campaigners, that the girl and her family were being manipulated by radicals, doctors and politicians keen to force a constitutional case challenging the anti-abortion amendment.

Hoping to discredit any criminal proceedings with a view to eventually challenging the Supreme Court decision, the smear campaign against the girl herself gained new momentum. Her friendship with the foreign boy 'A' was exaggerated into something far more sinister. He was wrongly described as an Iraqi, at a time when the Western world was still effectively at war with Saddam Hussein. Rumours were circulated around the Dublin newspapers that the girl had slept with a number of 'foreign' boys and that journalists should be wary of writing too much in her favour.

The family were racked with the added torment of the whispering campaign and felt powerless to prevent it. They pinned their hopes on their faith and sense of justice and hoped that eventually their daughter's name would be fully and finally cleared.

A thin paperback book – *The X Case: How Abortion was Brought to Ireland* – claiming a number of conspiracy theories was published by the anti-abortion organization Human Life International in America, and distributed around Dublin. With a cover representing a snake twisting through Ireland, it featured a foreword by veteran anti-abortion campaigner Father Paul Marx who wrote: 'This book delves deep behind the scenes of the Irish abortion controversy, exposing the lies and manipulation being used there to bring abortion on demand to yet another country.'

The book's author, Mr Clement Loscher, approached the girl's father at work, introducing himself as a teacher and asking for an interview. The girl's father refused and asked him to leave.

Mr Loscher, aged forty-two, of Clontarf, Dublin, a former part-time business studies teacher at Mount Temple comprehensive school, was dismissed from his job five days after the book came out, and later brought an industrial tribunal case against the school, claiming unfair dismissal. He claimed that shortly after informing the school about the book – which he suspected would attract adverse publicity – he was made redundant. Despite applying for up to thirty other teaching jobs since, he claimed to have been given only a few weeks' work in two schools. The tribunal panel ruled in favour of the school, which successfully claimed that it had selected Mr Loscher for redundancy only after the arrival of a permanent teacher who took over his duties. The panel said it found 'no evidence whatsoever' that he had been the victim of religious or political discrimination.

A number of parties interviewed by Mr Loscher in the book later threatened legal action against him for misrepresentation. The family took comfort from the fact that it was thought unlikely that any Irish bookshops or distributors would ever agree to handle such a controversial publication.

They were not so comforted by the fact that Mr Loscher continued to attend almost every court hearing, and promised a second publication on the case, exploring the backgrounds of each of the parties involved.

Growing calls for a new referendum on abortion followed the High Court ruling. The government publicly rejected this course of action, appealing to people to wait until the Supreme Court ruling, but there were rumours in the Dáil that a referendum might eventually be forced.

The Church did not know which way to turn. Its own clergy seemed confused and issued contradictory statements. Some even threatened to break ranks.

The Code of Canon Law adopted by the Vatican in 1918 and under which the Catholic Church still operated was unequivocal. 'Ensoulment', or the beginning of life, starts at conception and abortion is therefore a mortal sin. But this was not an unequivocal case. The senior bishops admitted that they were 'caught between a rock and a hard surface'. The leadership was anxious not to be seen to be meddling in politics, after their experience in 1983 when statements issued by Archbishop Ryan, and in the unsuccessful 1986 divorce referendum by his successor the late Dr Kevin McNamara, fostered the impression that the Catholic Church was trying to dictate to the politicians.

None the less, in 1992 this staunchly Catholic community

was being forced to examine its conscience on a range of moral, social and religious issues and the Church could not stand by and do nothing. Anxious not to lose control of the reins, the Pope issued an irrefutably clear statement from the Vatican urging all Catholics to reject abortion in any shape or form. He reminded them of the Code of Canon Law and the thinking behind the 1974 Declaration on Procured Abortion issued by the Sacred Congregation for the Doctrine of the Faith, which called for 'respect for human life from the time that the process of regeneration begins'. Some twenty-four years after the encyclical letter 'Humanae Vitae' was published at the request of Pope John Paul VI, banning contraception and bringing Catholic teaching into violent conflict with the customs of the modern world, the message was still the same.

Reiterating his 1991 message to his bishops, the latest Pope, John Paul II, pleaded: 'Stop the slaughter of the innocents.' He said that there could be no justification for spreading information 'to facilitate the killing of the unborn'. He denied that it was insensitive to Europe to enshrine anti-abortion principles into the constitution and he beatified seventeen Irish martyrs from the sixteenth and seventeenth centuries. The Irish bishops called on the prayers of the martyrs 'to protect the lives of unborn children'.

The Pope's response was to try to counter the growing trend for European Catholics to opt for what had been dubbed 'à la carte Catholicism', a dipping in and out of those aspects of the faith which suited them and ignoring those which did not.

David Lodge in his book *How Far Can You Go?* compared life for Roman Catholics to a giant game of snakes and ladders, with no snake more slippery than contraception, and no route more likely to send players plummeting to the bottom of the game board than abortion.

This view of life was widely reflected in the attendance rate at Sunday Mass in Ireland, as wave after wave of young Catholics rejected the Latin chants and incense in favour of their favourite programmes on cable television or a run round the Gaelic football pitch. Although some 93 per cent of the Irish population were Catholic, every week the number of church-goers was falling, most notably amongst the young. In the 18–25 age group only 56 per cent went to Mass each week (compared to 83 per cent in the oldest age group). The Irish Church was so short of novices to the faith that increasingly lay teachers were being employed at the Catholic schools.

The abortion issue brought matters to a head. Catholics who were used to listening to their own bishops rather than the hard-line Vatican were in inner turmoil and were desperately seeking some sort of guidance.

Pop singers and Irish cult heroes spoke out in protest at the repressiveness of the Church. The young people were far more likely to listen to Bono, lead singer of U2, or the controversial shaven-headed singer Sinead O'Connor, than the sermons of their local priest.

Irish Protestants also muddied the waters. The Church of Ireland Bishop of Meath and Kildare, Dr Walton Empey, said it was 'monstrous' that a young girl who had suffered so much should be subjected to further suffering at the hands of the State. He described the situation as 'a dreadful tragedy' and said many women in the Republic would be deeply concerned at its implications.

The Church of Ireland's submission on the proposed amendment of the Constitution in 1983, he said, had stressed its opposition to abortion, but had added 'save at the dictate of strict and undeniable necessity'. It drew attention to the 'possible medical and legal difficulties which might arise from the intended form of wording' and envisaged medical circumstances where a termination might be required. He said the Church of Ireland gravely doubted at that time, and now, the wisdom of 'using constitutional prohibitions as a means of dealing with complex moral and social problems'. He added: 'Unfortunately the sense of this was lost in the welter of emotionalism, political opportunism and self righteousness. As a result a young girl is suffering greatly.'

Unfamiliar with the wide-ranging opinions possible in the broad-based Anglican Church and accustomed to a monolithic vision of the clergy, many Irish people viewed such a statement as representing the views of all Anglicans in Britain and elsewhere. They sought a response from their own Church.

The Catholic bishops made no comment initially on the case at all. 'It is not the practice of the bishops to comment on particular court cases,' an unhelpful statement said. 'When an individual case is at the centre of public debate, especially a case so tragic and distressing as the present one, it is difficult to keep in view all of the important issues of principle which are relevant to the question of abortion.' A later statement added: 'When the legal issues raised by this particular case are clarified and the anguish of all those concerned may have become less acute, the bishops may feel it is more appropriate to comment.'

Behind the scenes, official sources within the Catholic Church were quoted as saying that the hierarchy did not believe it was necessary to follow 'the extreme position' adopted by Mr Justice Costello. The Church seemed to be implying that as long as abortion remained illegal in Ireland, it would not call into question those who travelled abroad for it.

The bishops later held an Episcopal Conference on the issue and came out with a surprising statement that could have been open to interpretation either way. Resisting the temptation to advise its flock how to vote if a further referendum on abortion were to go ahead, it accepted that both 'Yes' and 'No' votes were legitimate, provided the intention of the voters was to make clear their abhorrence of abortion.

It sparked tougher anti-abortion statements from several of the hard-line bishops, specifically urging Catholics to vote against abortion. Bishop Joseph Duffy, spokesman for the Catholic bishops, held a press conference in Dublin in which he said the Church saw the right to life 'as a God-given right'.

He added: 'There was adequate protection before for the right to life . . . of the mother.'

He said that despite the distress of the girl and her family, she should be forced to have the child. 'We have to acknowledge distress and to see it for what it is and to do all we can to eliminate it. But we have to, however difficult it is for us, draw attention, very respectfully, to the fact that there is another life involved – a tiny life, which is incapable of speaking for itself or defending itself. The right to life of the child.'

He agreed with Mr Justice Costello that abortion meant certain death for the child, but the threat of suicide meant possible death and that that should be the distinction. He later added that the bishops respected equally the right to life of both the mother and the child.

A carefully worded full statement on abortion issued later at the Irish Catholic Bishops Conference said:

When the pregnancy is the result of incest or rape the experience of the girl or woman is truly horrific. She may react with resentment, anger or rejection of the pregnancy, which she can feel to be a continuation of the violation of her body.

Nevertheless, however abhorrent or degrading the circumstances of conception, a new human life has come into existence. It is an innocent human life, a life given by God and called to live with God forever, a life which has a right to be welcomed into the human community. To end this life is a further violation of the woman's body and may only increase her distress.

Public opinion showed a waning of support for the Church in its rhetoric. An opinion poll in the *Irish Sunday Press* showed that between a quarter and a third of the population had 'less respect' for the Church's teaching on key moral issues.

It was a problem that the Church had already been trying to address prior to the 'X' case, by way of modernizing the religious services and teaching young clergy and laymen to present a more human face to their parishioners. Keen to move away from the traditional ideas of crosiers, incense and senile men, the Church was placed in a difficult situation. Whilst not wanting to lose the ground it had already clawed back, it could not forgo its basic moral teachings and advocate abortion for the girl.

Like the government, it sincerely hoped the matter would be taken out of its hands and that the girl would somehow be set free without the introduction of lawful abortion in Ireland.

Even Mother Teresa entered the 'X' case fray a year later in June 1993, when she arrived in Ireland for a visit sponsored by the pro-life movement to boost their cause. Interviewed on the 98 FM radio talk show hosted by the late Father Michael Cleary, the then populist face of the Irish clergy, the Calcutta-based nun told thousands of listeners, when asked about the case: 'Abortion can never be necessary because it is pure killing.'

A woman who had achieved world fame for her devotion to the Catholic faith, and whose strong anti-abortion views were well-documented, she blamed much of the world's disturbance and hatred on what she called 'a loss of love through killing'. She added: 'Every little child, every unborn child God created as a gift to love and be loved.'

Father Cleary – who had claimed the 'X' case was 'a model . . . planned deliberately to test the amendment' and said he suspected a great deal of organization behind it – told Mother Teresa that there was a danger that because of it abortion could be legalized in Ireland in rape cases. He asked her if she could ever accept that. 'No, never,' she replied. 'We must realize before the child is conceived whether we want or don't want the child, but if it is conceived then it has a right to live.'

Father Cleary said that, regardless of her views, Mother Teresa's simplicity of speech and sincerity of feeling had endeared her to a world embittered by war and hatred. 'She is not a great speaker and not a scholar, she is an old woman. But her views are heartfelt and represent what the majority of Catholics feel about abortion.

'It is not about Miss "X" or her family. It is about her child. We do not murder rapists in this country, so why should we murder their children? We have a terrible inferiority complex in Ireland about being this backward little country trying to catch up with the rest of the world. But why are we chasing the sort of societies where hundreds of thousands of babies are murdered every year, where nobody fights for marriage any more and where children carry guns to school? I think that if we just stood still for a moment, the rest of the world would want to catch up with us.'

After he had publicly expressed his views on the 'X' case, he said, he had letters and phone calls from almost a hundred girls and women asking for absolution for aborting their babies. 'Some of them had had their abortions more than ten years before, but still went to Mass every week to beg forgiveness. Now for non-Catholic women, the whole experience might be forgotten in a week, but if you have grown up in this faith, with these feelings and this is how it affects you for the rest of your life, wouldn't it be better to have the child and then consider the options?'

Those views were echoed later that year by the Pope in his papal encyclical 'Veritatis Splendor' released from the Vatican in October 1993, which reaffirmed 'the teachings of Scripture and tradition'. The Catholic Church's traditional ban on abortion, artificial birth control, sterilization, artificial insemination, premarital sexual relations, masturbation and homosexuality remained unaltered. Theological dissent on these issues was banned, because, it said, the moral teaching of the Catholic Church could not be founded on 'deliberative procedures' typical of a democracy.

Other clerics hoped for a more adaptable approach. The Bishop of Clogher, Dr Joseph Duffy, told the *Irish Sunday Tribune* newspaper that the Church must confront the changing social scene and adapt accordingly. 'There is no point ignoring what is happening, trying to evade it, or pretending life is like what it was in the past,' he said. The Church's role, he added, was to preach the gospel in a manner which was relevant to people's lives. 'What we have to do is to continue to confront changing fashions in society. First of all we have to try to understand them. Secondly, we have to address them.'

Some respected political commentators believed that this flexibility was the only way forward for the Church to remain in the lives of the vast majority of the Irish people. Writing in *The Times*, Clifford Longley said:

> Since the national shock at the 'X' case . . . there has been a remarkable turnaround on the issue, except by the bishops. There is a collapse in the mystique surrounding episcopal authority in the eyes of ordinary people and even among priests. People have not stopped going to Mass. But what they hear, they hear differently.
>
> Ireland is now backing out of the moral cul-de-sac of absolute Catholic doctrine imposed by law . . . Ireland is suddenly growing up fast, leaving the bishops far behind.

Mary Kenny, in the British *Sunday Telegraph*, wrote: 'Just as the Royal Family is being called to account in this country, and the House of Lords is denounced on all sides as the emblem of a class-ridden society, so in Ireland the Catholic Church finds itself more and more at odds with modern times, modern values and individual rights.'

Dick Spicer in *The Irish Times* said the Irish had evolved slowly from its religion-based family and clan cultures and needed 'more than most' a church which could help it cope with modernity without losing their ethical bearings. 'The tragic failure of the Catholic Church to come to terms with science and rationality is extracting a heavy price,' he said, and bringing about an 'abrupt social collapse'. He added: 'For many people, the Pope's stance against artificial contraception has reduced the Church to a vehicle for rituals and rites of passage devoid of any real ethical dimension.'

Others agreed, voicing the most frequently repeated criticisms of the Church that, having taken vows of celibacy, its clergy preached on matters of sex, and that while condemning women who sought abortions, they did little or nothing to remove the stigma attached to unmarried mothers.

In the words of the Northern Ireland Abortion Law Reform Association, campaigning to have abortion legalized in the north of Ireland (which was excluded from the British 1967 Abortion Act): 'The same groups profess to feel concern about the guilt women are said to feel after having abortions. It is public state-ments and propaganda put forward by these groups which increase the guilt and shame some women may endure and which drive them into positions of silence and isolation.'

Such a statement was made, in direct relation to the 'X' case, that anyone who had an abortion and anyone who helped them faced excommunication under Canon Law. Professor John McAreavy, head of Canon Law in Maynooth, warned that 'accomplices' to abortion included 'all those directly involved such as parents of a pregnant woman, the father of the child who pressed her for an abortion or who provided the means to enable her to have it ... and those who co-operate with or carry out abortions such as doctors and nurses'. The Catholic Church press office confirmed that this was not just the view of the professor. 'People should be under no illusions about the consequences of their actions,' a statement said. 'Abortion is a very grave matter, incurring the censure of excommunication.'

For the girl and her family, that way of thinking was no longer acceptable. Forced to closely re-examine their long-held beliefs, they continued as a family to go to Sunday Mass in a church near their new home until they were telephoned one week and advised to stay away.

'They were told that they were to be mentioned in a pastoral letter from the Archbishop of Dublin Dr Desmond Connell, to be read out to the masses, and that they should not attend church that week,' said one close friend.

The 67-year-old Archbishop's pastoral attacked as 'false reasoning' the view that abortion is an effective and reasonable response to unwanted pregnancies. In his first formal statement on the case, he told Catholics that they must be 'for life and not against it' and added that, even in a situation like 'X's, 'the outrage felt at the abuse of one child must not obscure obligations that exist towards that other child which is now present'. He said the anti-abortion stance was presented as 'bigoted, inhumane, lacking in compassion, cruel to women and consigning mothers to premature death'. But he warned people to make up their own minds whether they were in favour of abortion or not.

The effect of the publicly read letter was devastating for the family. A friend said: 'The mother was distraught and the father was furious. It was little less than public vilification. A little while afterwards the mother commented that she did not know why she was a Catholic anyway, because most of the people who had helped her and her family seemed to be Protestants.'

The alleyway in Williams Park, Rathmines, south Dublin, where the 'X' case foetus was conceived in December 1991. [Chris Taylor]

Harry Whelehan, Irish Attorney General, who first applied for the High Court injunction to stop the girl from having an abortion. [*Irish Independent*]

Mr Justice Declan Costello, High Court judge, who granted the Attorney General's application. [*Irish Independent*]

A rally against the High Court decision against 'X' in central Dublin.
[*Irish Independent*]

Protest demonstration in support of 'X' in O'Connell Street, Dublin.
[*Irish Independent*]

The Rotunda Maternity Hospital, Dublin, where the girl was first taken for treatment and diagnosed as suicidal. [Chris Taylor]

Candle-lit vigil for 'X' outside Leinster House in Dublin, the seat of Parliament. [*Irish Independent*]

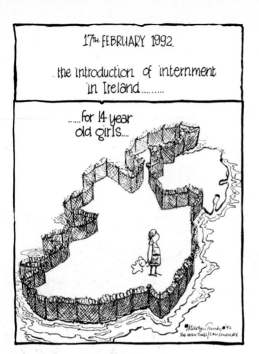

17ᵀᴴ FEBRUARY 1992.

..the introduction of internment in Ireland.........

.....for 14 year old girls....

Cartoon by Martyn Turner which appeared in the *Irish Times* and which he later gave to the girl and her family. [Courtesy of Martyn Turner, from *Politics Et Al*, Irish Times Books, 1992]

Mr Justice Hugh O'Flaherty, one of the Supreme Court judges who ruled that 'X' could go to Britain for an abortion. [*Irish Independent*]

Mr Justice Niall McCarthy, the late Supreme Court judge, who also overturned the High Court ban. [*Irish Independent*]

Mr Justice Rory O'Hanlon, High Court judge and ex-president of the Irish Law Reform Association, who resigned over the case. [*Irish Independent*]

Above right and below: Pro-choice rallies, central Dublin. [*Irish Independent*]

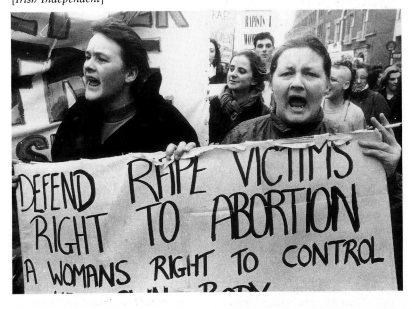

The Four Courts, Dublin, where the 'X' case began and ended. [*Irish Independent*]

Mr Justice Egan, one of the Supreme Court judges who allowed 'X' to go to Britain for an abortion. [*Irish Independent*]

Mr Justice Tony Hederman, who also overturned the High Court ban. [*Irish Independent*]

Anti-abortion rally in O'Connell Street, central Dublin. [*Irish Independent*]

Rathfarnham District Court, south Dublin, where the 'X' case girl made her first court appearance and testified against the defendant. [Chris Taylor]

The 'X' case defendant at his first court appearance. Detective Inspector Anthony Sourke shields him from the cameras. [*Irish Independent*]

TEN

The waiting went on for the family and those who were trying to help and protect them. Keen to do something positive to relieve the tension, DNA testing was again suggested.

Not commonly used in Ireland, the Republic hardly has any of its own DNA testing facilities, other than for paternity texts on greyhounds.

The medical authorities and moralists in the Republic were against such testing on anything other than normal body samples on the grounds that, if introduced for foetuses, it could be used to determine abnormality or gender in the unborn and raise sensitive ethical issues that Ireland was not yet prepared to face. But in the years immediately prior to the 'X' case, detectives were becoming increasingly aware of its possible implications in criminal matters and moves were afoot to introduce it in limited cases, and to train Irish officers and scientists in its technique.

At a meeting between senior officers in the case at Garda Headquarters in Phoenix Park, Dublin, it was decided that, even if such evidence were to prove inadmissible in an Irish courtroom, it would be worth taking as an added precaution. The family were, after all, breaking new ground on the abortion laws. They might as well be the ones to try to introduce DNA testing on a foetus into the Irish legal psyche as well.

It was arranged that, once the Supreme Court judgement had been given at the end of February or early in March – whichever way it went – the girl would be sent to a British hospital for the uncomfortable procedure of chorion villius or CVS sampling. Accompanied by her parents, who would have to pay their own

119

travel costs, and at least one of the six police officers now assigned to her case, she would have to endure the surgery as another factor in her ordeal.

To take a foetal biopsy for DNA sampling, either CVS or amniocentesis is used. In the latter, which until recently was the more commonly used, a needle is inserted into the mother's uterus and some of the fluid in the sac surrounding the foetus is siphoned off. The fluid is then cultured in a laboratory dish for several days or even weeks, so that cells can form and the chromosomal patterns be distinguished. It is a common procedure used to test for Down's Syndrome or other indications of mental or physical handicap. Its major disadvantage is the time delay involved.

In CVS sampling, a fine capillary tube is inserted through the stomach wall and, via micro-manipulation, a small sample of the villius – the tissue connecting the mother to the foetus – is removed from the womb lining to establish its genetic make-up. Not from the foetus itself, but from the tissue that helps feed it, the sample is fully established and does not need to be cultured.

Forensic scientists prefer CVS samples, but as both techniques carry a risk for the foetus – with CVS slightly higher – the decision is always left to the gynaecological consultant conducting the examination of the patient. Whichever way the sample is collected it is then matched against a blood or other sample from the suspected parent to provide evidence of parenthood.

Used widely in Britain and in the US since its discovery by an English genetic scientist Dr Alec Jeffreys in the early 1980s, such 'genetic fingerprinting' evidence had only ever been sought in a handful of cases in the Republic of Ireland.

Considered a forensic breakthrough akin to fingerprinting itself, the revolutionary biological technique – first tested in British courts in 1987 – replaced the traditional investigative techniques of blood group analysis or immunological tests. Genetic fingerprinting gives scientists a photographic representation of the chemical 'library' within each cell which goes to make up a complete human being. The blueprint information is carried by molecules called Deoxyribo Nucleic Acid (DNA) which are in the form of chromosomes in each and every cell.

Each individual is a composite of many small variations carried within forty-six paired chromosomes – twenty-three inherited from each parent – and by matching the 'libraries' of mother, father and child, direct links can be established.

DNA is remarkably stable and has even been extracted from Egyptian mummies. It is extracted from the blood, hair, semen, saliva or other samples and its fragments are separated into bands, according to their size. X-ray film of the vertical bands form a pattern of about a dozen black and white lines resembling a supermarket bar code.

Each DNA fingerprint is, like its namesake, unique to every individual. It has no exact match in the world. When Dr Jeffrey published his discovery in March 1985, he wrote: 'You would have to look for one part in a million million million million million before you would find one pair with the same genetic fingerprint. With a world population of only five billion, it can be categorically said that a genetic fingerprint is individually specific and does not belong to anyone on the face of this planet who has ever been or ever will be.' The recent questioning of DNA's infallibility in criminal trials relates more to human error when handling the samples and preparing the bands than to its evidential value *per se*.

Once prepared for comparison, the DNA patterns of each sample are placed side by side. Those belonging to the child will be analysed against those of the mother and father. The child's bands will match at least two of the mother's and two of the father's chromosomes in their respective lines. The odds of four bands from each sample matching are rated 250 to 1, of six bands matching 4,000 to 1, of 10 bands matching as 1 million to 1. The chance that a randomly picked man would accidentally match the bands of his child exactly has been estimated at between 200 million and 1,000 million to 1.

No two people (except identical twins) share the same chromosomal make-up, meaning that, once it was discovered that the bands of the 'X' case man matched with that of the foetus, unless the man had an identical twin brother who had also had sexual intercourse with the girl, only he could be the father of the child.

When he was first arrested, the accused had made great play of immediately agreeing to give a sample of his own blood, claiming that he had insisted upon doing so to prove conclusively that he was not the father. It was thought he must have believed at this stage that the girl was not really pregnant.

He may also have been aware that the tests would probably never be admissible as evidence – of ninety-eight such tests carried out for the Garda Siochana by British forensic scientists over the past few years, only one had ever come to court and that was ruled inadmissible because the prosecution was unable to prove the continuity of procedures to show that nothing had contaminated the samples.

The man's lawyers hoped that if the trial ever came to court they could seek to have the results of the tests on his blood and the foetal tissue proved inadmissible. One possible argument for this was that, as the defendant's samples had been taken in early 1992, before the 1990 Criminal Justice (Forensic Evidence) Act became law on 5 June that year, specifically dealing with procedures like collecting samples for DNA evidence, then they could be legally invalid. Under Section 2(4)(b) and (10)(a) of the Act, samples could be taken only with the consent of the donor, not compulsorily, in the presence of a doctor, and the suspect had to be made fully aware that they could prove his guilt or innocence. Inferences could be drawn by the court if a suspect refused to provide a sample.

A form such as the one opposite had to be completed, spelling out every detail to the defendant.

Consent by person aged 17 years or over to taking of sample from him.

1. I _____

of _____

being aged 17 years or over have been informed:

(a) of the nature of the offence in which it is suspected I have been involved

(b) that an authorisation has been given under section 2(4)(a) of the Criminal Justice (Forensic Evidence) Act 1990 for the taking of a sample from me for the purpose of forensic testing of the sample, the sample being one or more of the following samples, namely –

    (I) a sample of
      (i) blood
      (ii) pubic hair
      (iii) urine
      (iv) saliva
    (II) a swab from a body orifice mentioned in box opposite (tick box as appropriate)
    (III) a swab from a genital region mentioned in box opposite
    (IV) a dental impression

(c) that my consent is necessary for the taking of the sample;

(d) that the results of any tests on the sample may be given in evidence in any proceedings against me for an offence;

(e) that if I refuse without good cause to consent to the taking of the sample, then, in any proceedings against me for an offence, evidence of the refusal may be given and may result in offences being drawn against me and that the refusal may be treated as, or as capable of amounting to, corroboration of any evidence in relation to which the refusal is material, but that I shall not be able to be convicted of any offence solely on an inference drawn from the refusal.

2. I hereby consent to the taking of the sample.

Signed:

_____

Date:

_____

(Appendix A. Criminal Justice (Forensic Evidence) Act, 1990.)

The law regarding chain of custody also had to be rigorously applied – more so than in Britain – and it was on such a claim of procedural breaches that the judge had thrown out the evidence in the only previous case in Ireland where the prosecution had attempted to submit DNA findings.

Using a similar form to the accused, officers and medical personnel taking any samples had to complete the following.

Form to be completed by member or other person who took the sample under Section 2 of the Act.

1. Name and address of the person from whom the sample to which this form relates was taken:

_____

_____

2. Nature of sample:

_____

3. Garda station or prison at which sample was taken:

_____

4. Date on and time at which sample was taken:

_____

5. Manner in which sample was taken:

_____

I, the undersigned, took from the person named above at 1 the sample referred to at 2 above.

Signature of member or other person concerned.

_____

Date:

_____

(Appendix D. Criminal Justice (Forensic Evidence) Act, 1990 Regulations, 1992)

Before such fastidious procedures were brought in, a limited range of samples (mainly swabs) could be taken from suspects detained for sexual offences, or under the Offences against the State Act 1939, or the Criminal Justice Act 1984, for the purpose of testing for contact with firearms or explosives. Those arrested for drunk driving or related offences could also be required to provide specimens of blood or urine under the Road Traffic Acts.

Despite the claims made for DNA testing, it was not universally perceived as infallible and this was another area the defendant's lawyers were looking at. They studied closely newspaper reports from Britain and America that had begun to cast some doubt on the reliability of DNA testing. In one of the more celebrated cases, it was claimed that an innocent man had been wrongly convicted and had since been proved innocent in separate DNA tests. Sceptics wrote articles in various medical journals and publications expressing their concerns, which largely related to the age and quantity of the samples involved, and the rigorousness with which their handling was applied.

The vast majority of forensic scientists still believed, however, that genetic fingerprinting was the best technique available and claimed that its critics had been set up by defence lawyers hoping to publicly discredit the process so that a jury might not be convinced of its accuracy.

For those at Cellmark Diagnostics (part of the ICI group), the world's leading DNA testing laboratory which tests more than 12,000 samples a year and where the 'X' case samples were sent, the defence claims were nothing new.

Their long experience of court work had proved to them the importance of having the minimum number of people in contact with any one sample, so that the chain of custody was continuous and the integrity of the sample intact. Thus, once the frozen samples in the 'X' case were personally delivered by Detective Inspector Sourke and handed over to staff at Cellmark's grey, two-storey laboratory on an industrial estate outside Abingdon near Oxford, England, only three people were to come into contact with them – two forensic scientists and a supervising officer.

All three were later prepared to travel to Dublin for the trial and swear on oath that no procedural breaches had been made and that the test results were not only valid, but absolutely incontrovertible in their conclusions that the accused was the father of the foetus.

It would not have been viewed in any way as a personal triumph for the scientific staff. Like so many cases before this one, at the time of testing they would have only a code number rather than a name on each sample and know nothing of the case involved.

Dr Paul Debenham, head of international scientific services at Cellmark at the time of the 'X' case, said his staff could never hold a view on the result of a sample, because it could positively incriminate someone or prove his or her innocence – and either could be vitally important for those concerned. 'We generally test blind with no indication of what the case is about at all, which suits us fine. We sometimes never even find out what the conclusion was for those involved,' he said. 'And we can rarely relate stories we read in the newspapers to numbered samples we may have done many months or even years before.

'What was interesting about this case, though, was that for the first time we hoped to have hands-on experience of the Irish system and go to court and present our findings face to face.'

Cellmark found the process particularly fascinating because of the grey area of Irish law they had previously come up against with regard to DNA testing. 'The general impression we got was that people in Ireland didn't really know what DNA was or what it could prove,' said Dr Debenham. 'They were more likely to find out what it was all about by watching the Steven Spielberg movie *Jurassic Park* – which features DNA testing on dinosaur remains – than by familiarization with it in their own country.

'When we had made initial commercial approaches to family organizations and to the judiciary we found that they simply did not appreciate the possible uses of DNA testing and that they expected it to cost thousands anyway. When we told them the reality that we charged about £145 sterling for each sample tested, it shocked them. The only people we found who seemed to have any understanding of it at all were those at a small clinic in Dublin who do DNA testing to check the pedigree of sporting greyhounds.'

Some members of the Irish police and Technical Bureau *had*, in fact, recognized the importance of DNA testing and had prepared it to be used as evidence as early as 1988 in a murder case.

A 15-year-old schoolgirl called Carol Carpenter was found raped and murdered in the Dublin suburb of Tallaght. A few weeks later a 22-year-old neighbour was charged with her murder.

Detectives had found bloodstains at the house where the girl was killed. The defendant had been inextricably linked to that house and DNA testing proved that the blood was that of Carol.

The defendant pleaded guilty to the murder and was jailed for life. If the case had gone to trial it would have established a legal first in Ireland in introducing DNA testing as a technique of identification.

Following that case, DNA profiling was prepared for use in several criminal cases by the Gardai as a form of supporting evidence rather than a central argument and became a relatively accepted technique in non-controversial cases. It was used to eliminate a suspect in at least one case and is believed to have been a significant factor in the decisions of a number of defendants not to appeal against their convictions.

In July 1993 it was used in the trial of a 49-year-old Baptist pastor who had denied raping a 23-year-old woman who had arrived on the doorstep of his hostel looking for somewhere to sleep. Semen stains on the victim's underwear were proved by staff at Cellmark to have matched the pastor's genetic make-up almost exactly. A forensic scientist told the court that the DNA taken from the samples would match one in every 5,200 people. The man was convicted.

In light of the value of DNA at court cases, several members of the State Laboratory's forensic science department were later trained in the technique's uses by UK Home Office staff, and before the 'X' case came to public attention the DNA-specific Criminal Justice Bill had been passed in Parliament and was about to become law. More than IR £150,000 was eventually spent on installing specialized equipment to carry out DNA testing at Garda Headquarters and two molecular biologists were recruited to the task, first setting up a database of more than four hundred DNA samples from volunteers.

But no case had yet raised the issue of the interference with a foetal life to obtain forensic samples. The police and lawyers were concerned about the constitutional issues involved, particularly those relating to the wording giving the unborn the same right to life as the mother. It was unclear whether existing legislation allowed for DNA samples to be taken from a foetus without violating that foetus's constitutional rights.

For Cellmark, hoping to gain new business in the Republic, the evidence which would have been used at the 'X' case trial (half of which was necessarily taken from the foetal sac) could in their view have altered what had previously been a sensitive and somewhat difficult area. Their legal experts found that Irish law was, in essence, very similar to that in France, where the Napoleonic Code prevents any invasive technique to a child which may endanger its life. The difference is that in France abortion was legalized in 1975 and the largely Catholic community seems to have resolved its issues of Church and State.

'This case was certainly believed to be a breakthrough in Ireland as far as we were concerned,' said Dr Debenham. 'As worldwide sales of our techniques have increased, we have become quite used to dealing with different laws, customs and religions and adapting our sales pitch accordingly, but we just didn't know where we stood in Ireland.

'We had written to the Irish Justice Ministry to ask for clarification on the law, but got no reply. Although we realized that it was an entirely different ball game there when it came to interfering in any way with a foetus, we did not believe that there were really any moral or ethical issues involved in taking samples from a rape or murder victim.

'We have an ethical stance as a company that we will only take samples from CVS sampling or amniocentesis for parentage where a criminal case is involved. On this and the wider issue of checking the parentage of grown children, we have looked into the legal status ourselves and believe that Irish law could direct DNA tests under Part 7 of the Status of Children Act 1987, which states that a blood test can be required for paternity tests. Because it is called a blood test we feel that covers everything we do. But before this came up we were stumbling in the dark.'

He said the company viewed the situation after 'X' as one in which it hoped to educate and inform, although it would never actively seek casework. 'Whereas in the UK we would advertise in journals for people who specialize in family law, in Ireland we would now hope simply to quietly alert those sorts of people to the fact that our tests were used in the 'X' abortion case and were readily available for other cases.

'We believe that it could considerably improve the system of justice in Ireland and bring it into line with the UK, Europe and the United States in terms of scientific and forensic technology.'

Professor Simon Lee, professor of jurisprudence at Queen's University, Belfast, and member of the Standing Advisory Commission for Human Rights, said: 'The "X" case only ever really came to the attention of the Irish authorities because of the question of DNA testing. It is not something that had previously been possible in the Republic – although it will inevitably become widely available – and because of the parents' enquiry about it, they and their daughter were subjected to the full force of Irish law.'

Professor Lee, who has written a number of papers on the effects of the 'X' case on the abortion law in Northern Ireland, added: 'It would have been a first if the DNA evidence from the foetal matter had ever been brought before the courts, and in any other case it might have caused a backlash of indignation and upset from the public. But because it was this case, and this girl, and there was a tremendous feeling that everyone just wanted to nail the man who got her pregnant in the first place, I don't think it would have caused the outrage that it might otherwise have done.

'This has always been a no-go area in the Republic before. There is a kind of chill factor when it comes to abortion and all its surrounding areas. This case was remarkable in so many ways for raising people's awareness of the issues involved, even if they flew in the face of previous moral qualms.

'It had a ripple effect throughout Ireland, north and south, and in so many little unforeseen ways that could never have been predicted. I think the moral and legal status of the foetus and its related matter was just a small part of an overall situation in which people started coming to terms with issues they had not previously faced up to.

'Given a simplistic choice at that time, the Irish people would rather have had DNA testing introduced to the Republic than let the man concerned get away with it.'

For the girl, pale and wide-eyed as she prepared herself for her latest visit to hospital, the fact that she and the foetus she was reluctantly carrying might once again be the spearhead of a new phase for Irish legal history was of little practical comfort.

ELEVEN

On Monday, 24 February, three protracted weeks after the girl and her family were first thrown into the international spotlight, the Supreme Court hearing was held in camera. Two days later, on Wednesday, 26 February, judgement was delivered.

After three days of evidence, much of which related to the girl's state of mind and her right to travel, four of the five male judges decided after just a few minutes' deliberation to lift the High Court ban and let her at last cross the Irish Sea to England for a termination of her pregnancy.

The news was greeted with 'the utmost relief' by the girl and the family, who could finally make plans and start to contemplate a more hopeful future.

The judges' reasons were not delivered for another week, but when they were they caused a fresh furore because their decision had been based on the constitutional argument of health and life – effectively uprooting the Eighth Amendment – rather than the expected right to travel issue. This was shattering news to the pro-life movement.

It came as a further shock to the pro-choice lobby that, in spite of the judgement, three of the five judges had agreed that women who expressed the intention of going abroad for an abortion *could* be prevented from leaving the country and that the right to life of the unborn took precedence over the rights of a free citizen to travel.

Although their comments on this latter point were legally non-binding, they made for salutary thinking for the thousands of women travelling to Britain every year and for the many more who were horrified to think that they might need to.

The judgement was not without criticism of the government and of past governments which had failed to legislate on the abortion issue. One of the judges, Mr Justice Niall McCarthy, criticized the government for 'failing in its duty'. He said: 'It has been elected by the people to legislate, yet it cowers away from doing its duty when faced with any issue tinged with the least controversy.' (Sadly, Mr Justice McCarthy was later killed with his wife in a car accident while on holiday in Spain.)

The family's appeal to the Supreme Court to overturn the High Court decision had been made on the basis that Mr Justice Costello was 'wrong in law and fact' on a number of points.

Counsel for the family had claimed that it was not the Attorney General's duty to seek injunctions against the family; that such an order could not be made when Parliament had failed to enact any law on the matter; that the Eighth Amendment was unclear and ambiguous; that the balance of equality between mother and unborn had been misjudged; and that the right to travel, under European law, had been unlawfully revoked.

By finding in the defendant's favour and ruling that abortion was in fact legal in the State under Article 40.3.3 of the Constitution in certain circumstances, the judges were to have the most significant effect on the Irish population. Although there was widespread relief for the girl and her family, the ruling had further divided the nation and led to confusion in the public and legal mind about the precise state of the law.

The operation had been banned by the High Court, it was believed, on essentially the right to travel issue and yet the Supreme Court decision was interpreted as permitting abortion for the first time in certain limited circumstances where there was a threat to the life of the mother – all on the basis of a single psychologist's evidence.

The Supreme Court judgement also left questions over whether women were entitled to travel abroad for an abortion and to receive information about foreign abortion clinics. In many ways, although relieving the immediate plight of the family, it left more questions than answers for the nation as a whole.

The five Supreme Court judges were aware that their decision might have been the most important and influential of their judicial careers. A distinguished panel, they were led by the Chief Justice, Mr Justice Thomas Finlay, a 69-year-old Dubliner and father of five with a legal career spanning forty-eight years.

A former member of Parliament for the Fine Gael party in the district of Dublin South Central, he was nominated to the High Court in 1972, becoming its President in 1973 and Chief Justice in 1985. Three of his five children were involved in the legal profession, two as barristers and one as a solicitor. His manner in court was described as 'sympathetic and courteous' and he had a reputation for thorough analysis and patience.

Mr Justice Hugh O'Flaherty – at fifty-three, the youngest member of the panel – was born in Killarney, Co. Kerry, and was called to the Bar in 1959. A father of four, he became a Supreme Court judge in 1990. It was he who had helped to successfully represent the Society for the Protection of the Unborn Child in their case against the giving out of abortion information by the Well Woman Centre and Open Line Counselling in the High Court in 1986.

Mr Justice Niall McCarthy, sixty-six, was the son of a former circuit judge, and was called to the Bar in 1946. A father of four, he first came to prominence when he defended Mr Charles Haughey (later Prime Minister) in a 1970 arms trial. He was known as an exceptional speaker and a man of great legal stature.

Mr Justice Anthony Hederman, seventy, was a former Attorney General who was appointed to the Supreme Court in June 1981. A single man with a noted legal brain, he was the only judge to agree with the High Court decision.

Mr Justice Seamus Egan, sixty-seven, was the newest recruit

to the Supreme Court, having been appointed in 1991. He was said to have 'a grandfatherly manner' in court and was known for being highly principled. A father of seven, including five daughters, he had been involved in many prominent trials at Dublin's Four Courts and was appointed to the High Court in 1984. People who knew him socially said he was 'charming' and accessible.

Between their five wise heads, the judges had come up with a ruling which they must have known was going to cause as much of a furore as had Mr Justice Costello's a few weeks earlier – but this time for different reasons.

When the full transcript of the hearing was published, the extent to which they had questioned and mulled over their important task was evident. In between a series of short addresses by Mr John Rogers, SC, for the family and Mr Peter Shanley, SC, for the State, the judges had interjected and interrogated in a manner more familiar to a debating society than a hearing in a Supreme Court.

Mr Rogers opened by telling the court that he was instructed 'to advance every possible ground' that would permit the family to pursue the decision made for the girl 'in good faith and in all conscience'. He said she had a right under the Constitution to have an abortion and to travel abroad to receive such a service. 'Would it be right for the courts to second-guess the truly considered decision of parents which has been confirmed by medical evidence to assist and protect their child?' he asked.

Mr Justice Costello had been given 'no guidance' by Parliament on the clear meaning of the Eighth Amendment, and prior to it, Mr Rogers said, there had been a common law guideline of 'real and substantial risk to the life of the mother', which had survived the Eighth Amendment. 'If women die needlessly because their lives are only saved when there is imminent risk of death, this is going too far . . . The life of a mother will be needlessly lost.'

He referred to the 'balance of interests' used to decide the case of *Rex* vs *Bourne* (see next chapter), which similarly involved a 14-year-old rape victim. He said Mr Costello appeared to have taken on 'an absolute imperative to protect the life of the unborn', despite having made a clear finding that there was 'a real risk to the life of the mother'. He added: 'The nature of the evidence [in *Rex* vs *Bourne*] shows a very serious risk to the child's life, but the trial judge did not assess it accordingly.'

On the question of the detention of the girl in Ireland, he said there was no express law to prevent an individual from going abroad to procure an abortion which is lawful abroad. 'The right to travel is part and parcel of the right to liberty,' he said. 'My clients feel aggrieved that they are in some way being singled out for special treatment. There is nothing in the Eighth Amendment to justify or warrant the State restricting the individual from going abroad, just as it had no right to do so prior to the Eighth Amendment.'

He said that if the court could not order the State to ratify laws to protect the life of the unborn, then it could not order the girl either – or 'to do so would result in a hit and miss regulation of the constitutional protection and to allow this would be discriminatory'.

He submitted that the right to travel took priority over the right to life of the unborn, and cited the United Nations Declaration and European Convention on Human Rights.

Mr Shanley, for the Attorney General, said in reply that the State now sought to alter the original injunction to make it 'a less restrictive type of order'. He explained: 'The High Court order could now provide that "X" is prohibited from travelling abroad for the purpose of an abortion. It would remove the absolute prohibition on travelling actually ordered in the High Court. It now appears that a Community law issue is alive in this appeal.' He said that if the matter could not be resolved in the Supreme Court then his instructions were to refer it to the European Court.

'I should inform the court that the Attorney General felt

himself to have no discretion but to take the matter before the High Court. He felt it was not right or appropriate for him to sit in judgement himself or to deal with it on the nod.'

Mr Shanley said that the Eighth Amendment did not contemplate 'a probability of risk to the life of the mother – if it were so you would be asking the court to balance two wholly unequal consequences or risks, namely probability versus inevitability. If you adopt this approach you are not giving due regard to the life of the unborn.

'Lives are equal and due regard is to be given to the life of the mother where the mother's life is in imminent danger of death. If you do adopt the other standard you would need only to establish a substantial risk to the life of the mother. If this were permitted, you would not be giving due regard to the life of the unborn.'

Mr Justice McCarthy asked: 'Are you saying that there is only one answer: the child must be aborted if the mother is in imminent danger of death?'

In the most crucial question of the whole hearing, Mr Justice McCarthy added: 'If this is so . . . do you accept that the Eighth Amendment envisages a "lawful abortion" in Ireland?'

Mr Shanley replied: 'Yes, I accept that. The pregnancy may be terminated if, but only if, there is an inevitable danger to the right to life of the mother.'

Chief Justice Finlay said: 'Your formula is not a formula of absolute equality. It allows for tolerance. It is an equality until imminence of death. Who should survive?'

Mr Shanley replied: 'The mother.'

Chief Justice Finlay: 'Why? Would you agree that "due regard" in a broad sense would appear to rest on proper regard for the right to life of the woman?'

Mr Shanley: 'I do accept that. Possibly there are reasons for looking at the whole scheme of rights in the Constitution.'

Mr Justice McCarthy: 'But if the lives are absolutely balanced, why come down on one side or another?'

Mr Shanley made no direct reply, but added: 'In any event, neither the evidence of the psychologist nor the evidence of the child's mother is sufficient to satisfy the standard offered by Mr Rogers. As a matter of evidence, the test was not satisfied.'

On the third day of the hearing Mr Shanley addressed the court further on the legal meaning of the Eighth Amendment and its effect on the girl. He agreed that the rights of the girl's parents should also be weighed when favouring the mother's right to life over that of the unborn. He entered into a discussion of hypothetical cases with the judges, including that of a woman who would die if she carried her baby to full term. Mr Shanley said the State could intervene if death was inevitable.

'Medical knowledge can prophesy that death will follow if an abortion is not carried out,' said Chief Justice Finlay. 'But here we are dealing with a risk, which generally speaking, is quite different . . . Does your formula not appear largely inflexible with regard to the particular facts in this case?'

Mr Shanley replied: 'My formula does not take account of a mental or emotional factor which will possibly lead to the mother taking her life . . . The difficulty in allowing abortion where the death of the mother is not certain is that you push the test back and back.' On the right to travel issue, he said that it was not absolute and was subject to the exercise of all constitutional rights.

Mr Justice McCarthy asked: 'If an English citizen comes here, finds herself pregnant, can she go home to the United Kingdom for an abortion? Can this court restrain her?'

Mr Shanley said that each case would be decided on its facts, but that yes, such a woman could be detained in Ireland.

'Is everyone bound by these rights which derive from the Christian and democratic nature of the State?' Mr Justice Hederman asked.

'Yes. Even non-Christians,' replied Mr Shanley.

Mr Rogers said: 'On Mr Shanley's test it would be virtually impossible for any mother to satisfy that test. It leaves out of account psychiatric illness, which is a risk in waiting for the life of the mother. Suicide may come for many reasons and like a bolt from the blue. There is often no time for intervention. It may be brought on by panic. Quite often the physical expression and behaviour of the person is normal. It has been catalogued that this is so. Consequently we must take account of this as a matter of principle and common sense in addressing the risk to my client's life. To adopt Mr Shanley's test would fall short of the "due regard" requirement for the equal right of the mother. It has been demonstrated that there is a threat to the life of the mother. How, then, is it to be measured? There is an enormous responsibility on this court in fixing these boundaries. Mr Shanley's test seems not only to posit an imminent but also an immediate risk of death.

'The "inevitable test" puts the doctor in an impossible situation. He must be in a position to say that the mother's death was inevitable. How can he possibly say that with certainty? I have difficulty in accepting as a rational exercise how the State can police an intention. This is a very intimate aspect of the human person.'

Chief Justice Finlay asked: 'Surely where there is a stated intention to do a wrong the State has a right to injunct such criminal or unlawful intentions?'

Mr Rogers replied: 'That goes somewhat further. The injunction is against the act not the intention. A party may have the intention and change her mind.'

Mr Justice O'Flaherty commented: 'The woman may go to England with the intention of having an abortion and then change her mind and return home. There is also the likelihood that she will receive further counselling after arrival in England.'

Mr Rogers asked: 'Can this order be enforced? How are you to know what the parties did; where and when? Can the State ask a woman returning from the United Kingdom, "What did you do?" What is the effectiveness of such an order?'

Mr Justice McCarthy: 'If the court has the power to restrict travel abroad then surely it may have powers to have the woman examined?'

Mr Rogers: 'Exactly, that is why I am so reluctant to accept the right of restricting travel. If you do, it carries you so much further.'

Mr Justice Hederman: 'What if the woman goes outside the State for more than nine months? Is the State entitled to require the production of the child?'

Mr Rogers said there was established legal authority for the proposition that a court will not issue an order which is futile. Chief Justice Finlay agreed that the Supreme Court accepted this principle.

Mr Rogers: 'These are the authorities on which the court can rely in measuring the extent of the risk to the life of the mother in this case.'

Mr Shanley replied: 'I reiterate my submission that the psychological evidence led in the High Court was not sufficient to warrant a finding in favour of the mother.'

The five judges retired for less than an hour before returning. On doing so, Chief Justice Finlay announced: 'The court is satisfied that the appeal should be allowed. Reasons will be given later and counsel will be notified.'

With those two brief sentences amounting to just twenty words, the face of Irish constitutional history had been for ever altered.

A week later, on Thursday, 5 March, the five judges each gave their detailed reasons for their decision, on which they had not unanimously agreed.

Chief Justice Finlay defended the Attorney General and said it would have been 'quite incorrect' for him to 'take it upon himself' to decide on the case without bringing it to the courts. He rejected that part of the defendants' application. He also rejected their application that the courts were inhibited from exercising constitutional rights 'by reason of a want of legislation'.

On the interpretation of the Eighth Amendment, he said: 'I accept the submissions made on behalf of the Attorney General, that the doctrine of the harmonious interpretation of the Constitution involves in this case a consideration of the constitutional rights and obligations of the mother of the unborn child and the inter-relation of those rights and obligations with the rights and obligations of other people and, of course, with the right to life of the unborn child as well.

'Such a harmonious interpretation . . . leads me to the conclusion that in vindicating and defending as far as practicable the right of the unborn to life, but at the same time giving due regard to the right of the mother to life, the court must . . . concern itself with the position of the mother within a family group, with persons on whom she is dependant . . . and her interaction with other citizens and members of society in the area in which the activities occur.

'Having regard to that conclusion, I am satisfied that the test proposed on behalf of the Attorney General that the life of the unborn child could only be terminated if it were established that an inevitable or immediate risk to the life of the mother existed, for the avoidance of which a termination of the pregnancy was necessary, insufficiently vindicates the mother's right to life.

'I therefore conclude that the proper test to be applied is that if it is established as a matter of probability that there is a real and substantial risk to the life, as distinct from the health, of the mother, which can only be avoided by the termination of a pregnancy, such termination is permissible.'

He added that the girl's family had satisfied this test, saying they had established 'as a matter of probability that there is a real and substantial risk to the life of the mother by self-destruction', which could only be avoided by an abortion. He said the right to travel issue did not need to be officially commented upon in light of the ruling on risk to life, but added that as he felt that they were matters of 'considerable public interest' he wished to express his view. 'Notwithstanding the very fundamental nature of the right to travel . . . in a free society, I would be forced to conclude that if there were a stark conflict between the right of a mother of an unborn child to travel and the right to life of the . . . child, the right to life would necessarily have to take precedence.'

He praised the 'strikingly commendable attitude' of the family in returning to Ireland when the injunctions were first granted, 'notwithstanding the anguish which they were suffering'. He said there could be 'no question' of referring any of the questions about rights to travel under European law to the European Court of Justice and that it should be dealt with by Irish law only.

Mr Justice Hederman agreed with the first two main issues, on the actions of the Attorney General and the want of legislation. But he disagreed with the Chief Justice on the abortion issue and ruled that he would have upheld the order of the High Court.

Giving his reasons, he said: 'The right of life is guaranteed to every life born or unborn. One cannot make distinctions between individual phases of the unborn life before birth, or between unborn and born life.'

He said neither the High Court nor the Supreme Court had heard from or seen the girl and had instead to rely on 'the remarkable paucity of evidence' on the vital matter of the alleged threat to her life.

He acknowledged that the psychologist believed there was a threat to the girl's life by an act of self-destruction by reason of the fact of being pregnant, but said, 'This is a very extreme reaction to pregnancy, even to an unwanted pregnancy. The fact that pregnancy is unwanted is no justification for terminating it or attempting to terminate it.'

He added: 'Suicide threats can be contained. The duration of the pregnancy is a matter of months and it should not be impossible to guard the girl against self-destruction and pre-serve the life of the unborn child at the same time. The choice is between the certainty of the unborn life and a feared substantial danger of death but no degree of certainty of the mother by way of self-destruction.'

Mr Justice Niall McCarthy disagreed and voted to set aside the High Court order on the grounds that the girl should not be prevented from having an abortion because of the 'real and substantial risk' and her explicit right to travel.

He was the most critical of successive governments in failing to enact the legislation relating to the Eighth Amendment, describ-ing it as 'inexcusable'. He added: 'What are pregnant women to do? What are the parents of a pregnant girl under age to do? What are the medical profession to do? They have no guidelines save what may be gleaned from judgements in this case.

'The Amendment, born of public disquiet, historically divisive of our people, guaranteeing in its laws to respect and by its laws to defend the right to life of the unborn, remains bare of legislative direction.'

Mr Justice McCarthy, in the minority on the issue of the girl's right to travel, said: 'The reality is that each nation governs itself and enforces its own criminal law. A court in one state cannot enjoin an individual leaving it from wrongdoing outside it in another state or states.'

He said he could not disregard the fact that in the eight years since the enactment of the Eighth Amendment, 'many thou-sands of Irish women' had travelled to England for abortions. He added: 'It is ironic that out of those many thousands, in one case of a girl of fourteen, a victim of sexual abuse and statutory rape, in the care of loving parents who chose with her to embark on further trauma, having sought help from priest, doctor and Gardai, and with an outstanding sense of responsibility to the law of the land, should have the full panoply of the law brought to bear on them in their anguish.'

Mr Justice O'Flaherty agreed that the High Court orders

should be set aside. He said that the judges had brought 'all powers of concentration' to bear on the matters before them. He did not believe the Eighth Amendment had brought about any fundamental change to the existing law under the 1861 Act and said that that law provided 'enlightened' protection for the child in the womb. 'It treats the family with such respect and in language of such clarity and simplicity that any attempt to summarize or paraphrase it must be inadequate.'

He said that the State's role in dealing with women with unwanted pregnancies should be a positive rather than a negative one. 'No effort of heart or mind or resource should be spared by all citizens to provide encouragement for such mothers,' he added. In a Constitution which assures the dignity and freedom of the individual it could not be right to interfere with the authority of the family or freedom of movement.

He believed that abortion on demand was not something that could be legalized under the terms of the Constitution, nor could promotional propaganda about abortions abroad. But he added: 'Until legislation is enacted to provide otherwise, I believe that the law in this State is that surgical intervention which has the effect of terminating pregnancy bone fide undertaken to save the life of the mother where she is in danger of death is permissible under the Constitution and the law.'

Mr Justice Egan also agreed that Mr Justice Costello's order should be set aside. He said that the inclusion of the words 'with due regard for the equal right to life of the mother' in the Eighth Amendment recognized 'that an abortion will not in every possible circumstances be unlawful'.

He added: 'In my opinion the true test should be that a pregnancy may be terminated if its continuance as a matter of probability involves a real and substantial risk to the life of the mother. The risk must be to her life. But it is irrelevant, in my view, that it should be a risk of self-destruction rather than a risk to life for any other reason. The evidence establishes that such a risk exists in the present case.'

TWELVE

During the protracted arguments in the Supreme Court, the legal precedent set by the case of another 14-year-old girl which had caused as much public furore in polite English society fifty-four years earlier was repeatedly cited for its remarkable similarities to the girl's predicament.

In *Rex* vs *Bourne* [1938] – some twenty-nine years before abortions were legalized in Britain under the 1967 Abortion (NHS Family Planning) Act – a jury at the Old Bailey in London was essentially asked to consider the question of whether a young rape victim should be allowed an abortion if her mental health was at risk.

The trial hinged on the actions of an eminent London gynaecologist who had performed an abortion on a 14-year-old girl who had been violently raped by troopers of the Royal Horse Guards in their barracks in Horse Guards Parade, Whitehall, central London. The doctor, Mr Aleck Bourne, who deliberately chose to take on the case and to publicly declare his deed afterwards so as to challenge the existing law in the courts, claimed that he had a duty and an obligation to the girl because of her extreme distress.

According to the law reports of the case, the jury were told that the girl had been raped with 'great violence and in circumstances which would have been most terrifying to any woman, let alone a child of fourteen'. The court heard that the girl, with two older friends, had been lured into the Whitehall barracks one spring evening to see 'a horse with a green tail'.

'Foolishly, but innocently, she accepted the invitation and was taken up to a room where her clothes were ripped off and

she was then held down by five men who assaulted her twice,'
Mr Bourne was later to explain. The drunken troopers punched
and raped her, then set her free. Her friends, who had also been
approached by some soldiers, kicked them and ran away.

The girl staggered to Downing Street where she told a policeman what had happened. She was taken to Cannon Row police
station and then to St Thomas's Hospital, where she had to be
treated for her serious physical injuries.

Three soldiers admitted assault, but denied rape. They claimed
she had consented to sexual intercourse and that they thought
she was eighteen. They were later jailed for a total of ten years
for rape, attempted rape and aiding and abetting rape.

On falling pregnant the girl suffered 'extreme nervous symptoms' when she contemplated having to carry a child 'always
with her to remind her of the most horrible thing which could
ever happen to any girl'. Her respectable, middle-class parents
agreed that they could not let her go through with the pregnancy and promised to help her.

They first approached a doctor at St Thomas's Hospital, but
he refused to carry out an abortion, telling her parents that
because of the high breeding of the officers who had carried
out the attack, the child she was carrying might be a future
Prime Minister of England.

Her parents, who were 'so respectable they did not know the
address of any abortionist', then took her to Dr Joan Malleson,
later to become an energetic member of the Birth Control Movement and a founder of the Family Planning Association. Dr
Malleson wrote to Mr Bourne and asked for his assistance at
St Mary's Hospital, Paddington, west London, where he was
senior obstetrician and gynaecologist.

Mr Bourne, then aged fifty-one, had, it was known, previously carried out an abortion on a 15-year-old girl whose
physician had referred her to him. He had at first refused to
carry out the operation, but after the doctor told him he felt it
was necessary for the health of the young mother, he agreed.

Afterwards, he was criticized by some of those in his department at St Mary's, which seemed to him to be 'unjust'.

He later wrote: 'I decided that should another similar opportunity come my way, I would report what I had done to the police. The case of the girl in 1938 seemed to be a God-given opportunity as she had suffered the extremity of cruelty and horror and was, withal, an innocent child.'

Mr Bourne, the son of a Wesleyan minister and the father of three daughters, was a traditionalist in many ways – wearing a morning coat and top hat to work each day – but was also surprisingly anti-establishment. He once defended a colleague who had performed an abortion in Jersey in 1933, on a 28-year-old chambermaid whose four-month-old foetus he believed had died in the womb. His expert evidence denouncing claims that the foetus had been alive up until the abortion resulted in the doctor's acquittal on a charge of criminal abortion, and Mr Bourne was thereafter seen as sympathetic to the cause of women's reproductive rights.

He admitted the 14-year-old rape victim to a ward in St Mary's after learning from Dr Malleson that the police surgeon, the girl's family and her doctor all believed that the abortion, or curettage as it was referred to then, should be allowed her.

He wrote to Dr Malleson: 'I shall be delighted to admit her . . . and curette her. I have done this before and have not the slightest hesitation in doing it again. I have said that the next time I have such an opportunity I would write to the Attorney General and invite him to take action.'

The girl was admitted on 6 June 1938 and Mr Bourne watched her carefully for a week, 'to be sure of what type of girl' he was dealing with. He wrote later:

> The ward sister told me that, surprisingly, the girl seemed normally cheerful, and I remember at first being in doubt whether the operation should be performed.

But then on the seventh day it was necessary for me to examine her for the first time since I had seen her. It was a completely painless method ... to find out if the girl had been infected at the time of the rape, and it might have taken me ten to fifteen seconds.

But the occasion caused a complete breakdown of her morale. All her assumed cheerfulness disappeared and she wept beyond control. This decided me at once that she had to be relieved of her pregnancy.

In a report which bore remarkable similarities to the evidence of the psychologist who interviewed 'X' more than fifty years later, Mr Bourne later told a court that he found the young rape victim to be a 'sensitive, intelligent child, who was trying to hide her feelings behind a mask of courage'.

After careful consideration, he eventually performed an abortion operation on her on the morning of 14 June 1938, without charging any fee. The girl was six weeks' pregnant and he said he performed the operation to save her from mental collapse.

A few hours after Mr Bourne performed the operation, a chief inspector and another police officer from Scotland Yard called at the hospital to see him.

They told me that the operation must not be done, as they wanted the girl to give evidence as a witness at the Old Bailey against the guardsmen who had been arrested for assault [Mr Bourne wrote].

The Chief Inspector also said that in no circumstances could he countenance the operation 'on humanitarian grounds'. I made it plain to the Inspector that I could not recognize his right to dictate to me what I, as a surgeon, should or should not decide to do in the best interests of my patients, that I did not understand what he meant by 'humanitarian grounds', and that in any event I had already operated on the girl, and if he wished he could arrest me.

Mr Bourne was arrested and charged under the Offences against the Person Act 1861 section 58 (still enforceable in Ireland), with unlawfully using an instrument with intent to procure the miscarriage.

The section states:

> Every woman being with child, who with intent to procure her own miscarriage, shall unlawfully administer to herself poison or other noxious thing, or shall unlawfully use any instrument or any other means whatsoever with the like intent, shall be guilty of a felony and being convicted thereof shall be liable, at the direction of the court, to be kept in penal servitude for life or for any term not less than five years, or to be imprisoned for any term not exceeding two years, with or without hard labour and with or without solitary confinement.

Lawyers for the prosecution also relied on the Infant Life Preservation Act 1929 which stated:

> Any person who with intent to destroy the life of a child capable of being born alive or by any wilful act causes a child to die before it has an existence independent of its mother, shall be guilty of a felony, to wit, child destruction.
>
> No person shall be found guilty of an offence under this section unless it is provided that the act which caused the death of the child was not done in good faith for the purpose only of preserving the life of the mother.

If found guilty, Mr Bourne faced a maximum of twenty years' hard labour for his actions. He received hundreds of letters of support from all over the world, from as far away as China, and said that the only people who did not write were from Catholic countries or Hitler's Germany.

At his Old Bailey trial in July of that year he was defended by Mr Roland Oliver (later Mr Justice Oliver) and solicitors for the London and Counties Medical Protection Society.

Mr Bourne claimed in court that in his opinion 'the continuance of the pregnancy would probably cause serious injury to the girl, injury so serious as to justify the removal of the pregnancy at a time when the operation could be performed without any risk to the girl and under favourable conditions'. This was supported by the evidence of a psychologist Dr John Rees who interviewed the girl, and claimed that she was 'shaken to the core' and if she gave birth to a child would become 'a mental wreck'. Using the language of an era freshly emerged from World War I and about to enter World War II (and in words that could have equally been used in the case of 'X'), he told the court: 'The danger is mental, rather comparable to shell-shock. Like being wounded, blown up and buried. In this case she had been wounded and, one might say, blown up. Why should she be buried? If you are allowing the pregnancy to continue you are increasing the strain and you are bound almost certainly to have some form of psycho-neurotic or mental breakdown.'

Dr Rees said that the legacies of incest and rape in the young were terror and horror that would undermine long-term physical health. He said the victims of such acts often bore a long-term revulsion of sex and even marriage, and a general mental instability that could lead to schizophrenia.

He said that to him preserving life meant preserving health. He added that it was not possible to let a person drift into mental breakdown in the future and say one was preserving life. 'Surely it can be claimed that a serious mental breakdown is tantamount to mental death?' he asked.

Mr Bourne agreed. He said: 'The circumstances of her conception were such as to plant in her mind seeds of terror . . . I felt that the mental injury would last a very long time and there would be nervous psycho-neurotic and other troubles with their secondary physical illnesses perhaps all her life.'

The jury was directed that it was for the prosecution to prove beyond reasonable doubt that the operation was not performed in good faith for the purpose only of preserving the life of the girl. The surgeon had not got to wait until the patient was in peril of immediate death, but it was his duty to perform the operation if, on reasonable grounds and with adequate knowledge, he was of the opinion that the probable consequence of the continuance of the pregnancy would be to make the patient a physical and mental wreck.

The trial judge, Mr Justice Macnaghten, carefully distinguished between danger to life and danger to health and between the act of the professional abortionist and an operation openly performed by a qualified surgeon.

At a time when Britain was suffering from a plague of back-street abortionists, he told the jury: 'This is the second case at these July sessions at this court where a charge of an offence against that section (of law) has been preferred, and I mention that case only to show you how different the case before you is from the type of case which usually comes before a criminal court.

'In that case a woman without any medical skill or any medical qualifications did what is alleged against Mr Bourne here: she unlawfully used an instrument for the purpose of procuring the miscarriage of a pregnant girl. She did it for money – twenty-five shillings was her fee and she came from a distance to a place in London to do it. A pound had to be paid to make the appointment.

'She came, she used her instrument and within an interval measured not by minutes but by seconds, the victim of her malpractice was dead on the floor. She was paid the rest of her fee and she went away.

'The case here is very different. A man of the highest skill, openly, in one of our great hospitals, performs the operation . . . as an act of charity, without fee or reward, and unquestionably believing he was doing the right thing and that he ought, in the performance of his duty as a member of a profession devoted to the alleviation of human suffering, to do it.

'The question that you have to determine is whether the Crown has proved to your satisfaction beyond reasonable doubt that the act which Mr Bourne admittedly did was not done in good faith for the purpose only of preserving the life of the girl.

'This is a case of great importance to the public and more especially to the medical profession, but you will observe that it has nothing to do with the ordinary cases of procuring abortions. In those cases, the operation is performed by a person of no skill, with no medical qualifications and there is no pretence that it is done for the preservation of the mother's life.

'You have heard a great deal of discussion as to the difference between danger to life and danger to health. It may be that you are more fortunate than I am, but I confess that I have felt great difficulty in understanding what the discussion really meant. Life depends upon health and it may be that health is so gravely impaired that death results.'

He directed the jury to consider that the words 'for the purpose of preserving the life of the mother' should be given a 'reasonable' view of their meaning. 'I do not think that it is contended that those words mean merely for the preservation of the life of the mother from instant death.

'Apparently there is a great divergence of view even in the medical profession itself. Some there may be, for all I know, who hold the view that the fact that the woman desires the operation to be performed is sufficient justification for it. That is not the law. The desire of a woman to be relieved of her pregnancy is no justification for performing the operation. On the other hand, no doubt there are people who, from what are said to be religious reasons, object to the operation being performed at all in any circumstances. That is not the law either.

'On the contrary, a person who holds such an opinion ought not to be a doctor practising in that branch of medicine for, if a case arose where the life of a woman could be saved by performing the operation and the doctor refused to perform it because of some religious opinion, and the woman died, he would be in grave peril of being brought before this court on a charge of mansligence by negligence.'

The judge said that it was 'very undesirable' for a young girl of such tender years to be delivered of a child. He asked the jury to consider the evidence about the effect of the rape on a child under the age of fifteen.

'Here you have evidence . . . that the mental effect produced by the pregnancy brought about by the terrible rape . . . must be most prejudicial. No doubt you will think it is only common sense that a girl who for nine months has to carry in her body the reminder of the dreadful scene and then go through the pangs of childbirth must suffer great mental anguish, unless, indeed, she is a girl of very exceptional character . . . a feeble-minded girl, or one belonging to the class described as the prostitute class.

'In the case of an ordinary decent girl, brought up in an ordinary decent way, you may well think that Dr Rees was not over-stating the effect on her mind of giving birth to her child.

'So far as danger to life is concerned you cannot, of course, be certain of the result unless you wait until a person is dead. The difficulty that arises in the case of abortion is that by the operation the potential life of the unborn child is destroyed.

'The law of this land has always held human life to be sacred, and the protection that the law gives to human life extends also to the unborn child in the womb . . . which must not be destroyed unless the destruction of that child is for the purpose of preserving the yet more precious life of the mother.'

The judge said that the prosecution had accepted that Mr Bourne thought it right to perform the operation 'in view of the age of the girl and the fact that she had been raped with great violence'. He drew an analogy between the decision to abort a foetus and a surgeon faced with what appears to be an acute attack of appendicitis, but who finds that his diagnosis is mistaken because the appendix is normal. 'Is the surgeon to be blamed for performing the operation?' the judge asked. 'He used his best judgement . . . and if he, in good faith, thinks that it is necessary for preserving the life of the mother in the real sense of the words, not only is he entitled to perform the operation, it is his duty to perform it.'

After forty minutes' deliberation, the jury unanimously found that Mr Bourne was not guilty and exonerated him from all blame. The jury's verdict marked the first time that the health of the woman had been accepted in law as grounds for abortion.

Mr Bourne wrote some years later that he had 'never felt an atom of fear' about the verdict because of his inner conviction that he had done the right thing and 'had the support and sympathy of the vast mass of people'.

He said his defence had been based upon his claim that serious damage to either physical or mental health was 'indirectly as valid' as the certain risk of death if the pregnancy was allowed to continue.

The jury's decision was greeted with widespread approval and reflected general public opinion about the case, apart from those in Catholic quarters who now feared the worst. The British Medical Association expressed their enthusiastic reception of the verdict and newspaper editorials agreed that no other verdict was 'conceivable' in light of the 'revolting pregnancy'.

Legal experts considered the verdict a vastly more important event in the history of English law than the later Abortion Act itself. The legal precedent had been created which then took the form of case law.

Thereafter began the continued attempts to embody the court's decision in an Act of Parliament, which were repeatedly thwarted by the concerted efforts of Catholic and other members of Parliament, but which eventually succeeded in 1967.

Mr Bourne, who had single-handedly brought about the first reforms advocating abortion choice in extreme circumstances, was by no means an advocate of abortion on demand, and spent many years after his trial rejecting requests from women who thought he would readily relieve them of their unwanted pregnancies. In his autobiography, *A Doctor's Creed*, written in 1962, twenty-four years after his trial, he wrote: 'They called at my door at Wimpole Street, there were almost constant telephone calls for appointments, letters arrived from doctors and patients from all over the country. Needless to say I resisted every plea, but the nuisance persisted for months and then, in diminishing intensity, for years.'

He said he believed to be 'nonsense' the Catholic argument that a foetus is viable from the moment of conception (preferring instead the view that it was only viable once it was capable of independent existence), but he also believed that it would be murder to deliberately kill a viable child before birth. He also rejected the Christian doctrine that a foetus, as an unbaptized being, did not yet have a passport to heaven and therefore took precedence over the life of its mother, who – if baptized – would be a candidate for the life hereafter. 'The arguments about the foetus and its soul are of the same area of realism and intelligence as the schoolmen's discussions on how many angels can dance on the head of a pin,' he said disdainfully. He added: 'Despite the reputation I suffered after the trial . . . I have always been very strict in the interpretation of the law.

'Many times I have been asked if the law should not be radically liberalized . . . so as to permit abortion for almost any woman who wants the operation, even on the flimsiest of grounds.'

He said the proponents for such a change claimed that if the laws were relaxed the estimated 50,000 to 100,000 women who sought unlawful abortions each year at that time would suffer far less death and injury. Unable to foresee the massive growth of private medicine in abortion practice, he wondered where all the hospital beds would come from to cater for the expected influx of legitimate cases.

He also questioned the thinking of those who were unfamiliar with the emotional roller coaster a woman embarks upon when she discovers she is pregnant.

Those who plead for an extensive relaxation of the law have no idea of the very many cases where a woman makes an impassioned plea for the pregnancy to be 'finished' in the first three months, who, later when it is born, is very thankful indeed that it was not killed while still an embryo [he wrote].

During my long years in practice I have had many a letter of deepest gratitude for refusing to accede to an early appeal. During the first few months the distress of an unwanted pregnancy entirely blinds many women to the prospect of an actual baby being born so long ahead.

The threat of suicide, so common, is seldom implemented, but it is occasionally. A considerable difficulty is the assessment of the reality of the threat of suicide. Should a practical psychiatrist think that the danger is real and inevitable it is our duty to terminate pregnancy to preserve her life and thus the act is within the law.

He said that many women suffered feelings of remorse when they did go through with an abortion. Others often asked for a second or third abortion on demand, and would place the doctor who carried out the original abortion in a difficult moral dilemma.

Whenever he believed an abortion could not be justified Mr Bourne said he would urge the patient not to run off to an abortionist, offer to see her as often as she wanted, arrange hostel accommodation if necessary and even speak to hostile parents or husbands on her behalf.

'I have always felt that if I cannot help them by abortion then the least I can do is to try to help them through their pregnancy and after.' He said many women asked him to help arrange to have the baby adopted once it was born, but very often found that they could not bear to part with it after all.

In the case of young rape victims, however, he was still adamant of his view. 'With no reservation I would include as an unquestioned justification the termination of a pregnancy which has followed the rape of a girl below the age of consent. I wonder how many of those inflexible bigots whose own daughters conceive after rape would retain their harsh attitude when the disaster came into their own homes,' he commented.

A remarkable man for his time and a lifelong socialist, Mr Bourne later retired to Ashstead, Surrey, where he died in 1974 aged eighty-eight. The fate of the celebrated victim who – if she had survived – would have been in her seventieth year at the time of the Irish abortion 'X' controversy, was never further documented.

As one legal adviser to the 'X' case said afterwards: 'The similarities between the Bourne case girl in 1938 and "X" in 1992 were astonishing. Both were 14-year-old innocents from utterly respectable families, both were the victims of serious sexual assault, and both were reluctant partners in the legal processes that were to bring about abortion reform in their own countries.

'The fifty-four years that passed between their pregnancies counted for nothing at all in Ireland, where time had virtually stood still until "X"'s foetus started the clocks ticking again.'

THIRTEEN

The Supreme Court ruling offered the first glimmer of hope in a long dark tunnel of despair for 'X' and her family. The girl's appearance was, for the first time, described as 'serene' on hearing the news. The family had gone through the mill and come out the other side, all those around them hoped.

Friends, anxious at the now strained relations between the girl's parents, hoped that the news would bring the family closer as a unit than they had been since the beginning of their ordeal.

The parents were still finding it hard to come to terms with all that had happened to them. One of them commented that they would never have believed it if someone had told them a few months before that one day they would be almost ecstatic at the news that their child could have an abortion.

Reprieved from the burden of having to take their case to the European Court of Human Rights – which would almost certainly have been unable to hear it before the 24-week UK time limit for the abortion to go ahead – the family were determined to 'get it over with' before the courts changed their minds or before a pro-life group slapped a new injunction on them.

Officially under the now clarified Irish law, they would have been allowed to have had the abortion done in Ireland (the first time it would have ever been legally possible in such circumstances) but in practical terms it would have been impossible. Considered a matter of professional misconduct by the Irish Medical Council, abortions other than to save the life of the mother were simply not allowed. Even if they had wanted to spare their sick daughter the ordeal of travelling to England again for the operation, they had little choice and were not prepared to wait a moment longer.

Almost immediately they put into action their plan to have the DNA sampling done under police supervision in England, at the same time preparing once again to travel across the Irish Sea to have the pregnancy terminated.

Their doctor referred them to St Mary's Hospital in Manchester, and they embarked on their journey on the afternoon of Tuesday, 3 March. With them was Detective Inspector Anthony Sourke, ready to personally transport any foetal matter for DNA testing to Cellmark's laboratories in Oxfordshire. The girl, nearly thirteen weeks pregnant, was admitted to the sprawling Victorian red-brick building in Whitworth Park, Manchester, for the delicate DNA-extracting procedure to be conducted.

St Mary's, founded in 1790 and by the 1990s part of the Central Manchester Healthcare Trust funded by the British National Health Service, was famous for its care of women and children. Dr Brian Lieberman, the South African-born consultant obstetrician and gynaecologist who was also the co-ordinator of the regional in-vitro fertilization centre, saw personally to his new young charge and prepared her for the procedure ahead.

'She needed some special care because of her age and the circumstances in which she became pregnant,' he said. 'She was referred to the gynaecology department as a straightforward medical referral from Ireland. This was not a police matter but a medical one.

'She came along for the procedure of chorion villius sampling, to extract material from the placenta for DNA testing. This is a relatively simple procedure that takes a matter of minutes and is done under local anaesthetic.

'Once this was done, we prepared the girl for the next stage of her care and attached a foetal monitor to her to assess the state of the foetus. That is when we discovered that there was a problem.'

Dr Lieberman quickly realized something was wrong when he could find no trace of a foetal heartbeat. He broke the news to the girl and her family that fate seemed to have intervened in her case.

He explained to the girl's bewildered parents that she had suffered what was described in medical terms as a 'missed abortion' but was later described in court as 'a spontaneous and natural miscarriage'. He further said that on examination of the girl it was his opinion that the foetus would never have survived to full term.

The news was a tremendous irony for the girl and her family, having been the catalyst for one of the most important and publicly debated constitutional changes in Irish history. But it was also regarded as a blessing and an end to their grief. A friend who saw them shortly afterwards said: 'They felt as if God had personally intervened to ease their suffering. They had been completely against abortion before this terrible thing happened to their daughter and going through with the termination was the ultimate – and perhaps the most traumatic – part of this whole distressing episode for them.'

The parents and doctors, fearing the girl might suffer from further depression and feel long-term guilt and remorse after the abortion, also regarded the miscarriage as being much easier to handle psychologically.

It was a well-known risk of the process to withdraw material from the foetal sac through chorion villius sampling (CVS) that the foetus might miscarry afterwards. Statistics put the chances of it happening at about 1 in 1,000.

Dr Lieberman said: 'We just don't know if the CVS caused it or whether she would have had this miscarriage anyway. At the end of the day, in this particular case, it didn't really matter.'

Dr Paul Debenham, of Cellmark, said the risk increased depending on the age of the mother, the stage of pregnancy and the type of sample taken. 'In such a case the testing is generally done between fourteen and twenty weeks, well within the time zone to allow for the results to get back and be checked and for an abortion to then go ahead within the legal limit of twenty-four weeks.

'It is the same type of sampling as is done for Down's Syndrome tests and the risks are always clearly pointed out to the mother,' he added.

After the miscarriage was discovered, the medical procedures necessary to purge the girl of the dead foetus were conducted. The sampling process also complete, the girl was kept in over-night before being allowed to leave hospital care. Relieved and emotional, the family flew home to the tearful embrace of their family and friends.

Reluctant to be cast as heroic legislation-breakers, they told everyone that they had always just wanted what was best for the girl and now wanted to try and return to some sort of normality.

They were little prepared for the emotional ordeal still ahead of them. Psychologists who help victims of child sex abuse and their families come to terms with their experiences say that many of the most serious problems occur when the victims and their families are least suspecting them. 'It is when the dust has settled and friends and supporters start to drift away and leave them to get on with their lives that some of the worst problems emerge,' said Caroline Ainscough, consultant clinical psychologist and author.

'Left to their own devices and without the drama and tension and constant support and succour of friends and family, victims and their relatives can suddenly feel utterly deflated and defeated by events. It is at times like these that they need support the most, but it is exactly at that time that those who have been around them day and night for weeks feel it is best to leave them alone.

'The victim and her family are expected to be getting on with life and coping, when in reality that is generally far from the truth. It is generally at this time that tensions and problems previously submerged by events, tend to come to the fore.'

The accused and his family had their own tensions to deal with as the interest in the 'X' case remained high. For weeks they had read about the girl and her family in every newspaper and seen almost daily reports of their suffering on television. They could hardly believe the international coverage the case was getting or stomach the sympathy being generated for someone whom they regarded as the chief culprit.

Insisting on his innocence to everyone, the man continued to go about his business and tried to carry on as normal a family life as possible. But the strain in this household was also beginning to show and as all but their closest friends and relatives stayed away, the seeming injustice of it all caused deep family rifts.

The girl and her family had moved well away from the district. They had not yet decided whether it should be a permanent move, but for now they were the chief witnesses in a possible prosecution and the police did not want them being interfered with by the accused man or anyone who supported him. The question of whether or not the family should sell up and move permanently was a vexing one. Why should they be forced out of their home, they agonized. Was not the man's family eventually likely to move away anyway once he was in prison?

Their minds were made up after an incident in a Dublin supermarket which left the girl further traumatized. On one of their first outings back into the community in an attempt to return to normality, she and her mother rounded the corner of an aisle in the store and almost bumped into the man's wife and daughter. An uncomfortable confrontation ensued. The look on the face of the man's daughter – the girl's former best friend – upset her dreadfully. Leaving the store, she begged her mother to take her away from the area. Her parents conceded. Their house was prepared for sale, and they stayed in accommodation on the other side of Dublin.

Their son, a bright child and a talented singer, had to change schools, but seemed to be taking the tremendous upheaval in his life remarkably well. 'Maybe it was because he was still too young to really understand all that was going on, but he turned out to be the most resilient one of all,' commented a friend of the family. 'He had suffered a total change in his family circumstances, moving house and home, having a sick sister and a mother and father who were behaving unusually. He had to leave his school and the singing group that was so dear to his heart, but he seemed to take it all in his stride, and it was often his sense of humour and wish to keep things normal that kept the rest of them sane.'

The girl was enrolled at a new school for whenever she felt able to restart her education and her parents meanwhile investigated the possibility of hiring a private tutor for her.

The staff at the new school were fully briefed about the girl's circumstances and were said to have been 'marvellously supportive' of her and her family. At first she attended only a few classes to see how she could cope, and then gradually built up her attendance. Inquisitive fellow pupils, who might otherwise have been suspicious at her regular absences, were told that she suffered from poor health and would occasionally need time off.

Her father returned to work full-time and her mother tried to start to come to terms with all that had happened to her family and her marriage. It was to be a most difficult period for her, as she tried to get back into the routine of a normal life, parted from those she had never wanted to let out of her sight again. 'She got herself into an understandably agitated state,' said a family friend. 'She felt strangely alienated from normal life and just couldn't cope at all. She needed a great deal of love and support at this time.'

The girl, meanwhile, was starting to cope quite well for the first time. In a series of counselling sessions during this time she was interviewed again by the psychologist who had first seen her. She was a different person. 'She was immediately relaxed, totally different,' he said. 'That vacant, panicky look had gone.' He was delighted to report that she was making the first tentative steps towards happiness.

Dr Mary Henry, a close friend of the family who kept in touch regularly, reported that the family were 'coping remarkably well' under the circumstances. 'They were such nice people – good, clean, decent, middle-class people – and the children were just the same,' she said. 'They were the type of children to have impeccable table manners and to jump up and clear the table away after dinner without even being asked. That never changed, even in the middle of all this upset.'

The girl's grandmother grew particularly close to her, and took her away for a short break with her uncle and aunt. 'It was a welcome breather for all of them,' said Dr Henry. 'The mother, I felt, was particularly under pressure. She was understandably being a bit overly protective towards the girl and was always at her side. They needed to get away from each other for a while, although the girl was still very reluctant to go out on her own or with friends.'

Dr Henry recalled one of the rare lighter moments during a visit to the family home, during which she told them of a new play in town called *Love Child* in which the illegitimate son of Bishop Eamonn Casey – whose clandestine sexual relationship had just become public – grew up and married Miss 'X'. 'I think it was one of the first times in a long while that I really heard them laugh,' said Dr Henry. 'And God knows they needed to.'

For the accused man, there was no such light relief. He took his family on a foreign holiday in April in an attempt to get away from the pressure. But he was disturbed to discover that the police had been to his house while the family were away.

A few months later, at 7.40 on the morning of Saturday, 25 July 1992, after a warrant issued by Judge Brian Kirby at his office the previous night, the officers rang his doorbell once again. In the presence of his family he was formally charged with nine offences against the girl, a legal minor – four of having unlawful carnal knowledge of her, the Irish legal wording for statutory rape. After replying 'Definitely not guilty', he was taken to the local Garda station where, two hours later, each of the charges against him were read out by Sergeant John Connolly. In the presence of his solicitor, Mr Garret Sheehan – a likeable and well respected Dublin lawyer renowned for taking on difficult cases – the accused man replied 'Nothing to say' to each charge.

At a special weekend sitting of Bridewell Court in south Dublin that day he appeared before Judge Gillian Hussey and was remanded on his own bail of IR £500 with an independent undertaking from a businessman friend of a further IR £2,000 as security.

A week later he appeared at Rathfarnham District Court, dressed in a dark grey pin-stripe suit and accompanied only by his solicitor. Members of the girl's family were in the courtroom to see him.

He strode out of the court smiling after the brief hearing and thanked the 'gentlemen' of the press as they jostled for position to take his photograph. With reporters and television cameras all around him he walked purposefully forward and into a waiting car. He even waved at the people watching him drive away.

At his next appearance, in September, he was accompanied by his wife. Tempers were running high. There was a fracas outside the court when he left. A photographer from the *Irish Press* newspaper had his camera snatched as he attempted to take pictures of the defendant. The camera was later returned by a man accompanying the defendant, with the film unravelled. The police were asked to investigate the incident, but no further action was taken.

For the government at least, the political controversy appeared to be over and the criminal law system was dealing with the relevant issues. Just when the dust seemed to be settling and providing a welcome breather from the abortion issue, a further potentially explosive incident lurched to the fore.

In the first week of May 1992, police were approached by a young man from Co. Londonderry, Northern Ireland, but living in the Republic, who told them that his former girlfriend, a Dublin woman, was ten weeks pregnant and planning to travel to Britain for an abortion.

The man, who was twenty-four and living in Co. Donegal in the north-west of the country, went into Kevin Street Garda station in central Dublin one Saturday and told police he wanted to use whatever means were possible to stop his girlfriend aborting their baby.

The request could have plunged Attorney General Whelehan into a fresh controversy and led to a spate of private actions for travel bans against other women in similar circumstances.

The authorities were understandably reluctant to get involved. The police contacted a legal assistant in the office of the Director of Public Prosecutions, who simply told them that it was not an offence under Irish law for a woman to have an abortion in Britain. She instructed them to submit a report to the Chief State Solicitor, who would pass it on to the Attorney General.

The pregnant woman, who was separated from her husband and in her mid thirties with four children, was said to be planning to travel abroad imminently and her boyfriend was desperate to stop her.

Hoping to test the suggestions made by the country's highest courts that the moral issue overrode travelling rights, the case could not have come at a more inopportune time for the government. Prime Minister Albert Reynolds had ten days earlier announced that the Attorney General had advised him that he would not seek any further state travel injunctions if the forthcoming Maastricht Treaty on Economic and Monetary Union was approved.

The police and the boyfriend's own legal advisers told him he was 'very unlikely' to succeed in the current climate. He then made tentative enquiries about seeking a private injunction against the woman on constitutional grounds, invoking the right to life of the unborn enshrined in the Eighth Amendment.

Already under counselling from a Dublin pregnancy advisory service, the woman was said to be 'horrified' on hearing of her boyfriend's actions and the possible ramifications for her. She had suffered complications after the birth of her last child, her marriage was in ruins, she was unemployed and had recently split up with her boyfriend. Primarily she did not want the child on health grounds, but there were other pressing factors against her having another child.

Temporarily reunited with her estranged husband because of the row, she left with him for England and had an abortion in London before the Chief State Solicitor had even been alerted to her plight. Her husband said later she had been 'very distressed' and had 'panicked' when she read in a newspaper that her boyfriend was trying to stop her having an abortion. 'It had been a nightmare for her,' he told the *Irish Sunday World*. 'One minute she wanted to have the abortion, the next minute she didn't. She was in a terrible state.'

The couple stayed with friends in London and the woman remained in the clinic for a number of days after the operation. When it was over, she telephoned a British newspaper to tell them that she had had the pregnancy terminated. 'She wanted to get her side across, to tell people that she did it for medical reasons,' her husband said.

He had hoped that he would be reunited with his wife after the abortion, but his wife and children moved into a Dublin hostel and she later told him the marriage was over.

The case sank without trace. Some journalists said they suspected the whole thing may have been a set-up by pro-life campaigners. But a spokeswoman for the Irish Family Planning Association said that the case was 'very real' and could have become as controversial as the 'X' case. 'Had it preceded "X", there might have been just as much furore. It placed the woman in a very difficult situation, and she and the boyfriend were irrevocably split by the issue,' she said.

A doctor at the south Dublin practice where the woman was a patient said: 'It caused her a great deal of further distress at an already distressing time. It made many who knew her aware that despite "X", a woman could in theory be dragged back from England or prevented from going in the first place. She was very, very alarmed.'

(Interestingly, the case bore similarities to that of two Oxford students in England a few years before, when the boyfriend unsuccessfully launched a High Court bid to stop his girlfriend having an abortion on the grounds of his rights as a father. The girl won the case, but eventually carried the pregnancy to full term anyway. The baby was believed to have been given up for adoption.)

Later that same month in a further outcry over abortion 2,000 copies of the *Guardian* newspaper were withheld from sale in Ireland by distributors because they carried an advertisement for Marie Stopes Clinics. In a move calculated to embarrass the government, Irish opposition MP Mr Proinsias de Rossa stood in the Dáil and read out the words of the banned advertisement, including the telephone numbers of two London abortion clinics, thereby consigning them for ever into the parliamentary records and enabling the media to report on them under the rules of privilege which allow reports of statements made in Parliamentary debates to be published or broadcast without fear or favour.

Mr de Rossa, leader of the Democratic Left group, told the Prime Minister that the move to withhold the newspaper was 'the latest ludicrous consequence of the Eighth Amendment'.

The Irish media agreed. An editorial in the *Irish Press* said the incident would be almost humorous 'if it did not provoke tears'. It added: 'It is time for Mr Reynolds and his government to say publicly this nonsense has to stop, that this is a democracy, not a dictatorship of self-appointed Ayatollahs.'

The Irish Foreign Affairs Minister Mr David Andrews said he was 'personally seriously embarrassed' at the withdrawal and shredding of the newspapers by distributors unsure of the legal position.

The farce continued when it was learned that the police, alerted by the anti-abortion lobby, had descended on the independent radio station 98FM and demanded copies of their transcripts after they had repeated the words of Mr de Rossa in the Dáil. They were apparently unaware of the rights of privilege.

A month later more than 2,000 copies of the *Guardian*, carrying a similar abortion advertisement, went on sale in the Republic. There was no comment from the office of the Attorney General and the distributors and bookshops said they had received no complaints.

There was little else to allow the government a respite from the topic of abortion. It quickly became apparent that despite the obvious relief for the family and their hope that everything would now return to normal after the miscarriage, the Supreme Court ruling had so shocked those who vehemently opposed abortion that a fresh uproar was about to begin in its wake. Even the pro-choice lobby were concerned at the meaning of the judge's decision, particularly in regard to travelling rights, and the debate which had gripped Irish attention for over a month raged on. A national referendum offering voters a straight 'Yes' or 'No' vote on abortion was called for by those on both sides who were determined to overturn the Supreme Court ruling.

The founder members of the Pro-Life Amendment Campaign, who had disbanded nine years earlier and returned to their usual line of work, regrouped after a series of hasty phone calls. 'We were scattered to the four winds,' said one senior member. 'Some of us had been working abroad, others were untraceable and many took a lot of tracking down. But most were still living and working in Dublin, and we gathered together as quickly as we could afterwards to discuss the implications of the ruling.'

Shocked enough to think that abortion could ever be legally allowed in Ireland, they had expected the judgement to have been based on the 'as far as practicable' wording of the Eighth Amendment, with the judges believing that it simply was not practicable to prevent someone from travelling abroad.

'When the judgement was published and it was on the basis of the danger to the mother's life, we were flabbergasted. The affirmative answer given by Peter Shanley to Mr Justice McCarthy when he asked "Do you accept that the Eighth Amendment envisages lawful abortion in Ireland?" seemed to us to be an incomprehensible concession by the State that should never have been made.

'No doubt the national mood was to get everyone off the hook and to let the girl go because we were nationally embarrassed by it, but we could not believe that that would be sufficient for a patron of the Constitution to let such a hard-fought matter just slip away.

'In that one admission, he might as well have altered the Eighth Amendment to say "due regard to the *greater* right to life of the mother".'

The group reformed as the Pro-Life Campaign five days after the Supreme Court judgement was delivered and began to campaign for a new referendum and the clarification of the Eighth Amendment. Likened to terriers in the fight for a ban on abortion in Ireland, they were not about to loosen their grip on the government.

FOURTEEN

In this hostile climate of indignation and retribution against what was regarded by many right-wingers as a mood of moral decline, the revelations about the private life of the Bishop of Galway Eamonn Casey were an unwelcome intervention.

Discovered to have secretly fathered an illegitimate child through an American divorcee Ms Annie Murphy, the popular 66-year-old bishop was also found to have 'borrowed' just over IR £70,000 of church funds to secretly pay towards his son's education.

In May 1992, just three months after the 'X' case, while the Irish Catholics were still reeling from its effects, Ms Murphy approached the Irish media and told them everything about her relationship with the bishop. She said her affair with the bishop started shortly after she went to stay with him in the 1970s to recover from a troubled marriage. Their son Peter was born in 1974 and the bishop paid her regular maintenance sums between 1976 and 1992, after she had returned to live in America.

When the news of the scandal broke, the bishop fled to the US and on to Ecuador, where he took up work as a missionary priest. A later investigation into the diocesan funds found a discrepancy in a loan from a reserve fund, for a single payment 'loan' to a third party.

The bishop later acknowledged that he had acted inappropriately, but said he had not acted illegally. He claimed he had repaid the loan with interest, thanks to the donations of several kind friends. He said in a statement: 'I acknowledge that Peter Murphy is my son and that I have grievously wronged

Peter and his mother Annie Murphy. I have also sinned grievously against God, His Church and the clergy and the people of
the dioceses of Galway and Kerry.

'Since Peter's birth I have made contributions, such as they
were, towards my son's maintenance and support. All payments
came from my personal resources except for one sum of IR
£70,669.20 paid to Annie Murphy in July 1990 through her
American lawyer.

'I have confessed my sins to God and I have asked his forgiveness as I ask yours. Prayer, guidance and dialogue are clearly
necessary before final decisions are reached about how I can set
about helping to heal the hurt I have caused.

'I have already set out on that road and I am determined to
persevere. I trust that you will respect my need for some time
and space to reflect and pray so that, with God's help, I can
again hope to serve Him and His people, especially Peter and
Annie in my new situation. Pray for me.'

The bishop then lay low during the worldwide publicity that
followed the publication of *Forbidden Fruit*, Annie Murphy's
best-selling book on their relationship.

The case caused as much uproar as the 'X' case had done, if
not more. One commentator said: 'Just as everyone remembers
where they were the day President Kennedy was assassinated,
so everyone in Ireland remembers what they were doing when
they heard about Bishop Casey.'

A year later the Bishop gave a series of interviews to the *Irish
Sunday Tribune* newspaper, in which he spoke of his shame and
humiliation at the scandal. Responding to a series of questions
and answers from his jungle home 5,000 feet above sea level
near Quito, he expressed his sorrow at breaking his vows of
celibacy and lamented the harm and shock he had caused across
Ireland. He spoke of his homesickness and expressed a wish to
return to Ireland one day to retire. He said he regretted not
having been a better father to his son, and now hoped to see
him regularly to make it up to him.

For many of the young of Ireland, the case merely confirmed their scepticism of the Church's right to eulogize on moral matters. 'At least he observed one law of the Church,' the comment went around Dublin. 'He didn't use a condom.' Others said there was never a better time to go to confession and off-load the sins of several years' standing. 'You could get a load off your chest this week,' observed one Dublin columnist.

One of the most popular T-shirts at the time in Ireland summed up the irreverence with which most young people regarded the whole affair. Combining the call for free availability of contraceptives and action on unwanted pregnancies, the T-shirt's emblazoned logo read 'WEAR A CONDOM — JUST IN CASEY'.

The pro-choice campaign, bolstered by all this pioneering liberal expressionism, prepared to capitalize on the shock and indignation felt over the 'X' case and that of Bishop Casey. They continued to rail against the hypocrisy of the Church and the State and argued for the legislation for abortion choice to be enacted.

In the midst of the fray, the outspoken behaviour of one of the most powerful pro-lifers epitomized the high emotions generated by the issue, which forced their way to the surface at the cost of all else.

Mr Justice Roderick 'Rory' O'Hanlon, a 69-year-old High Court judge and newly elected President of the esteemed Law Reform Commission, was a devout Catholic and father of twelve when he first read about the 'X' case in the Irish newspapers.

A former professor of criminal and constitutional law at University College, Dublin, he was perhaps best placed to understand the legal context within which the girl's plight had been placed. Also a member of Opus Dei, a secretive Catholic organization whose members express their unquestioned allegiance to the Pope and his bishops and meet regularly to discuss how best to implement (rather than merely express) their faith, he had deeply held beliefs about the abortion issue.

Moved particularly by a series of books he had read two years earlier by a former abortion doctor who had become an ardent anti-abortionist, and by the American psychologist John Powell who wrote *The Silent Holocaust* about abortion in the United States, Mr Justice O'Hanlon decided the time had come to speak out. 'I had always felt that if I could do anything to help the anti-abortion campaign I would feel obliged to do so, but I honestly never really thought the need would arise,' he said, speaking from his comfortable wood-built home on the outskirts of Dublin.

'Then the "X" case came along and I felt suddenly that we were faced with a similar crisis to that the United States had in another Supreme Court decision [*Roe* vs *Wade*].'

A widely respected man with a remarkable peacefulness about him, the judge added: 'I felt that if I remained silent and said nothing about it and the same results followed in this country then I would never forgive myself if I had done nothing to halt its progress. I could foresee that there was a possibility that I would be removed, but I felt so strongly about abortion as a practising Catholic that I had to fight against it regardless of the personal consequences.'

Initially reasonably circumspect, albeit not altogether tasteful, he wrote an article for the *Irish Law Times* in which he compared the 'X' case to that of a celebrated cannibalism trial. In *Rex* vs *Dudley & Stephens* (1888) a British court had ruled against two shipwrecked sailors who murdered a dying cabin boy in order to feed on his flesh. A jury found the men guilty and seven judges from the Queen's Bench ruled that a life could never be lawfully taken to save another life.

Categorically stating that the views were his own and not put forward as those of the Law Reform Commission, Mr Justice O'Hanlon wrote:

At this stage we are back to where we started, with the decision in the only other case decided in these islands where the issue was a life for a life.

I think we are safe in assuming that it would be unthinkable that any court in modern-day Ireland would ever hand down a judgement the effect of which would be to bring about the death of an innocent human being . . . on the grounds that it was necessary to preserve the life of another human being.

But such a judgement can now be given which has the effect of bringing about the death of an unborn child. The judge may do so having due regard to the constitutional right to life of the unborn child, but is it the equal right to life of the unborn child?

He suggested a constitutional amendment giving a foetus 'from the moment of conception' the same rights as a child born alive. It was a move which he knew could lead to the loss of his new five-year contract as President of the Commission – a post he had been chosen for by one of his former law students, the Attorney General Harry Whelehan.

'The article received a great deal of publicity, but I refused to give interviews about it,' said the silver-haired son of a journalist. 'I think I might have got away with that, but then the *Sunday Tribune* asked if they could do a profile on me and I gave them a lot of material, including the information, which I volunteered, that I was a member of Opus Dei and had been since before I was a judge.

'They converted the story into a front page newspaper feature, picking up on that and a remark that I had made that in my opinion if European law requires us to adopt moral standards which are not acceptable to the Irish people then we should reject them.

'That was converted into the headline "Judge Said EC Not Worth It If It Means Abortion", and that at a time when the government were trying to pilot through the Maastricht Treaty.' Another newspaper which picked up on the story ran the headline: 'Secret Society Judge Speaks Out.'

It was more than the government could stand. Judge O'Hanlon was summoned to see the Taoiseach and the Attorney

General Mr Whelehan. During a terse meeting, he said that he could not promise to keep quiet on such matters in the future.

Mr Reynolds then wrote to the judge and said: 'Such a public expression of views by a person in your position can only be calculated to attempt to influence public opinion about the policy the government should adopt.' For the first time in the history of the State, the Taoiseach asked a judge to resign his position as President of the Law Reform Commission.

The judge told him that the government was in breach of its contract – 'which had no strings attached and no prohibition against saying anything I liked about changes in the law, which effectively was what I was talking about.' The government demanded that he leave his post, and he eventually felt that he had no choice but to agree. After taking a few days to clear his desk at his office in St Stephen's Green, he moved back to his chambers in the Four Courts, where he resumed his former job as a High Court judge.

Mr Justice O'Hanlon was inundated with letters from all over the country, expressing anger at his removal and praising him for his 'courageous and conscientious' stand. The majority of the government, however, supported Mr Reynolds for removing him. They said they believed his membership of Opus Dei was incompatible with his position.

One cabinet minister claimed that the judge had moved into the political arena and the government had lost confidence in him as President of the Commission. Others pointed out that he was only removed because his views were at odds with the government's and pointed to the lack of action against Miss Justice Mella Carroll, whose name appeared on a statement issued by the Council for the Status of Women (which she chaired) recommending a particular course of action after the 'X' case. 'While the government took action against Mr Justice O'Hanlon . . . the Executive was silent in response to the public stand of another High Court judge whose views did not conflict with the government,' wrote Mr Bart Daly, editor of the *Irish Law Times*.

Mr Justice O'Hanlon seemed to be undaunted by his dismissal and refused to remain silent on the issue. He became less guarded about some of his views, which were considered in several quarters to be extreme. Submitting a series of articles to the *Irish Law Times* – whose circulation he undoubtedly boosted – he further explored the legal issues surrounding the 'X' case judgements and called for the Supreme Court judgement to be overturned. He never tried to defend his membership of Opus Dei, or hide it, and believed it to be a guiding force in his life.

'I was fascinated by Opus Dei early on because it advocated living a normal, professional life, whilst having something approaching a clerical concept in your life,' he said. 'It is regarded with suspicion as being a secret organization, but there is no prohibition on a member from frankly acknowledging he is a member, as I did. It is just that there are no member-ship lists published, and it is considered a matter for the individual.

'Their philosophy is not that you are sanctimonious, but that if you take on any job – be it professional or personal – then you do it to the utmost ability, in the presence of God all the time.'

With this faith behind him, he felt that he had been placed in the very position where he could continue to actively express his views on abortion, as those of the Pope and the Catholic Church, in the final years before he retired or until he was sacked.

'We are at a turning point in history here and yet the Irish media are a closed book on the subject. All I have achieved is, by being somewhat outrageous as a judge, I have been allotted a number of column inches in the Irish press that would not have reached the people otherwise.

'And as I believe that at least 60 per cent of the population are opposed to abortion but have no outlet in this country to express that view – which is why I would ask for another refer-endum with a straight "Yes" or "No" vote – I intend to continue to speak out on the matter. If I simply resigned or retired I would no longer be newsworthy.'

In his final years as judge before he was due to retire in 1995 aged seventy-two, he said would have liked to see the 'X' case judgement go back to the Supreme Court and overruled on the grounds that it contravened the 'natural' or 'moral law' of the Constitution. 'Abortion has become permissible in this country for the first time ever by reason of a judgement in the Supreme Court and never by a decision either of the people or Parliament,' he said. 'There is a very strong argument for this not being right and if it were ever accepted then it would mean that abortion could not come in now and could never come in in the future, unless we scrapped the entire Constitution.'

He also held strict views on the interpretation of European law and believed that no pregnant Irish girl or woman should be allowed to travel abroad if she intended to seek an abortion in another country. 'Whilst in theory I wouldn't prevent anyone from travelling, you cannot . . . guarantee a right to travel for the purposes of having an abortion. It is totally inconsistent with the guarantees of the right to life of the unborn.'

He expressed 'every sympathy' for Miss 'X' and her family, who, he said, were trapped by 'an error of judgement' made by the Attorney General in the first place. But he believed that once caught in the legal net, she should have been legally forced to have her baby, and – nurtured by counsellors and her family – could even have grown to love it. 'It may have been the happiest of endings to the most terrible of tragedies,' he added. 'But now none of us will ever know.'

Mr Justice O'Hanlon continued to speak out for the next two years and planned to do so until his retirement. In one separation case between a couple with five children he said that the use of contraceptives could have been an element leading to the disintegration of a troubled marriage. He even quoted from a book written by an Opus Dei priest, Monsignor Cormac Burke, who wrote: 'Contraception . . . turns the marital act into self-deception or into a lie . . . It tends to take the very life out of love itself. Within the hard logic of contraception, anti-life becomes anti-love.'

There were several further calls for his removal from the bench, on the grounds that he was becoming 'bizarre and irrational', but he successfully resisted them all. Considered scrupulously fair and an advocate of press freedom, he was popular with all who knew him, even if they did not always agree with his views. The government were aware that in spite of the criticism he attracted, he also engendered considerable admiration from many quarters for his devout convictions and his determination to express them.

The controversial judge was not the only party vehemently fighting for what they believed on the abortion issue. Few can have been as determined as the Society for the Protection of the Unborn Child (Ireland) Ltd who embarked on a lengthy legal battle against those advocating freedom of abortion information.

Where the Pro-Life Campaign had been at the forefront of political and public lobbying, SPUC had chosen to concentrate instead on the legal and constitutional questions and their initials became a familiar entry on the High Court lists.

Funded by private donations, they had successfully banned the Dublin Well Woman Centre and Open Line (Open Door) Counselling from assisting Irish women to travel abroad for abortions in 1986 and 1988. These pre-referendum judgements were later upheld in the Supreme Court in 1993 on a legal technicality despite the national mood for change. The only dissenter was the youngest and newest judge in the Supreme Court, Mrs Justice Denham, who made a 'passionate' appeal for the injunction to be lifted but who was defeated four to one. Three of the four other judges were those who had ruled on the 'X' case.

The defendants, who had been wandering through the maze

of Irish law for more than fifteen years, promised to take their battle on to the European courts. They regretted the 'waste' of time and money that could instead have been spent on women's health.

SPUC welcomed the decision that would stop the centres from 'referring women to Britain to have their babies killed by abortion'. They said they were confident that when legislation came it would not include any provision allowing centres to refer women, only to give out basic information.

Politicians on all sides said the legal morass had been caused by the government's failure to act sooner on legislation. 'The courts will continue to maul the law in this and other complex social issues until the Parliament acts,' commented Charles Flanagan, the Fine Gael spokesman on health.

The basis for the legal ruling in 1993 had been forged in the 1980s and in 1992, when SPUC had two major battles on their hands. The first, in which the Dublin High Court listened to four days of evidence, was an attempt by SPUC to suppress fourteen named leaders from the Union of Students in Ireland (USI) from distributing details on UK abortion services.

Representing the students, Mr John Rogers SC, fresh from his success in the Supreme Court with the 'X' case, told Mr Justice Morris that a woman wishing to have an abortion should have a right, based on bodily integrity (secured by the Irish Constitution), to have it in the best circumstances and to know which was a good clinic – 'given that if she went to a back-street clinic she may well suffer injuries of a very serious nature'. The information the students were giving out was on pregnancy advisory clinics in Britain who present 'all the options' to women, including keeping the child, fostering and abortion, the court was told.

For SPUC, Marie Vernon, assistant secretary and public relations officer, said: 'The information is assisting women to have an abortion. In my view it is much better that (a woman) did not have the information and had the child.'

Counsel for SPUC, Shane Murphy, said that none of the rights cited by Mr Rogers could balance or exceed the right to life of the unborn. 'If extinguished it cannot be replaced, and if ended it cannot be compensated for,' he said.

Mr Justice Morris ruled in favour of SPUC and granted permanent injunctions against the USI. He also referred the papers in the case to the Director of Public Prosecutions. The USI lodged an appeal with the Supreme Court, which they later lost, but – despite their statement of intent to appeal – the judge set a legal precedent by awarding costs (amounting to tens of thousands of pounds) against them.

To add to the confusion over what was right in law, in October 1992 – two months after the students' original case – the European Court of Human Rights awarded damages and costs of almost IR £200,000 against the Irish government for violating human rights by ordering the Dublin Well Women Centre and Open Line Counselling to stop giving out abortion information. To the government's political embarrassment, the Strasbourg court accused it of breaching the Convention for the Protection of Human Rights and Fundamental Freedoms when in 1988 its Supreme Court ordered the two counselling organizations to stop.

The Supreme Court had, in response to an application by SPUC, issued wide-ranging injunctions against the two agencies forbidding them to tell Irish women 'the identity and location' of abortion clinics in Britain. The services officially closed, but unofficially their staff continued to provide information on the telephone from their homes, in defiance of the ban. The information they gave out was also still available in telephone directories for the UK and in several magazines that slipped past the censors.

The European Court awarded IR £25,000 to the Well Woman Centre for loss of income, and IR £100,000 in costs. Open Door received IR £68,986 in costs. The court acknowledged that the injunctions had legitimate aims, but said they were 'over-broad, disproportionate' and not 'necessary in a democratic society'. Mr Rolv Ryssdal, the Norwegian chairman of the court, added: 'There can be little doubt that following ... counselling there were women who decided against a termination of pregnancy. Accordingly, the link between the provision of information and the destruction of unborn life is not as definite as contended.'

Representatives from both counselling services hailed the decision as a long-awaited victory. They said the decision put the Dublin government under increased demand to press for travel and information clauses in the proposed abortion referendum, leaving them open otherwise to a direct and unwelcome clash with Europe on matters of law.

Mrs Vernon of SPUC condemned it, saying: 'It is unprecedented that the European Court of Human Rights should interfere in the Constitution of any of their member countries.' Critics countered that this was only because Ireland's laws on abortion were unprecedented within Europe.

SPUC battled on. Having won a judgement on costs, they pursued it to the end. Mr Justice Declan Costello, the judge who had first granted the injunction to stop 'X' travelling to Britain for an abortion, granted SPUC's application in February 1994 to appoint a receiver over the USI and Trinity College Students' Union funds, after they failed to pay the IR £29,000 awarded against them in 1989. The students protested vociferously. They marched on the Dáil calling on the government to pay the costs of their court battles, which they claimed had only been necessary because of the government inaction on abortion information.

Fees estimated at more than IR £100,000 were being sought by SPUC, who claimed they had no funds of their own other than the IR £2 annual fee their 4,000 members paid. A Student Support Trust was set up for public donations. Trustees included Senators Mary Henry and David Norris. On the instructions of the receiver, however, Trinity College Dublin paid SPUC IR

£14,000 from money due to have been made over to the union, which would now have to find alternative funding services.

A month later the students came up with a novel fund-raising idea. They set up a stall selling condoms at the Virgin Megastore in central Dublin. Given the nickname 'Spuckers', the condoms were sold at IR £2 for a packet of three to raise the money the students needed. Young people brought them in their hundreds.

The students announced, with some relish, that they would be forcing SPUC for the first time to accept funds derived from condom sales. Mrs Vernon of SPUC responded: 'If they want to be that vulgar there is nothing we can do about it. We don't mind where we get the money from as long as they pay their costs.'

FIFTEEN

After the Supreme Court ruling Prime Minister Reynolds had little choice but to agree to hold a national referendum on abortion. Deciding on a nine-month gestation period, he called it 'an option of last resort' and promised it would decide the complicated issues once and for all.

But first there was the even hotter issue of the Maastricht Treaty on Economic and Monetary Union to be decided upon – an issue on which the Irish people were constitutionally obliged to vote in a referendum.

The far-reaching treaty signed in Maastricht, Holland, in December 1991, advocated a more federalist system and decreasing sovereignty for member states. It had to be ratified by all twelve signatories before it could become law. The British government had initially expressed its whole-hearted support for the treaty and agreed to ratify it through Parliament, as had nine other states. Denmark, France and Ireland were the only countries to hold referendums and the European heads of state threatened disunity and isolation if all EC members did not agree. Denmark was due to vote first before Ireland put the Treaty to its 2.5 million voters, and Mr Reynolds and his government were determined to see it through, not least because of the billions of pounds' worth of EC aid promised to deprived areas of the Republic.

Traditionally staunch Europhiles (the country had voted 5 to 1 in favour of joining the EC in 1972), the Irish had always regarded the rustle of foreign money as a strong incentive. Europe represented the opportunity to move away from being a relatively poor country overshadowed by Britain and the 'thorn' of Northern Ireland, to the promise of wealth, jobs and travel. EC subsidies had already substantially benefited agricultural and industrial areas and Ireland had been delighted to have been given centre-stage in the international diplomatic arena, culminating with the presidency of the EC in 1990. Even something as seemingly unimportant as Ireland's hosting (and eventual three successive wins) of the Eurovision Song Contest swayed the Irish towards Europe. Here they were, the people of this little green country on the outskirts of the EC, holding court for all to see.

Ireland also had long and proud relationships with Spain and France dating back several hundred years. The Irish felt closer to the former enemies of the British – with whom they had once shared a common hatred – than to the UK.

The Maastricht Treaty, although not in any way altering Ireland's already strong position within Europe, was seen as the symbol of its embrace of further integration. To reject it would be the equivalent of cutting Ireland from its moorings and letting it float out into the Atlantic to sink, the people were told emphatically. 'The Maastricht referendum is the most important question the Irish people have to answer this year,' said Mr Reynolds. 'It is not about killing babies. It is about the social and economic welfare of this nation for the next decade and many beyond it.'

Thousands of booklets were produced by the government to explain the Treaty. It was hailed variously as: 'a good deal for Ireland . . . closing the prosperity gap . . . working together on foreign and security policy . . . and making it possible for Ireland to go on enjoying the considerable economic benefits of EC membership'.

The Bill proposing the Treaty was set to go before the Dáil on Tuesday, 5 May 1992. The Treaty's referendum was set for Thursday, 18 June. But it was only a few months after the abortion controversy had exploded, and one was to become inextricably tangled with the other.

When the details of the Maastricht Treaty were first being worked out in Holland in 1990, Charles Haughey was in his final term as Ireland's Prime Minister. The Irish pro-life movement, who viewed the Treaty with the utmost suspicion, had studied it carefully, fearing that under its wide-ranging clauses Ireland could become subject to rulings from the European Court of Human Rights (as authority of the 1950 European Convention of Human Rights) which would directly contravene the wishes of the people who had voted for the 1983 Amendment.

Although the Pro-Life Amendment Campaign (PLAC) had been officially disbanded nine years earlier, there were those still in Dublin who maintained a vigil for the rights of the Irish unborn. They were later to reform as the Pro-Life Campaign after 'X', but prior to their official relaunch there were still those with influence. It was they who decided that a special guarantee by way of a protocol specifically for Ireland needed to be inserted as the only way of escaping the possible consequences of federalist influences.

After several private meetings with government ministers dealing with the Treaty, a draft proposal for such a guarantee was taken to Charles Haughey. Gerard Collins, then Foreign Affairs Minister, admitted afterwards that he had been pressured into the move, but insisted that such a protocol had already been on the political agenda and the pro-life lobby simply reinforced the government's view of a need for it.

Eventually, a wording was agreed, despite the fact that there had been no consultation with the electorate or those who represented them. It was taken to the EC summit in December 1991 where foreign ministers were persuaded to accept it into the Maastricht Treaty on European and Monetary Union. The final wording read: 'Nothing in the Treaty on the European Union, or in the treaties establishing the European Communities, or in the treaties or acts modifying or supplementing those treaties, shall affect the application in Ireland of Article 40.3.3 of the Constitution in Ireland.'

Neither the press nor those in political opposition knew anything about the protocol until the Treaty had been signed on Friday, 7 February 1992 – the day X had been forced to return from England and five days before her plight was to become public knowledge.

As it had all taken place prior to the 'X' case – when people did not yet conceive how it could possibly make any difference to the hard-line abortion law as they believed it already stood – there was little widespread reaction to the news. After 'X', however, the protocol took on a whole new meaning for both sides of the debate. Those who had pushed for it suddenly realized that in light of the Supreme Court ruling in the 'X' case, it could be used to defend the legalization of abortion in Ireland. Those who were advocating choice on abortion saw it as a way for the judges' suggestions about bans on travel and information to be legally locked into Irish and European law, with no recourse to the European courts.

One critic, feminist Ailbhe Smyth, described it as 'an attempt to ensure that Ireland would not be polluted by the stench of reality – by abortion.'

A Repeal the Eighth Amendment Campaign was launched by the pro-choice lobby, who believed that the only way of fighting the protocol was to demand the introduction of legislation to provide for abortion in specific circumstances. The Campaign statement declared:

The Eighth Amendment is inhumane and unworkable. It allows no exceptions in cases of rape, incest, severe deformity of the foetus, or of a threat to the health of a pregnant woman.

This Campaign asserts that the bodily integrity, freedom of movement, health and dignity of Irish women can never be guaranteed so long as the right to life of a pregnant woman is equated (in the Constitution) with that of the foetus she is carrying.

Lawyers expert on EC law also entered the fray, arguing that the protocol could cause a direct clash between the European Court and the Dublin High Court on what Mr Justice Costello had referred to as the 'moral issues' to be decided by each member state. Both sides called for a referendum before the Maastricht Treaty vote – the re-grouped Pro-Life Campaign calling for a statement to the effect that no direct abortions could ever be carried out in the State to be inserted into the Constitution, and the pro-choice lobby calling for an amendment to the protocol.

The government issued its suggested new wording for the protocol, allowing both travel and information under Article 40.3.3, but the EC leaders fiercely resisted any moves to reopen the protocol at a time when the Treaty itself was on increasingly shaky ground internationally.

In light of that rejection, the government promised separate referendums on travel and information later in the year, after the Maastricht referendum. In a separate booklet entitled 'Some Basic Questions Answered on European Union and Abortion', the government assured voters that an early referendum on abortion was 'illogical and unreasonable'. It said that each EC state had the power to derogate from European law where it was in conflict with public policy, adding: 'Public policy in Ireland is clearly anti-abortion . . . our EC partners have indicated clearly that they regard our stance on abortion as our business.'

The public debate intensified. Feminist and pro-life groups were for once in agreement – they could not be expected to vote on the Treaty as it stood. The Catholic Church weighed in with a statement a month before the referendum giving a clear message that voters should not support the Maastricht Treaty if it meant that the right to abortion in Ireland was secured under European law. The Catholic bishops expressed their 'alarm' that the right to life of the unborn did not appear to be on the government's agenda. They neither advised a 'Yes' nor a 'No' vote to Maastricht because they said that acceptance of the Treaty would jeopardize the unborn, whereas rejection would leave the problem unresolved. The Church demanded a new referendum on abortion and said that the overturning of the Supreme Court's decision would be 'one of Ireland's most distinctive contributions to the soul of Europe'.

The pro-life lobby held rallies and demonstrations demanding a referendum on abortion first. Their posters warned voters: 'Don't be Mass-tricked'.

In the face of all this opposition, the European Parliament felt they had little choice but to pass a resolution – backed by an overwhelming majority of their members – calling for a revision of the protocol to make explicit allowance for Irish women to travel abroad for abortions. This resulted in a Solemn Declaration (signed on 1 May 1992) that the right of Ireland to have special laws on such moral matters must be offset against the fundamental right to freedom of movement. It also stated that the EC would respect any future changes to Article 40.3.3. passed by any later referendum.

The declaration, however solemn, meant little in the Republic. Described in Parliament as 'words writ on water', it was considered little more than a pious statement. Many felt that Irish politicians were merely trying to get the politics right and then juggling the law around afterwards.

Irish feminists and the rest of the pro-choice lobby were concerned that it was simply not specific enough and could still mean a ban on travel in light of the Supreme Court wording. They feared that pregnant women could be prevented from obtaining information about abortion and from travelling abroad for the operation, with no right of legal redress in the European Court of Justice. One commentator asked: 'Will they stand at the mouth of the gangway, moving in with rosary beads and pregnancy-testing kits to pick off the women of child bearing age?'

Then Denmark stunned Europe by voting 'No' to Maastricht two weeks before the Irish referendum. The EC was incensed and the Danes were publicly castigated and threatened with ostracism (forcing them later to overturn their decision). Faced with such opprobrium and after some earnest lobbying and firm reassurance on both sides, Maastricht was, in the event, overwhelmingly approved by the Irish people by a majority of seven-to-three.

With a 'Yes' vote of 69 per cent on a 57 per cent turnout, Mr Reynolds and his supporters breathed a collective sigh of relief. 'This is a great day for Ireland and a great day for Europe,' he said. He announced 'a day of national celebration' and added that the vote was 'a tribute to the maturity and wisdom of the Irish people'.

Mr Jacques Delors, President of the European Commission, praised Ireland for 'choosing active participation in the construction of Europe rather than isolation without perspective'. Within a year 'buckets of Euromoney' were being rained down on Ireland. It originally negotiated around IR £8 billion (more than any other EC state), and eventually received IR £7 billion. Critics warned that it was far from a 'free gift' and accused voters of selling Ireland's soul to Europe at any price. It was a debate that was set to rage on.

Not long after the Maastricht vote, Ireland's coalition government began to teeter on the brink of collapse, with the junior partners, the Progressive Democrats, already at loggerheads with Albert Reynolds over other issues, threatening to withdraw from the administration. Both parties denied that they wanted a general election on the same day as the proposed referendum on abortion, but sources on both sides admitted that there might be no alternative.

As the referendum date approached – set for 3 December (but later brought forward a week under a little-known nineteenth-century law) – the Irish government was facing yet another crisis in a year of unprecedented upheaval.

Four months after the Maastricht vote, in October 1992 – during the week that the clocks were to be set back to mark the official end to British Summer Time – the Irish satirical magazine *Phoenix* printed a cartoon which read: 'Have you remembered to set your clocks? Please put all clocks and watches back nine years to Referendum Time.'

Just over a month later the people of Ireland were asked – for the second time in less than a decade – to go through the wringer again on the most controversial issue of all: abortion. One historian called it 'another ghastly national game of foetal ping-pong'.

After so much national grieving for 'X', the nation was once again to be forced to face up to this deeply uncomfortable issue. The Constitution was paralysed, the Maastricht Treaty had been jeopardized and the country traumatized. Politically, the country was in a mess as the 1983 referendum which had enshrined the unborn child's equal right to life with that of the mother was once again put under the microscope. The banner and placards were dusted off and once more brought out of the cupboards. Those on both sides prepared their battle plans as they took to the streets and urged the people to vote one way or another.

Police had to separate campaigners for both sides when they clashed at rallies in Dublin in the weeks leading up to the referendum. At one 5,000-strong anti-abortion parade, headed by a car with a statue of the Virgin Mary tied to its bonnet, demonstrators handed out leaflets which declared: 'Induced Abortion is Today's Holocaust.' Their opponents chanted: 'Pro-life, it's a lie. They don't care if women die.'

The pro-lifers, marching through Ireland with their small children waving gruesome posters of mutilated foetuses, demanded rights for the unborn. Their militant wing, Youth Defence, mounted intimidating late-night pickets outside the homes of known opponents and were later publicly denounced by the mainstream pro-life campaigners because of their controversial tactics. Dubbed the 'Celtic Hezbollah', and operating from scruffy offices above a pub in Dublin, Youth Defence advocated no abortion under any circumstances. The organization claimed to have 5,000 members nationwide, and tried unsuccessfully to field a candidate in the 1983 general election. They urged a resounding 'No' vote in the referendum, insisting that abortion was murder.

Their less vociferous colleagues, occupying powerful positions in the government, the judiciary and the medical profession, quietly applied pressure behind the scenes. The new-look Pro-Life Campaign was launched in Buswell's Hotel in Dublin by Senator Des Hanafin, who outlined the offensive. He declared that the Supreme Court had gone against the wishes of the people, as expressed in 1983. 'After nine years the clear objective of the Amendment, and the clear consensus of the people, have been defeated by a Supreme Court judgement.

'Let us make no mistake about it, this is a remarkably permissive finding: it is not an exaggeration to say that the judgement leaves the way open for potentially widespread abortion, because it would be impossible to sustain a prosecution against someone arguing that he had acted in good faith in believing that a suicide threat constituted a substantial risk to the mother.'

The Catholic bishops stated: 'Abortion has now been declared legal in Ireland. Experience has shown that laws permitting abortion even in restricted circumstances rapidly lead to abortion on demand. A particularly urgent challenge now faces our legislators as they seek to exercise their responsibility to protect the lives of unborn children.'

Mr Justice Brian Walsh, a former Supreme Court judge and current member of the European Court of Human Rights, warned in a lecture at University College, Galway: 'Any proposal to alter the Constitution should only result from a careful and extensive examination of the need for such a change. In the present case there are all the appearances of an over-hasty and superficial reaction without regard for the right of the electorate to be offered a choice. The only choice now on offer is a little abortion or extensive abortion, and even within that Hobson's choice there are dangerous ambiguities.'

The Prime Minister, who three weeks before the vote lost control of the coalition government and declared a snap general election for the same day as the referendum, rode the waves of criticism. He was keen to tighten up the Constitution rather than face this potentially explosive situation again.

He and his supporters knew his country had been torn between its past and its future ever since the 'X' case erupted almost exactly nine months before and was now being put on the rack once again. Appealing for one-party unity after eleven years of turbulent coalition and minority governments, he made his personal opposition to abortion clear. 'There is an Irish ethos that we all recognize,' he said. He called the ballot the Pro-Life Referendum and claimed that it would correctly amend the wording of the Constitution. 'This government does not accept that suicidal tendency is a reason for abortion,' he added.

He hoped to avoid the wrath of the Catholic Church and the anti-abortion lobby by putting the outright constitutional ban beyond doubt again and effectively nullifying the legal precedent set in 'X'. But he also hoped to placate liberal opinion with the two major safeguards on travel and information.

More than two million 'explanatory' booklets were produced by the government. Critics said they made the issue more confusing than it already was. The proposed re-wording specifically ruled out consideration of any risk of 'self-destruction' or references to the mental health of the mother. Neither did it countenance abortion in cases of rape or incest. On the substantive issue, it declared: 'It shall be unlawful to terminate the life of the unborn unless such termination is necessary to save the life, as distinct from the health, of the mother where there is an illness or disorder of the mother giving rise to a real and substantive risk to her life, not being a risk of self-destruction.'

The wording of the travel clause said: 'Sub-section 3 of this section shall not limit freedom to travel between the state and another state.' The wording of the information clause (virtually redundant anyway after the European Court of Human Rights ruling a month earlier) said it would 'guarantee freedom to obtain, or make available, information relating to services lawful in another state, subject to such conditions as may be laid down by law'.

If all three proposals were passed, it would mean that a girl like 'X' could, in the future, legally obtain information on abortion and lawfully travel to Britain for it, but could never have a termination in Ireland on the grounds of her mental health. The Pro-Life Campaign praised the government for making a genuine attempt to give the electorate a chance to reject abortion.

Women's groups opposed the substantive issue wording on the narrowness of the grounds for abortion. The Council for the Status of Women said 'this complex and difficult issue has once again been reduced to a few words insulting to the integrity of women as individuals and mothers. The very notion of differentiating between the lives and health of women citizens in the Constitution is simply unacceptable.'

Doctors too were unhappy with the distinction between 'life' and 'health' and opposition parties accused the government of trying to be all things to all people. The Irish Council for Civil Liberties warned that a result giving priority status to the foetus and preventing women from travelling abroad would treat them as 'no more than breeding machines'.

The Catholic Synod of Bishops made a surprising announcement that people should make up their own minds on the issues even after the Pope had urged Ireland to remain 'a beacon of Christian faith and virtue in a corrupt world'. Realizing that it might be counter-productive to take the hard line on such an emotional issue, and in a watershed ruling which was to incense the pro-life campaigners, the Synod said that in all good conscience, Catholics could vote either way – provided they registered their abhorrence of abortion. 'Many actions which are immoral are not prohibited by the state,' the Synod said in a statement, 'because attempts to prohibit them could lead to an unacceptable infringement of the personal liberty of citizens in a free society and could bring the law into disrepute.'

Padraig Flynn, then Minister for Justice, addressing the Dáil, said that Ireland had 'a long and proud tradition' regarding the right to life of the unborn and that the proposed Amendment was 'most emphatically not an abortion amendment'. He added: 'What we are proposing here is that a provision be inserted in our fundamental law that is likely to remain unaltered for the foreseeable future. We must do all we can to get that provision right and we would be failing in our duty to women and to their entitlement to protection where there is a risk to their life if we refused to take account of the fact that cases may arise, however infrequently, where the woman's life would be endangered by continuation of the pregnancy.

'If there were only to be one case in one million, or even ten or more million, we would have to take account of it. There is a duty on all of us to ensure that nothing is put into the Constitution which might, even in the remotest possible case, mean that action that was necessary to save a woman's life would not be taken.'

Faced with the complicated tripartite set of proposals, the population plunged the government into turmoil when they rejected by a 2 to 1 margin the proposed rewording on the abortion issue, but voted in favour of the travel and information clauses.

After a 70 per cent turnout of the population despite icy weather, 66 per cent rejected the main abortion proposition, 67 per cent approved the travel clause and 64 per cent the information proposal. Both sides claimed victory. The difficulty came in deciding how much emphasis could be placed on the interpretation of the outcome.

On the general election vote, the surge in support of the social democratic Labour group at the expense of Mr Reynolds's more central Fianna Fail and of Fine Gael, the right-wing opposition party, marked a historic watershed in the country's political history. For the first time Ireland seemed to be moving away from the historic civil war politics entrenched by the Anglo–Irish Treaty of 1921, and towards a system similar to that in the United Kingdom, with a clearer right–left divide.

With the new current of transition sweeping the country, and a growing resentment of the troubles of Northern Ireland that had always dogged the nation economically and politically, the voters expressed their views at the ballot box. The two old men of politics, still staunchly supported by the older generation, the Church and in the counties, were swept aside in favour of a popular party whose key words were reform and change.

With one of the youngest electorates in Europe, better educated and well-travelled, the importance of the abortion issue could not be under-estimated in the cracking of this mould and the demand for liberal change. Europe was beckoning, Mary Robinson was President (nominated by Labour) and the youth of Ireland wanted to break the ties with its austere and archaic past.

Their votes left those who failed to keep up with the times stunned and confused and those who correctly identified the new mood amply rewarded. From this election on, it was considered that the Roman Catholic Church and the parties it had long endorsed would be fighting a rearguard action.

The votes gave Fianna Fail sixty-eight seats, Fine Gael forty-five and Labour thirty-three. The Progressive Democrats, former junior partners, won ten seats. A total of eighty-three seats are required in the 177-seat Dáil to form a majority government. Fianna Fail had 39 per cent of the vote, its lowest level in seventy years, while Fine Gael slumped to its worst position in more than thirty years. Dick Spring's Labour doubled its seats and the former rugby international and barrister became the unexpected pivotal force in Irish politics.

After much behind-the-scenes negotiation, a historic centre–left coalition was formed between Fianna Fail and Labour in which Mr Reynolds held on to his position as Taoiseach by his fingertips and the hugely popular Mr Spring became Tanaiste, or Deputy Prime Minister, and Foreign Minister – giving him a key role in talks on Northern Ireland. The new government promised a strong programme of liberal reforms which would 'leave no area of Irish life unchanged'. Unemployment, a burning issue in Irish rural communities, would be tackled head-on, with the help of European money.

Labour commanded almost half the cabinet seats, but Maire Geoghegan-Quinn, one of the brightest and most liberal lights in Fianna Fail, was appointed Justice Minister. Making no secret of the fact that she had set her cap at being the next Taoiseach when Mr Reynolds retired or left office, she set about her first task, to decriminalize homosexuality, and was expected to have an important influence on abortion and divorce legislation, when the government eventually got round to it.

Mr Reynolds, it seemed, had merely survived this round of the abortion debate to face the prospect of an issue that simply refused to be aborted.

SIXTEEN

Public opinion was closely measured as, during the year that followed, a gradual shift in the consciousness of the Irish people grew more and more evident, and the trend towards more liberal policies gathered strength.

The promised programme for reform steamed on. In June 1993 Parliament rejected last-minute pleas from the Catholic Church and passed a Bill making condoms readily available to everyone. The move ended more than twenty years of controversy over family planning and allowed people to buy condoms over the counter rather than have to go to their doctors for prescriptions.

The law had been amended seven years earlier to allow sales of condoms to people over eighteen other than married couples (it later lowered the age restriction to seventeen or over). Limited to 'approved medical outlets', which included chemists, sexually transmitted disease clinics, surgeries and family planning clinics, it was an offence for anyone else to sell them. As a consequence, the Irish Family Planning Association had been charged in 1991 with unlawfully selling contraceptives from its Condom Counter at the back of the Virgin Megastore in Dublin and fined IR £500. The popular Dublin rock band U2 were incensed at the decision and paid the fine.

On 24 June 1993, a few weeks after the condom legislation, the Irish Parliament finally voted to legalize homosexuality – ratifying the right won by Senator Norris which had remained on the statute books for more than three years. The coalition government defied the objections of the Catholic Church and opinion polls to pass unopposed the second reading of a Bill to allow homosexuality over the age of seventeen.

Justice Minister Maire Geoghegan-Quinn insisted that the Bill was not an encouragement to homosexuality. 'It is to leave those of homosexual orientation free to come to terms with their own lives and to express themselves in personal relationships without the fear of being branded and punished as criminals,' she said. This statement came despite a controversial claim from one opposition politician in Parliament that homosexuals were 'left-hand drivers driving on the wrong side of the road'.

In what was viewed by many devout Catholics as a frightening decline into the moral quagmire of Europe, these radical rulings were further followed by pledges to tackle the two other major social issues that had caused such bitter division in Ireland – divorce and abortion.

A referendum on divorce – also illegal in Ireland – was originally set for 1994. The first national vote on the issue since the option was rejected by referendum in 1986, it was – at this time – widely expected to be carried, and with the government's support.

Mr Reynolds, in a newspaper interview in 1992, said he had high hopes of the consequences of such social reform. He even believed it could lead to the disarming of the terrorists on both sides of the community in Northern Ireland, 'as part of an agenda aimed at removing inequalities and the causes of friction and distrust, between the North and the South'. He added: 'I honestly believe that the balance of advantage lies with Ireland being part of the mainstream of Europe and European integration.'

It was clear that the abortion referendum vote was part and parcel of Ireland's new taste for European Community membership in contrast to its insular, conservative past. Mr Reynolds's critics argued that, while closer European ties may have been promising six Irish punts for every punt Ireland contributed to the Community, they would also lead to a flood of modern secular beliefs and a further undermining of Catholic moral values and traditional culture.

He countered that the European repercussions for Denmark after its rejection of the Maastricht Treaty were something Ireland could not afford. For this last frontier of Catholic morality, always in the shadow of Britain and on the western fringes of Europe, Maastricht had represented the crucial breakthrough it craved. Its people enthusiastically embraced it as a symbol of the freedom of choice and the way of establishing its true independence.

Conor Cruise O'Brien wrote in the *Irish Independent* just before the referendum: 'If the Irish people are offered the choice between God and Mammon, the outcome will be Number One: Mammon. Number Two: God.'

The journalist Cal McCrystal, in the London *Independent*, said: 'Europe . . . propelled Ireland from its earlier dedication to economic nationalism into a situation in which much of its past was jettisoned in the interests of swift growth. The smell of success overwhelms incense and peat smoke.'

The girl and her family had been out of the news for months. Little was known about their new whereabouts or how they were coping. Many of those in the Irish media felt it was a subject best left alone. Few had even followed up on whether or not she had ever had the abortion and were shocked to learn much later that year that she had miscarried.

It was at a pre-trial deposition hearing in the former school-house that was converted into Rathfarnham District Court on Friday, 13 November 1992, that her remarkable progress from those dark days in February was made clear. In the presence of a·small number of reporters who were allowed by Judge Sean Delap to remain in court and record every word she spoke, she felt strong enough to make her vitally important deposition for the Book of Evidence personally.

With the love and support of her family, and counselling from police officers and rape crisis advisers – one of whom sat right behind her, a hand gently patting her back – she was able, for the first time, to describe publicly her experiences at the hands of her best friend's father.

Had she carried his baby to full term, it would have been born three months earlier, some time in August shortly after her fifteenth birthday, and there is little doubt that she would have been unable to face the child's father in a courtroom so soon afterwards. But eight months after the miscarriage and without shedding a tear, she turned and stared at him directly when she was asked to point him out in court. 'That man there,' she said softly, her steady finger stretching towards him.

The accused – charged with nine offences of unlawful carnal knowledge, sexual and indecent assault alleged to have been committed in four separate places on six separate dates between June 1990 and January 1992 – could only hold her gaze for a moment before looking away.

It would be another eighteen months before he would be locked up in a Dublin prison cell. But at that moment, in that tiny blue-painted courtroom with the morning sunlight pouring in on him through the mullioned windows, he knew he could no longer escape the consequences of his crimes. The special secret he had ordered her to keep was utterly uncovered and her calm deliverance of it was the death-knell for his three-year masquerade.

Throughout her testimony she had sat neatly on the edge of her seat. Feet together, knees clamped shut, her fingers clasped tightly on her lap. The wide collar of her crisp white blouse was laid carefully over the bottle green jumper of her school uniform and matched the predominant colour in her knee-length plaid skirt. A tiny crucifix on a fine gold chain dangled over the lip of her collar and shimmered with her every tremble, sending flashes of light dancing around the walls and ceiling.

Slim, petite and pale, her glossy brown hair was neatly combed and clipped back under a bow at the back of her head, before falling over her shoulders and half way down her back.

Eyebrows unplucked, face without a trace of make-up, her brown eyes opened wide and then shut tightly as she recounted each sordid detail of her eighteen months of abuse at the hands of the neighbour who lived a few doors away from her respectable, middle-class home – a man she had considered a father-figure and trusted family friend.

Her small voice with its lilting Irish accent carried across the courtroom as the girl sat less than ten feet from her assailant and told the secrets he had sworn her never to tell.

Fixing her eyes on the large windows of the old schoolhouse far above the head of Judge Delap, she told how the accused, a man she had known since she was 'very small', had started by fondling her breasts under her school uniform in the back of a car that summer afternoon in the Dublin mountains and ended up having intercourse with her in the alleyway behind the swimming pool car park.

She showed little sign of being aged beyond her years, forced into pregnancy and a harsh re-examination of her simple Catholic faith. Steadfastly nurtured and encouraged by her parents and the counsellors who had become her closest confidantes, she had somehow managed to survive it all, after veering close to suicide, suffering chronic depression and ultimately a miscarriage.

Her parents sat on a church pew a few feet behind her. Her mother was in a smart jacket and skirt and had carefully groomed hair. Her father wore a crisp suit and sat bolt upright and taut. They were pale with sadness as they watched their daughter relive her ordeal. Her father never took his eyes off his daughter, as if he were willing each word out of her. Her mother sat trembling and wringing her hands.

In an adjoining room outside the court, their friends and family had gathered to offer their support. Barred from the courtroom during the girl's evidence, they sat clustered together on a bench in the chilly former vestry and whispered their thoughts to each other.

Across from them on the other side of the small room was another group of people. Supporters of the accused and his family, they avoided eye contact with their counterparts just a few feet away. A police officer stood in the corner just in case of trouble.

Outside, a film crew from the Irish television station RTE stamped their feet in the cold as they waited for the proceedings to end and another shot for their files. Unable to broadcast anything that showed pictures of either the accused man or the girl at this stage, they none the less wanted to catch the expressions on the faces of the other people coming out of the courthouse, and that of the judge who was to hear the girl's evidence.

A long-suffering local policeman, who had arrived by bicycle earlier to open up the court and turn on the bar heaters suspended from the ceiling, stood chatting amiably to them as they all waited.

Inside the warm courtroom and far from the emotional furore that erupted on to Ireland's streets at her plight, the barrister for the Director of Public Prosecutions, Eamonn Leahy, gently led the girl through her evidence with a series of questions and answers. Momentarily touching the cross at her throat and glancing at her parents sitting stiffly behind her, she replied in the simplest terms.

Mr Leahy led her carefully through her evidence, stopping only to ask her if, when she was staying with the defendant while her parents were in Lourdes, she had tried to stay away from him.

'For the remainder of the week did you take any steps to make sure that you weren't alone with him?' Mr Leahy asked.

'Yes. I stayed with his daughter or else his wife,' she replied.

On another occasion, after detailing a further sexual assault on her in the man's car, the girl was asked by Mr Leahy: 'How did you feel when he was doing this?'

She replied softly: 'I was trapped. I couldn't get out of the car.'

On Saturday, 7 December 1991, the night she became pregnant, the girl said the man gave her a lift to the local video shop to return a film. The accused's son and his girlfriend were also in the car and the group stopped at a pub for a drink. The boy and his girlfriend were dropped off and the accused suggested that the girl moved from the back seat of the car to the front when the vehicle emptied.

She said it was after nine o'clock when the man drove to a quiet spot in an alleyway behind the swimming pool in Rathmines and locked the car doors. He told her to partially undress, then reclined her seat, before kissing her 'very hard' and having sex with her.

'When it was over, what did he say or do?' Mr Leahy asked.

'He told me to be careful putting on my tights in case I put a ladder in them. He got out of the car and fixed his clothes and then we went home.'

'Was anything said in the car on the way home?' Mr Leahy asked.

'Yes, he asked me did I tell anybody and I said no.'

'And what did he say when you told him no?'

'He didn't say anything.'

The girl's final testimony related to New Year's Day, 1992, when the accused and his wife were invited to her family house for a drinks party. She said she remembered that she had been having a minor argument with her family because she wanted to go to a local Christmas funfair and her parents wanted her to stay and help with the party. Later that evening, she said, the man's wife and her own mother called her into the lounge and asked her to fetch something from the defendant's house. The girl said the defendant was already there, fetching replacement batteries for a Christmas toy.

'I didn't want to go down to the house and I asked if his daughter could come with me because I knew if I went down to the house something would happen . . . I didn't want to go on my own, but his wife insisted that I go on my own,' the girl said dolefully.

When she got to the house, she said, she found the defendant in the conservatory leading into the kitchen and he started to abuse her. When it was over, he returned to her house and said nothing.

Mr Leahy asked: 'While the matters that you described were going on, did he ever say anything to you about telling anyone else?'

'Yes, he told me never to tell anybody.'

'Did he say what would happen if you did?'

'He said I would be the reason for putting him in jail and that his family would split up if I did.'

The accused man, wearing a blue check jacket, blue shirt and grey slacks, had been sitting expressionless alongside a female relative until that moment. He looked up and held the girl's gaze momentarily before looking away.

Judge Delap smiled kindly at the girl and thanked her for her time. She had been giving evidence for more than ninety-five minutes. He asked her to sign her deposition before she walked past the defendant to where her parents were sitting. They hugged her emotionally and sat squeezing her hand and repeatedly patting her shoulder.

The man did not attempt to leave the courtroom hurriedly when the hearing was over. He stood smiling and chatting to his solicitor for a while, and almost brushed shoulders with the girl's father as both groups gradually moved towards the door. Neither man acknowledged the other and the defendant left the courtroom first. Hailing a welcome to his supporters in the ante-room, he was driven off smiling in a friend's car.

The girl waited inside. Her family members flooded into the courtroom and congratulated her on her performance. 'She was brilliant, wasn't she?' enthused a woman police officer with her. Her mother and father nodded and stroked their daughter's hair affectionately. One of the most harrowing parts of her three-year ordeal was over, they told her.

Flushed pink and close to tears, she almost managed a smile as she was led from the court surrounded by them all. Right from the outset, she had told her family and the police, she desperately wanted people to believe her story, afraid that the defendant would somehow persuade them otherwise.

It had been vital to her therapy that she should go through the important rituals and ceremonies of the due legal process, so that they could act as landmarks for her slow recovery. Psychologists and counsellors have long recognized the importance of such a moment in a victim's recovery. Akin to the importance of attending a funeral after a death, the court case can often signify the official laying to rest of the grief and distress that has been caused.

Just over 200 miles north in Belfast, not long after the girl's court appearance, another 14-year-old pregnant girl was about to be the subject of a controversial court hearing.

The girl, known as 'K', who became pregnant through consensual sex at a discotheque with a young boy, was living in a children's home in Co. Antrim in the care of the local authority and did not want to have the baby.

Legal under British law to anyone of any age if a doctor decided it was necessary, but unlawful in Northern Ireland, the termination could only have been possible to such a ward of court with the permission of her guardians, the Northern Health and Social Services Board.

Perhaps with the 'X' case in mind, her supporters – including her invalid father who was estranged from her mother – claimed that she would commit suicide unless she were allowed an abortion. The girl had already tried to cut her wrists with broken glass, had declined all food and repeatedly punched herself in the stomach. The local authority agreed that she would kill herself and applied to the Belfast High Court for an order allowing the operation to go ahead. Her mother, who had had little or no contact with her daughter for ten years, strongly objected to abortion in principle and to it particularly in this case, and fought the action in the High Court to no avail.

The judge, Mr Justice Shiel, eventually ruled that the girl could have the abortion in Northern Ireland because of the medical evidence that to allow the pregnancy to continue to full term would result in her being 'a physical and mental wreck' – using the words of Judge Macnaghten in the 1938 *Rex* vs *Bourne* case. He quoted extensively from that case and cited Mr Justice Macnaghten's interpretation of the law regarding the use of the term 'unlawfully' in the legal wording of the crime of abortion.

After being told that there was no surgeon to be found in Northern Ireland who would carry out the operation, the court gave permission for the girl to travel to Liverpool with a social worker for the abortion.

The court had heard evidence from doctors and social workers that there was a substantial risk of the girl committing suicide if the pregnancy continued. The judge ruled: 'From the moment that she was first informed that she was pregnant she has stated on numerous occasions that she will commit suicide if the pregnancy is not terminated, or she will kill the baby if it is carried to full term. I have no doubt that these threats are genuine and that the minor is not merely being manipulative of the doctors and social workers.'

The judge added that he could not see 'any ground upon which any proceedings, criminal or civil, could successfully be brought against any doctor who in good faith carries out the operation to terminate the minor's pregnancy'.

But a consultant obstetrician told the court that, in view of the uncertainties of the law, neither he nor any of his colleagues were prepared to carry out the operation because of the possible risk of legal proceedings – particularly in light of the objections from the girl's mother.

The girl, who was fourteen weeks pregnant and recovering from an operation to remove her appendix at the time, was thus removed from one hospital and taken across the Irish Sea to another to have the operation, even though the law had allowed her the convenience and less stressful course of having the operation on her own soil.

Abortion in Northern Ireland has always been a sticky subject for British politicians. Whilst vociferously defending their stance that Northern Ireland was British territory and under British sovereignty, its delicate religious make-up meant that, when it came to allowing abortion elsewhere in the United Kingdom, Ulster could not be included.

It was not just the sensitivities of the Republican community which were at stake. The fundamentalist Protestants in the North were just as much against abortion as any of their Catholic neighbours.

In any event, the special moral nature of Northern Irish society meant that it was not included in the 1967 Abortion Act and was still subject to the 1861 Offences Against the Person Act as was the South. Women with unwanted pregnancies from the North (an estimated 2,000 a year) had to find the money and the time to travel to Britain for abortions along with their southern counterparts.

The 'K' case reopened old wounds. The Abortion Law Reform Association hailed it as the North's 'X' case and called again on the British government to review the law. Doctors spoke of their fears at carrying out what they regarded as lawful abortions under the strict medical grounds which allowed them in the North, only to have a Catholic nurse or theatre assistant report them afterwards.

Professor Simon Lee, head of law at Queen's University, Belfast, wrote two papers on the situation for the Standing Advisory

Commission on Human Rights. Called 'The Twilight Zone' and 'Abortion on Remand', his papers railed against the inadequacies of the law as it stood in the North. He cited the 'K' case and the later 'A' case as examples.

In the latter case in January 1994, lawyers on behalf of a 23-year-old severely mentally handicapped woman called 'A' who claimed to have been raped by a workman at her family home, applied for her to have an abortion in Northern Ireland. The court heard that she was born handicapped and had an IQ of sixty-one. A ward of court, she suspected she was pregnant and a friend helped her carry out a home pregnancy test which was positive. A doctor confirmed that she was just over ten weeks pregnant and the woman immediately became very upset and wanted the pregnancy terminated.

A consultant psychiatrist who saw her said she was 'emotionally very immature and suggestible, with poor impulse control'. He said she was emphatic that she felt unable to care for a child and he felt that her mental state would be seriously affected if she carried the baby to full term. She had mentioned stepping out into the path of a car and was threatening impulsive self-injury, which could not be prevented even if she were admitted to hospital.

A consultant gynaecologist, who said he was prepared to risk prosecution and carry out the abortion in Northern Ireland, told the court: 'If ever there was an indication of a lawful abortion under the 1861 Act this must come very close to being a perfect example of it.'

In an unprecedented ruling, the court ruled that she could have an abortion in the North and the operation was carried out to save her further mental anguish. The Northern Health and Social Services Board secured a declaration from the Belfast High Court that it would be lawful for a medical team to terminate the pregnancy.

In making his ruling, Lord Justice MacDermott said the state of the law on this matter was 'unsatisfactory and uncertain'. He added: 'It is a position which in the best interests of not only the medical and legal professions, but more importantly of the public at large, ought to be remedied. The Abortion Act 1967 may have its faults, but it presents a much more coherent and understandable position than that which continues to prevail in this jurisdiction.'

Professor Lee commented:

Both these case came in the wake of the 'X' case and in the latter case the judge gave a very liberal interpretation of the Bourne ruling, relating to the emotional suffering of the victim. Once the legal precedent has been set, the danger is always that other cases will follow and I made it clear that the law was chronically uncertain in Northern Ireland.

I was slated by the pro-life lobby for saying so, but then they got their comeuppance when, as predicted, these two similar cases came before the courts, which showed the law to be flawed.

In the light of the two cases, the lobbying for a change in the law in Northern Ireland gathered new momentum and campaigners hoped that the 'X' case would bring about legislative changes in the North sooner than they would be made in the South.

SEVENTEEN

Legislation on abortion in the Republic was slow in being formulated throughout 1993. The pace of change set by the dramatic events of 1992 became markedly sluggish the following year. The campaigns for both sides took stock and regrouped. A flurry of letters and private meetings urging further consultation kept government ministers busy.

Most people expected the travel and information issues to be dealt with fairly easily, after the overwhelming vote in their favour in the referendum. The main abortion issue, however, was going to take a great deal more thought. Not that there was any shortage of suggestions from all sides.

The government floated the idea of setting up an ethics panel of specialist consultants who could adjudicate on suicidal mothers as candidates for abortion. This led to questions on how the panel would be chosen to represent a balanced view.

Some recommended that the government should take a lead from Spain, a culture which was profoundly anti-abortion, where legislation condemned it in principle, but provided a substantial list of exceptional circumstances in which it was legal. The pro-life lobby saw this as a non-viable proposition.

Much play was made of the high moral example set by a woman in Italy that year, where abortion under dire medical circumstances was also legal. The Irish newspapers were full of the story of a 28-year-old cancer victim Carla Ardenghi who had refused an abortion to save her life. Her son Stefan was born a few hours before she died, but did not survive. Mrs Ardenghi was nominated for beatification as a saint in a year in which the Pope had already beatified a woman who gave up her life in similar circumstances in 1962.

The Pro-Life Campaign employed some of Ireland's leading constitutional experts, along with lawyers and barristers to carefully examine case-book history and see if there was a legal challenge possible to the Supreme Court ruling. What they feared most was a *Rex* vs *Bourne* type of case in which an Irish doctor might carry out an abortion on a suicidal or otherwise psychologically distressed woman and then test its legality through the courts. Although officially leading to a charge of professional misconduct – if such a course were ruled as lawful in the Irish courts – any doctor in such circumstances could then have strong grounds to challenge the Medical Council's ethical stance and reinstate his or her professional reputation.

Under such a cloud, the debate on Church, abortion and the State did not lessen in intensity. The pro-life lobby pointed an accusing figure at the increasing abortion rate in Britain where some three million abortions had been carried out since the 1967 Act was passed – almost 170,000 in 1991 alone – amounting to the termination of one in five pregnancies.

The British 1991 Human Fertilization and Embryology Act reduced the time limit from twenty-eight to twenty-four weeks, but permitted abortions up to birth if there was a risk of permanent injury to the woman's health or if the child was found to be seriously handicapped.

The anti-abortion organizations countered horror stories of women like Sheila Hodgers with tales of women who treated abortion as a consumer item – just another form of contraception payable across the counter. In one such commonly told story doing the rounds in Dublin, a 38-year-old London professional woman with three children and a 'marvellous nanny' who accidentally got pregnant allegedly sought an abortion for no other reason than that it would interrupt her annual ski-ing holiday. A GP was said to have refused her request, but other doctors agreed to sign the necessary forms and her baby was aborted.

· The pro-life groups also relied heavily on their claim that women who have abortions are haunted for the rest of their lives by images of their dead baby. Better to have the child and take the responsibility, they said, than to regret killing it for the rest of your life. Their opposition groups claimed that the so-called 'post-abortion syndrome' was an invention of the pro-life camp, designed to terrify women into going through with their unwanted pregnancies.

In such a heated climate and on the issue of abortion legislation in Ireland, discussions with all sides continued to be protracted and divisive. Some thought they might never see fruition.

Health Minister Brendan Howlin, entrusted with the formidable task of formulating the proposed wording of any legislation, struggled on behind the scenes and promised that his intention was to 'ensure that lives are saved and not to set up abortion clinics'. He said that the new laws would place time limits on when abortions could be carried out, as well as setting out the criteria constituting a real and substantive risk to the life of the mother. A panel of medical experts could be established to rule on abortion cases.

His home, shared with his 70-year-old mother, was picketed by extremist members of the pro-life lobby. As time went on, he sincerely hoped that his promises of far-reaching social reform by the end of 1994 would come to fruition.

Brendan Howlin's task was further complicated when in March 1993 the Medical Council of Ireland surprised everyone by announcing that doctors who performed abortions in Ireland would be acting unethically and could be struck off. Despite the Supreme Court ruling, a majority vote of the ethics committee led by chairman Professor Padraig Keane said that such doctors would be open to a charge of professional misconduct. Professor Keane announced that there was 'no evidence to show that abortion was a necessary part of any medical treatment'. He added: 'It should not be carried out.' He also commented directly on the 'X' case and said that if information now available had been available at the time of the Supreme Court judgement then the 'learned judges' might have reached a different conclusion.

The committee drew up abortion guidelines and said that it was the 'ethical imperative of all doctors to preserve life and health'. Its statement added that there were now new methods available to treat conditions without aborting a foetus, whereas in the past abortion had been considered an accepted part of treatment – referring to the 'double effect' clause written into the Irish Constitution.

Mr Howlin condemned the Medical Council's decision and said that he did not think a doctor should be struck off for acting within the proposed abortion laws.

Feminist groups and the pro-choice lobby described Professor Keane's statement as 'three steps back into time'. They said it was 'a disaster for women's choice'. The 150-member Council for the Status of Women said it was 'deeply disturbed' at the confusion caused to doctors by the statement. 'For some women, even in the most serious situations, a termination would not be an option they would consider. However, we know from the debate in 1992 that not all women agree. Faced with a lack of unanimity among the medical profession and practical knowledge that the euphemism of "current medical practice" may already, albeit rarely, involve termination of pregnancy, other women will not passively accept a blanket ban when it could be their health, if not life, that is jeopardized.'

The Council requested an urgent meeting with the Medical Council to discuss women's rights during pregnancy. The request was not responded to. Doctors for Freedom of Information also sought clarification of the guidelines and asked Professor Keane to release the research data on which the Medical Council had based their claim that there were no medical grounds for a termination of pregnancy.

It later emerged that members of the Medical Council had disagreed with the decision and that there had been a split in the ranks and Doctors for Freedom of Information called for an open debate on the subject before it became sacrosanct in the Council's ethical guide and constitution.

The Institute of Obstetricians and Gynaecologists claimed that under the new guidelines even a restricted form of abortion sanctioned by legislation would be 'inoperable' because the doctors involved could be struck off the medical register.

The recently formed Association of Irish Humanists urged that abortion should be available for women at risk to their health or in a crisis situation. They strongly advocated abortions only before twelve weeks' gestation, however, relying on 'consensus scientific opinion' that the development of the central nervous system does not begin until twenty weeks.

The effect of the Medical Council ruling was that, whatever the 'X' case did in achieving rights for women travelling abroad for abortions, it would still be extremely unlikely for a girl in a similar situation to be allowed an abortion in her own country.

Not everyone agreed that the Medical Council's stance was a backward step. The Pro-Life Campaign welcomed the statement as 'hugely significant' and said it 'served to underscore the tragedy of the "X" case and the handling of it by the Supreme Court'.

A letter to the *Irish Times*, signed by thirty-two nurses, criticized those who 'failed to recognize the crucial ethical and legal distinction' between abortions and life-saving operations. It added: 'Surely in pregnancy the doctor has two patients and a duty to care for them both?' It criticized the dictionary definition of abortion as 'the termination of a pregnancy before the child is viable', which, it said, 'cloaks a horrific reality: the intentional destruction of a human being'. The letter went on:

As nurses and midwives we are not willing to assist in such destruction. Abortion is carried out variously, by suction, by dismemberment and crushing to enable the contents of the womb to pass through the cervix, so tightly closed in pregnancy; by poisoning with concentrated saline solution leading to the delivery of a dead child; or, later in pregnancy, by labour-inducing drugs ... possibly following an injection of urea to avoid the 'complication' of a live baby.

To linger on such facts or, say, to produce the photographic evidence, might be considered distasteful or insensitive. But how else are we to dissuade legislators apparently determined to give the blessing of the law to procedures which have no place in the care of mothers and their babies, and which are rejected by an overwhelming majority of the medical, nursing and midwifery professions in this country?

(*Irish Times*, 12 July 1992)

Despite what was seen as a setback for Irish women, elsewhere the mood for change allowed developments unimaginable a few years before. The Irish Family Planning Association (IFPA) heralded a major breakthrough for the provinces by announcing the opening of three new regional pregnancy counselling centres in Galway, Cork and Limerick. Tony O'Brien, Chief Executive, said it was no longer acceptable that women outside Dublin should have to travel half-way across the country for pregnancy counselling and family planning advice.

More than a hundred general practice doctors sympathetic to the aims of IFPA joined a register so that any woman in a crisis pregnancy in a rural area would not have to travel further than ten miles to see a doctor after IFPA counselling, whether or not that advice resulted in an abortion.

The IFPA also issued a Profile Report, a statistical analysis of the first one hundred clients at its newly opened counselling centre in Dublin between October and December 1992. The survey found that the vast majority were aged 16–24, single, in professional occupations and between nine to twelve weeks pregnant. For most it was their first pregnancy, and all had used contraception (the pill or condoms being most popular) which had failed.

Asked their attitude to the pregnancy, 85 per cent said they felt 'distressed, upset, unhappy and confused'. Ninety-five per cent would not consider adoption, and 80 per cent said abortion was the only option in the situation. Seventy-six per cent had told their partners of the pregnancy, of which 48 per cent said they had been 'generally supportive'. Of partners, 35 per cent said they were 'confused'. Those women who had not told their families amounted to 67 per cent, but of those who had, 95 per cent said they were supportive whatever the outcome.

Ruth Riddick, now a driving force at the IFPA and its education officer, said it was hoped the research would stimulate further deliberation at public policy level. 'Without understanding of the human dimension of this controversial issue, of the women behind the statistics,' she said, 'no progress will be possible.' She hailed the new regional centres as 'a significant development' while Maxine Brady said it would 'make a major contribution to the well-being of women seeking professional counselling and abortion information'.

The pro-life lobby rallied on. Described as 'militaristic' in their approach to campaigning by their opponents, and with advice from their intimidating and highly organized counterparts in America, they vowed to continue the battle. 'We are up and running,' one group announced. 'As far as we are concerned we have some unfinished business to attend to.'

Leading American pro-life campaigners from the controversial organization Rescue America announced a planned tour of Ireland in the summer of 1993.

America had witnessed a tumultuous period in which more than 70,000 Christian activists had been arrested for picketing abortion clinics since 1987, making them the biggest movement of civil disobedience in America this century. With an estimated 1.6 million abortions every year and President Bill Clinton committed to upholding the constitutional right to abortion for a generation to come, the pro-life lobby had effectively lost the political struggle.

The bitterness which followed led to a total of four abortion surgeons being shot dead in Florida, and another being seriously injured, as well as riots, physical assaults, acid attacks and fire bombings.

Many of these attacks were made by individuals waging a one-person war against abortion. Others were affiliated to groups like Operation Rescue, a branch of Rescue America, which comprised a group of Catholics and evangelical Protestants formed into a highly trained force, capable of waging prolonged warfare. Volunteers or 'abortion abolitionists' as they liked to be known, gave up their jobs to work full time and train secretly for up to three months at a time. They picketed people's homes after tracing the number plates of their cars parked outside clinics, and did all they could to block the work of the abortionists.

Their actions eventually led to the passing in 1994, for the first time anywhere in the world, of a law which made it a direct criminal offence to picket an abortion clinic, its patients or its staff. Anti-abortionists described the Freedom of Access to Clinic Entrances Act as a dire infringement of their rights to freedom of speech.

Focusing their attention on Ireland, which must have seemed refreshingly ripe for rallying, the American anti-abortion groups sent across shock-tactic posters and manuals to some of the more extreme fundamentalists. Whilst their war against abortion in the Republic had not yet fully developed, and was never likely to be widespread in light of the general assumption that the abortion traffic would still be diverted to Britain, some in the pro-choice lobby felt that it was only a matter of time.

Many of the most controversial US campaigners were banned from Britain, but some diverted to Europe before leap-frogging to Ireland. Others, who were considered 'safe' by the authorities, were to follow. In March 1994 Mr Joseph Scheidler, a leading US anti-abortion campaigner, held a conference at

Malahide, Co. Dublin ,and declared Ireland as 'the last great hope of civilized society'. Speaking at the end of a four-day event staged by the American organization Human Life International (who had been responsible for the earlier publication of the controversial book on the 'X' case), and attended by 600 people, Mr Scheidler urged anti-abortion activists to 'go after politicians who are soft on abortion and get rid of them'.

An executive director of the Chicago-based ProLife Action League, Mr Scheidler insisted that he used only non-violent means to shut down at least twelve abortion clinics in Chicago alone.

Father Paul Marx, the event's organizer, who also attended, told the audience: 'Ireland is in a very bad way, morally and spiritually.' He claimed there was a direct link between contraception and abortion, but complained: 'The priests here don't preach about it and the bishops say nothing.'

In the liberal camp, various new organizations sprang to life to counter the anti-abortion threat. Two, Frontline and its affiliated organization the Campaign to Separate Church and State, were preparing for what they described as 'a long haul'.

Frontline, which was set up as a direct response to the 'X' case, was a coalition of organizations dealing directly with the issue of crisis pregnancy, including Doctors/Psychologists for Freedom of Information, the IFPA, Union of Students, Open Line Counselling, Cherish and the Well Woman Centre. It was committed to campaign for 'the development of an open, supportive and informed society within which to reduce the level of crisis pregnancy in Ireland'.

Its chairman, Dr Mike McKillen, a Trinity College biochemistry lecturer, claimed lobbying by the organization led directly to Ireland's first ever Patients' Charter, meaning that, although the case of Sheila Hodgers had been 'most dramatic and terrible', it would be unlikely to happen again.

'We have come a long way in the past decade, and I think

the medical profession has had its consensus altered by Sheila Hodgers and by "X",' he said. 'Patients are also much more aware of their rights and would perhaps be more questioning now about second opinions or moving to another hospital in that situation.

'What we need is more education, information and research into crisis pregnancies, and legislation to stop another "X" case from happening. It is a tragic fact of Irish life that there will always be rape victims. As a society, if we can't prevent it, we can at least offer them every possible support.'

The Campaign to Separate Church and State had quite a different, although affiliated, aim: to dilute Catholic religious control over matters of law, health and education.

A self-styled 'tribal Presbyterian', Dr McKillen, a 50-year-old father of two from Belfast, started off down the Church versus State path in 1978 when he claimed to have witnessed the control exercised by the Church over his children's education in Ireland. He and his supporters hoped to challenge directly the State's relationship with the Church, which they claimed was in breach of Ireland's Constitution, by preparing two big test cases for the High Court.

In the first case, in which the Church was enjoined as a co-party with the State, the CSCS contested that by paying approximately IR £1 million annually to some forty-seven chaplains at community schools, the State was in breach of its constitutional vow 'guaranteeing not to endow any religion'.

The campaign won a motion of discovery in the High Court in spring 1994, forcing the State to hand over documents on the matter, and were hoping for a full hearing of the case by the end of the year.

In the second case, which was taking longer to come to fruition, the CSCS hoped to test the rights of parents and children not to have religious instruction intermingled with secular studies, as advocated in a Department of Education teachers' handbook.

'As an organization we did not come out fighting on the already emotionally charged abortion issue after the "X" case, but we did decide to look, quietly and rationally, at ways to bring about major social change elsewhere through litigation, lobbying and the raising of social consciousness,' said Dr McKillen. 'By using the prosecution system, we hope to separate the Church from the State and, as a consequence, vindicate the rights of women in health matters, so that they become matters only between the doctor and patient, without the ethical control exerted by the Catholic Church on the majority of our hospitals.'

Two further *causes célèbres* in 1993 – the Kilkenny incest case (which proved to many just how little progress the country had really made in the area of child abuse), and the case of Lavinia Kerwick – focused the nation's mind once again on matters of rape and sexual abuse.

Lavinia Kerwick, aged nineteen, who also came from Kilkenny, was 'date-raped' by her immature 17-year-old boyfriend after an initially consensual heavy petting session on a riverbank went too far. Reserving judgement for a year when he first heard the case in 1992, the judge brought the young defendant back before him in 1993 and gave him a nine-year prison sentence, suspended for six years, after hearing that he had no previous convictions, he had got a job and had expressed deep remorse at his crime.

The sentence led to an outburst of criticism of the judge, who had described Lavinia (who had gone public the year before) as a 'remarkable and resilient young woman'. His critics said that in truth her anorexia nervosa eating disorder had worsened and she had to be led screaming from the court. (Though she later recovered enough to give interviews to almost every newspaper in Ireland.)

The Irish press published page after page on the case and activists fumed at the 'chauvinism still ruling our legal system'.

Lavinia was hailed as an 'emblem for wronged Irish women and a martyr for emancipation'.

But many commentators and those in legal circles felt that, in this particular case, the sentence had in fact suited the crime. The flood of indignation was, to many, an alarming signal that those in Ireland who had recently found a voice might just have started to alienate their own cause by jumping on every feminist bandwagon. As the respected journalist Sam Smyth wrote in the *Sunday Independent* a few days after the trial: 'It is disappointing to see women who usually have an instinctive compassion, and often describe themselves as liberals, unable to make the imaginative leap over the gender barrier and confront lynch-mob mentality.'

In a far more serious case in the same year, which also came before the Circuit Criminal Court, a man from Castlecomer, Kilkenny, was jailed for seven years for systematically raping and beating his daughter (then twenty-six) over a period of sixteen years.

The woman told how, from the age of ten, she had been the victim of violent physical and sexual assault and had borne her father's son at the age of fifteen. Apart from raping and buggering her, he had broken her fingers with a lump hammer and blinded her in one eye after kicking her in the head.

She had been treated in hospital dozens of times for injuries which she was bullied into saying had been caused by accidents around the home. When she did tell her doctor, social workers and the police in a series of anonymous calls and secret visits, nothing was done about it as her father always denied it and threatened her and her mother with further violence if they made an official complaint.

Each time she ran away from home and found lodgings in a hostel her father dragged her home again for further abuse. It was only after her father's last and most serious assault on her, after which she ended up in hospital, that the police began an investigation.

Her father pleaded guilty to six specimen charges (of an original fifty-six) and was sentenced to seven years' imprisonment. The maximum sentence he could have faced was life. His victim claimed he would find her and kill her when he got out and would take her son, then aged twelve, away from her.

The case led to calls for tougher sentences in incest cases and to a 'Stay Safe' programme introduced nationwide in schools, with teachers encouraging abused children to speak out about their abuse, even if it was at the hands of a neighbour or relative. The campaign immediately came under attack from what one writer in the *Irish Times* called 'misguided zealots' who threatened legal action against schools for promoting what they called 'anti-Daddy, anti-male' philosophies. One American psychologist who toured Ireland specifically to lobby against the campaign told an audience: 'Children are being told to tell teachers if anyone interferes with them, even if it is their father. This is a direct attack on parental responsibility.'

It did not seem to occur to him that the 'X' case might never have happened if the victim had felt able to tell her teachers of her own long-term abuse under such a 'Stay Safe' campaign.

EIGHTEEN

'X', meanwhile, was continuing to receive counselling and was being prepared for her eventual freedom from the treadmill of her unhappy past. No longer living in quite such dread of not being believed, even though the criminal trial was still to come, the time had come to finally start looking to the future.

As part of her recovery and therapy, she had been taken to the third floor offices of the Irish Family Planning Association in Lower Ormond Quay, Dublin, and shown the four volumes of press cuttings which had been amassed on her case. Turning the pages of the scrap books with a counsellor, she was to start to come to terms with her unwelcome fame and gradually to accept it.

'No one could expect to go through what she went through and come out of it unscathed,' said one counsellor. 'But she could not have had more love and support from her family and from all those who have spent time with her, coaxing her to move on and start her life from where it was interrupted.'

The trial had long been set for Monday, 5 July 1993, at the Circuit Criminal Court, a few weeks before the girl's sixteenth birthday. The final weeks of the criminal court's summer session were set aside for what was expected to be the most keenly anticipated case in Dublin. But two weeks before the case was due to open before a jury, rumours started circulating of an application by the defence lawyers to have the matter . postponed.

Based on a claim that the accused could never get a fair trial after all the publicity about the case and the much-cited quote from Mr Justice Costello, calling him 'an evil and depraved man', the defence lawyers were hoping to postpone the case indefinitely.

They went to the High Court to argue that if it were to go ahead, it should be held in camera, without any of the attendant publicity, so that a jury might not know that this was the high-profile 'X' case and would not be prejudiced against the defendant. If a jury was troubled by any of the highly emotive issues underlying the whole case, the lawyers argued, they might not treat it as a straightforward sexual assault trial and would condemn the defendant before they had even heard the evidence against him.

The suggestion from the Attorney General's office to journalists at the time was that if a judge ruled that it were to be held in public, with the expected publicity, then the defendant might be persuaded to plead guilty to lesser charges to get the matter quickly dealt with by a judge and not a jury.

In any event, on Wednesday, 30 June, less than five days before the trial was due to start, the case was officially adjourned. Judge Michael Moriarty – who had once been the senior counsel in the Kerry Babies Tribunal – was told that the trial could not proceed because of the High Court application made at the last minute by the accused's defence lawyers.

Prosecution barrister Mr Eamonn Leahy told the court that the State was applying for an adjournment and asked that the case should be put into the court list for mention on Friday, 23 July – the final week of the session before summer recess – effectively postponing it until at least the autumn. The defendant was remanded on continuing bail to that date and the lawyers concerned said the matter was not likely to be dealt with before October.

The news came as a body blow to the family. The continual strain of the previous eighteen months and the waiting for the hearing had been too much for her parents to bear. The family were devastated to learn that the trial had been postponed. One friend said: 'It really shook them. When I went to see them shortly afterwards, the girl looked completely washed out and the parents just seemed beaten down by it all.

'Here they were, eighteen months on, at a time when they should have been just about getting over all that they had been through, and instead they still had it all hanging over them. They couldn't plan a holiday, they couldn't plan a birthday party for their daughter, they couldn't think of anything but the trial and it did nothing for the girl and her recovery or for them.

'She felt again as if she had somehow not been fully believed. That this was the reason for the delay and that the defendant might never come to trial and be proved guilty.

'The family had already been greatly upset by the controversial pro-life book about the case at about this time. They had told the girl about it and she thought that everyone would believe it was true.

'By this time she had started at her new school, but did not dare tell any of her new friends who she was or what she had been through. Only a few of the staff knew and had been terribly supportive, but the girl needed to be close to people her own age again.

'The postponement of the trial was just a prolonging of the agony for all of them. The family kept saying over and over that it seemed so cruel. Cruel to them all, and most of all to their daughter, who was by then not really looking very good at all.'

Dr Mary Henry recalled seeing the family at this time and said she genuinely feared for their full recovery. 'When I had seen them before, a few months earlier, they had been trotting along quite nicely and building up to the trial. The girl wanted to give evidence, she wanted to testify and see the legal process through. Then they heard that the case had been put back, possibly indefinitely, or that there might not be a trial at all.

'They were shattered by that. It seemed the unkindest cut of all. They had always co-operated with the police and played everything strictly by the book and here they were not being treated as fairly as they felt they had behaved.

'I was reminded at this time of what someone had once said about ours being courts of law, not justice, and I felt that this is exactly what had happened in this case. I felt very sad for them indeed.'

Soon after hearing the news of the adjournment at the end of June 1993, and a few weeks before his daughter's birthday, her father told his family he could not take any more and was leaving home. He packed a few belongings and walked out on his wife and children, moving in to live with his sister.

There was no one else involved and nobody was to blame, he told his distraught family, but he could no longer face the daily stress of living with the pain and guilt of all that had happened.

'Everyone had thought that he was the mainstay of the family and was coping so well,' explained a friend of the family. 'He seemed to be much more in control than his wife was. But it seems that inwardly he hadn't been coping at all.'

The girl was devastated. Her younger brother, too, felt lost without his father. The middle-aged businessman kept in touch with the family and did not rule out the possibility of a reconciliation, but for now he said he needed some time on his own.

The girl's sixteenth birthday fell on a Thursday. Her father sent her a bunch of flowers and a pair of earrings. There was no family party. She spent the day quietly with her mother and brother.

Three days later the news that the family had split up was splashed all over the tabloid *Sunday World* newspaper. A reporter had knocked on their door the previous day to get a quote. The mother slammed the door in his face and then drew all the curtains for fear of photographers with tele-photo lenses. The police were called to remove him from their front garden.

'It brought everything back for them, the fear of being exposed,' said a friend. 'They thought their new address was a secret from the press. They were not listed in the telephone book and had tried to find a safe haven for the girl. They were terribly upset.'

The injustice of their situation seemed intolerable to the parents. Their daughter, their marriage and now their privacy had all been violated by the actions of the defendant, while he and his family remained intact and as yet untouched by the law. The girl, already pushed to the threshold of her emotional endurance, was now plagued with the added worry that she may somehow have inadvertently caused her parents to separate.

One close family friend said at the time: 'However much anyone told her that it was not her fault, she could not help but think that the separation must have been caused by the pain she had unintentionally caused.

'I had always liked to imagine her when she is about thirty years old as being happily married to an understanding husband with children of her own and leading a life that she is quite content with. But that seemed a very long way off from the reality of how she was at this time. First, she had been repeatedly abused by this man and then she was repeatedly abused by the legal system. Many of us thought then that she might never get over it.'

At the next court hearing on 23 July, amid the bustling cattle-market style of Irish criminal courts, the matter was adjourned for four days so that a hearing for the High Court judicial review could be set. Hardly able to hear the request for an adjournment over the hubbub of barristers, police officers, criminals and members of the public milling around the scruffy courtroom, the judge agreed.

Three days later, in the equally informal atmosphere of Court Ten of the High Court, Judge Miss Mella Carroll set the date for the judicial hearing of the defence application for 14 October. The defendant, chief perpetrator of the 'X' case, was referred to as 'Z' on the court listings.

The following day, back in Court Fourteen of the Circuit Criminal Court, a provisional trial date was set for 15 November, with the case coming up for mention three weeks earlier, on 22 October, to see whether it was likely to go ahead.

'Z' did not attend any of the hearings and waited at home to be telephoned and told of the latest developments. It was exactly eighteen months since the girl had fallen pregnant and his crime had first been exposed. It would be another ten months before he was to face the courts. He had spent the entire time living at home with his family and continuing with his normal routine while he waited for the trial to go ahead.

The girl, in the meantime, was blossoming into womanhood as she reached sixteen. As time went on, she could only present an increasingly mature image to any jury who would have to force themselves to imagine her as a 12-year-old child when her abuse first began.

There were to be many more delays. The judicial review, which the family had hoped would be heard in October, was postponed three times from 14 October to Monday, 18 October, and again to 25 October before Mr Justice Kinlan. It was finally set for 19 November.

On that date, on the first day of the hearing before Mr Justice Liam Hamilton, President of the High Court, the judge first ruled that the attempt by the defendant to stop his trial should be heard in public. He rejected the application to have the case heard in camera, but warned newspapers that the case should be referred to as the 'A' case, with no publication of names or addresses which could identify those involved.

Ralph Sutton, SC, for the accused, told the judge that there had been 'massive publicity' on radio and television, in newspapers, books and parliamentary reports about the case. He said that it would be impossible for the accused to get a fair trial. He said it would be 'most undesirable' that there should even be publicity about the application.

His appeal to have the case heard in camera was supported by Maurice Gaffney, SC, for the DPP. He said the DPP was conscious of the fact that there would be a criminal trial and he was concerned that publicity about the case might affect the minds of potential jurors to an extent that they might not properly contribute to a fair trial.

But Mr Justice Hamilton said that he had no discretion under Article 31(1) of the Constitution to direct that the case be heard in camera. He said it stated that justice should be administered in courts in public, save in special and limited cases as prescribed by law and he ruled that the case should be heard in the open.

Following that ruling, Mr Sutton began his application in which he explained that his client had been charged in July 1992 and returned for trial in November. He had not been arraigned. He had indicated that he was pleading not guilty and the trial had been postponed because of the current application. Mr Sutton further stated that no attention was attracted to the case until the publication of the High Court and the Supreme Court judgements in a 'related matter'. There had then been 'massive' publicity about the pregnant girl and her situation.

Although the judgements had dealt with what he called a 'different situation', some expressions used in them were taken up by the newspapers and given greater publicity and emphasized in a way that the judges never intended.

Mr Justice Hamilton asked if it was not for the judge trying the case to decide whether or not the accused could get a fair and impartial trial. Mr Sutton replied that he hoped to prevent the case even going to the Central Criminal Court because the High Court had the power to prohibit it. He referred to the publicity regarding DNA testing and said the whole business of the abortion injunction arose because the parents of the girl went to the police and asked whether a foetus could be used in the course of a DNA test. Reading passages from several newspapers, he said the publicity about the DNA test led to a 'build-up in the public's mind' about it. He claimed the media had reported that the test had turned out positive and that this was very prejudicial to his client.

Mr Sutton also said the use of the word 'rape' in media reports would have a damaging affect on the trial because it suggested a violent crime, adding that there had been 'a high degree of excitement' over the case because of the related proceedings. He said his client was now seeking the 'exceptional remedy' of an abandoned trial because of the 'exceptional heat, indignation and passion generated'.

Remarks made, he said, by public representatives and other persons in authority would carry 'very considerable weight' and were likely to carry potential weight with a jury.

Garret Sheehan, the defendant's solicitor, supported the application. He said in an affidavit: 'The extraordinary and prejudicial pre-trial publicity in this case is such that it is unrealistic for [the accused] to expect the members of any criminal jury to be impartial and unbiased concerning the issue of fact determined by them.'

He said the details of the criminal proceedings were 'so notorious that they had permeated into virtually all quarters of Irish life'. He believed that it would be difficult to find any person on the court panel of jurors who had not been adversely influenced as to the facts and circumstances of the case.

The defendant, in an affidavit and his first testimony in a court since his arrest, said he believed that there was an atmosphere in Ireland – particularly in the broadcast and print media – that was 'very aggressive' towards persons who found themselves the subject matter of a criminal allegation in respect of any sexual criminal offence.

He said he firmly believed that 'certain elements' of the media fostered a view that any person charged with a sexual offence must be guilty of that offence, and that any subsequent acquittal arose from an inadequacy of the course of the trial and/or the approach of the legal personnel involved.

For the DPP, Mr Gaffney argued that the trial *should* go ahead in spite of the publicity. He cited a number of foreign cases to support his claim and Mr Justice Hamilton interjected and said that the Mike Tyson and Kennedy cases were other similar examples.

Mr Gaffney said that if it appeared that a jury might be over-borne by outside influences, a judge could postpone the trial until the impact of the publicity had died down.

When talking about publicity, they were necessarily speculating how many people had been reached and affected by it, he said. It was not enough to speculate when asking the question whether there was a real risk of unfairness in this case.

Mr Gaffney added that he knew of no case in Ireland where pre-trial publicity had led to the prohibition and abandonment of a trial. There were no cases in which jurors were found to have acted perversely in criminal cases. He said that for massive publicity to endanger a fair trial, it must be massive in its relevance to the trial.

Mr Justice Hamilton commented that he did not think the trial could be held without the jury knowing that the accused was the man in the 'X' case. Mr Gaffney disagreed. He said that if any juror heard the accused being arraigned, there would be no reason why the details would bring the other case to mind.

Reserving judgement on the application for one week, Mr Justice Hamilton pointed out that the accused had been described as a rapist in a newspaper and added that it was 'the height of irresponsibility' to presume the guilt of a man before he was found guilty. He added that a number of members of parliament had also not shown discretion in relation to the case. He warned that it was necessary to exercise vigilance with regard to the protection of people's rights. 'The only question I have to ask myself is this: is there a real or serious risk that the trial would be unfair if allowed to proceed?' he said, before retiring to consider his judgement.

A week later, on Tuesday, 30 November, Mr Justice Hamilton gave his decision and ruled that the trial should go ahead. He said that it was clear that this was a case of 'massive national coverage and of media saturation – a case where a story had been told and retold in all forms of media'. Such publicity, he said, was sympathetic towards the plight in which the young girl found herself and antagonistic to the person alleged to have been responsible for her plight. He had variously been described as 'a rapist' or 'alleged rapist'.

Mr Justice Hamilton said that any person reading or hearing such material would be likely to feel a sense of outrage and prejudice against the person alleged to have been responsible. He agreed that it was fundamental that he should have a fair trial in accordance with fair procedures.

But, he said, the jury should reach its verdict by reference only to the evidence put before them at the trial and not by reference to facts alleged or otherwise, statements or opinions gathered from the media or some other outside sources.

He said that after eighteen years as a member of the Bar and nineteen years' service as a judge, he had confidence in juries 'to act with responsibility in accordance with the terms of their oath, to follow the directions given by the trial judge and true verdict give, in accordance with the evidence'. He added: 'It is the duty and obligation of juries to act with complete impartiality, complete detachment and without letting matters of sympathy, prejudice, sentiment or emotion take any part. And it is the obligation and duty of the trial judge to so instruct them.'

He cited a similar case in which the Appeal Court had said it 'could not conceive of circumstances which would entitle an accused person to demand the abandonment of his trial'.

As to the nature and extent of pre-trial publicity, the judge said that 'more than the usual care' would have to be taken in the empanelling of the jury, in the conduct of the trial and in the giving of directions to the jury. 'If this care is taken,' he said, 'then I am not satisfied that there is any real or serious risk of an unfair trial in this case. I dismiss the application for prohibition.'

On Thursday, 2 December, at the Supreme Court, Mr Sutton, for the accused, applied for a stay to prevent the trial going ahead, pending an appeal against Mr Justice Hamilton's decision. Mr Gaffney, for the DPP, objected to the stay. He said there had already been 'considerable pressure, anxiety and strain' on the people involved.

Mr Justice Thomas Finlay, the Chief Justice, said it was clear that it was 'simply not possible' to permit a trial to be held, and then for the Supreme Court to be asked whether it should have been held or not. That would not be consistent with justice, he said, and the matter should not be approached on a superficial basis. He said the Supreme Court would hear the appeal as soon as possible, and granted the stay pending that appeal.

The Supreme Court hearing was later heard in camera and judgement was delivered on Wednesday, 16 March 1994. Cited as the case of Z vs *Director of Public Prosecutions*, it was heard by five Supreme Court judges, Chief Justice Mr Justice Finlay, and Justices O'Flaherty, Egan, Blayney and Denham – the first three of whom had presided in the original 'X' case appeal.

Chief Justice Finlay delivered the judgement in open court. He said 'Z's application hinged on his claim that the original judgements of the High Court and Supreme Court relating to the girl's abortion constituted 'an adjudication of his guilt or innocence' and prevented him from having a fair trial. He secondly claimed that publicity about the taking of DNA samples and references to the tests yielding a positive or conclusive proof of his guilt rendered a fair trial impossible. Finally he said that the 'sensational and emotive' publicity surrounding the whole

'X' case constituted 'a real and serious risk of an unfair trial, incapable of being avoided by a trial judge'.

The judges said that the onus of proof was on the applicant to prove a real risk that he could not obtain a fair trial. They cited the importance of the 'public requirement of the trial and conviction of guilty persons committing criminal offences' balanced against the rights of the accused and attempts to ensure 'as far as practicable' a fair trial.

Chief Justice Finlay said the trial judge would be able 'in a specific way and with considerable specific detail' to tell the jury that the trial was that of the man accused in the 'X' case, and would be able to direct them that the controversy, publicity and commentary arising from the case and subsequent issues were 'wholly irrelevant' to the trial and must be completely put out of their minds.

He said he was satisfied that a jury so instructed would be able to bring an impartial mind to the case and would be scrupulous in preventing themselves from being swayed by such publicity.

On the question of the DNA testing, Chief Justice Finlay said that although there were at least forty newspaper references to the tests, and several references made on television and radio, only three or four referred to the positive results, and he did not think potential jurors would have retained memory of the details of the publicity.

He said it was also possible that the DNA test results might not even be allowed as admissible evidence during the trial, but that if they were the judge would properly direct a jury to ignore anything they had seen or heard in the media and concentrate on the evidence as put before them.

Even if the evidence were not allowed, the judge admitted that there could be some danger to the defendant that a member of the jury might remember that there had been DNA testing and would resent not being told about it. To avoid that happening, Chief Justice Finlay said that he believed, because of the unusual circumstances of the case, that the trial judge could specifically point out the DNA publicity to the jury and make it clear to the jurors that they must 'try the case on the presumption that whatever DNA testing took place did not in any way implicate the accused in the offences with which he was charged'.

With these provisos, the judges dismissed the defendant's appeal and said that the trial date should be set as soon as possible.

Eight days later, on Thursday, 24 March, the Supreme Court's promise of a speedy conclusion was fulfilled. The trial date, so long awaited, was set for six weeks later, starting on Monday, 9 May. The girl and her now divided family prepared themselves once again for battle.

NINETEEN

Liberal legislation, discussed and promised for so long, had still not been enacted by the summer of 1994, more than two years after the 'X' case. The mechanics had been set in place but not completed, said the politicians. The most commonly used excuse for the delay was the complicated nature of the beast.

The European elections in June were an additional hurdle for the government. Anxious not to endure a repeat of the Maastricht fiasco, all controversial matters were conveniently put back until after vital Euro matters had been resolved.

Then there was the possibility of a general election in 1995. Would it not be best to wait until after then to push through any contentious legislation? advisers asked.

The Abortion Information Bill, dealing with the less emotive issues of information and travel, had been drawn up at the end of 1993, ready to go before the Dáil, but was continually delayed. Originally due to be published in January 1994, it was designed to give life to the vote of the November 1992 referendum. Allowing for names and addresses of abortion clinics to be given to women in crisis pregnancies and provision for non-directive counselling, the new laws were also expected to permit doctors, clinics and magazines to provide information on abortion services available in other countries, but not any direct referral to clinics.

The pro-life campaign was most concerned about the question of referrals in the Bill and urged the final legislation to allow only for non-directive counselling. The government countered that the Bill had been drawn up after extensive consultations with all the concerned parties, and with the wishes of the populace foremost in the minds of the legislators.

Albert Reynolds warned that the substantive issue on whether abortion could ever be constitutionally lawful in Ireland would take much longer to achieve and would need further care and consideration. Privately, many said that it would be a brave government to take on such a divisive issue and that the matter would probably be indefinitely postponed.

The near conclusion of the criminal proceedings in the 'X' case rekindled the debate and led to renewed calls for action on the abortion issue, which had almost faded from the public memory. John Cooney, in the *Irish Independent*, who penned an analytical report on why the 'foetus factor' was still unresolved in Ireland, wrote: 'The famous "X" abortion case is heading for a final verdict . . . through the normal judicial procedure. However slow the legal system might be, it appears to move towards an ultimate resolution, in contrast to the immobility which can shroud the political arena.' He called the lack of political progress in the area 'a constitutional cul-de-sac' and warned that the governmental inaction on abortion and divorce would encourage the conservative lobbies in Ireland to 'press the advantage of a more fundamentalist climate of opinion'. He was quickly proved right.

Two days after his article appeared, the Pro-Life Campaign held a press conference in Dublin's Buswells Hotel. Announcing a new spearhead aimed at the government, Caroline Simons, one of the campaign's brightest young stars, claimed that the government would be acting unconstitutionally if it permitted information on abortion clinics in Ireland.

The Pro-Life Campaign said that the provision of names, addresses and telephone numbers amounted to an abortion referral and that the government would be acting 'in flagrant disregard' of its constitutional duty to protect life if it allowed for the free circulation of such information. Ms Simons said that the withholding of such information was not censorship but life-protecting and could be compared to the official secrecy surrounding the whereabouts of death-threat author Salman Rushdie in order to save his life. She added: 'It cannot have been the purpose of the government in bringing forward the Information Amendment, or the intention of the people in enacting that Amendment, to set aside . . . the decisions [of the High Court and Supreme Court in the 1980s].

'Throughout the Dáil and Senate debates in 1992 . . . there was a constant emphasis on a continuing commitment to protect unborn life. To propose at the same time that it might be lawful to provide assistance in bringing about the destruction of that life outside the jurisdiction would be unthinkable and absurdly hypocritical.

'There is no question of there being in any sense a constitutional right to an abortion outside the State and to act as if such a right existed would be seriously to undermine the protection of that right within the State.'

The Pro-Life Campaign said that any legislation on abortion information should only include factual information – about the procedure and its medical implications – and not anything which amounted to abortion referral. It urged the government to 'honour the law laid down in the Constitution' and continue to protect the life of the unborn 'to the fullest extent'.

Professor William Binchy, another leading member of the campaign, an expert in medical ethics and the brother of the author Maeve Binchy, insisted that the campaign's argument was not political. He said it was based 'on the legal parameters of the Constitution and the findings of the Supreme and High Court cases'. He said the campaign would not be taking any further action until the legislation on abortion had been published.

The same day as the Pro-Life Campaign held its press conference, a government source told *The Irish Times*: 'The people voted for the right to travel and the right to information in that referendum. If people have been given the constitutional right to go somewhere, they surely have the right to know where to go.'

The newspaper claimed that, although the Bill regulating the availability of abortion information had been finalized for a number of weeks, it would not be published until after the European elections to keep it away from the political campaign.

The findings of an opinion poll published in *The Irish Times* had shown no alteration of the public view that abortion should be available in limited circumstances. Of those asked, 71 per cent voted for legislation to allow abortion. Out of these, 41 per cent said the legislation should permit abortion in all circumstances where there is any threat to the life of the mother, including the threat of suicide; 30 per cent believed legislation should exclude the threat of suicide from the circumstances in which abortion should be permitted and limit terminations to women who face a physical threat to their lives solely.

Only 24 per cent were totally opposed to legalizing abortion in any circumstances, a figure which rose to 33 per cent in rural areas and among the over-fifties. There was substantial support (71 per cent) for the introduction of legislation to provide access to abortion information, while 23 per cent were opposed to it.

The Prime Minister read the poll results and said there was no deliberate delay on the part of the government on the information legislation. He said he hoped it would be enacted by the end of 1994.

A week after it was announced that the legislation would be delayed, Human Life International, the world's largest anti-abortion organization based in America, opened a permanent office in Dublin from which it planned to launch a concerted campaign for a third referendum on abortion.

Peter Scully, its executive director in Ireland, who admitted that its advisers included a member of Youth Defence – the militant anti-abortion organization – said the office's funding would come from Irish-American sources. 'Since the events of October 1992, there has been no unified effort for a referendum, until now,' Mr Scully announced. 'The possible postponement of the divorce referendum would provide an opportune time for a pro-life referendum.'

He said the 13-year-old organization, set up by Father Paul Marx and to be located in Dublin's central Mountjoy Square, would provide educational material, including leaflets and videos, for like-minded organizations. It was the first time that an American anti-abortion organization had set up a permanent base in Ireland and its arrival filled many with dread.

The divorce referendum, so long expected, was facing prolonged setbacks. Although nothing in the polls had suggested anything but that it would be voted for in the immediate aftermath of 1992, campaigns against its passing gathered momentum and the tide of opinion slowly started turning back to pre-1992.

An opinion poll in the *Irish Independent* in June 1994 claimed that 57 per cent of the population were still in favour of divorce, and said that the 32 per cent of those against had dropped by four points. But the 11 per cent who said they did not know had increased from eight per cent a few months earlier.

The poll confirmed, as if there had ever been any doubt in anyone's minds, that there was an absolute majority against divorce in the farming communities outside Dublin and people who represented those voters marshalled their forces in the face of the continuing delays.

Sean Haughey, TD, grabbed headlines in 1994 when he declared that Labour's 'steam roller approach to the liberal agenda of divorce, abortion, homosexuality and the Church's role in education has led to constitutional blunders and a re-awakening of the silent majority.' He added: 'We should assert our identity on every issue and continue, as we did in the past, to represent the ordinary, decent people of the silent majority.'

A delegation of bishops, headed by the influential Archbishop of Armagh, Cardinal Cahal Daly, met with senior government ministers and restated their opposition to divorce.

Government statistics showed that at least one marriage in eight ended in separation or breakdown in the Republic, with at least five marriages breaking up every day. In the absence of divorce – as defined by the Constitution's Article 41.3 which stated 'no law shall be enacted providing for the grant of a dissolution of marriage' (and endorsed by 63 per cent of the electorate in a referendum in 1986) – more and more Irish couples were living apart and embarking on illicit sexual relations with third parties.

Many separated and deserted spouses depended on social welfare payments or lone parents' allowance. More than 22,000 people (of an estimated 55,000 who were separated) were living on such State benefits in 1993.

The Catholic Church's nullity courts also dealt with a record number of annulments, their number having tripled in the ten years between 1979 and 1989. More than 2,500 couples had also taken advantage of the Judicial Separation Act of 1989, which gave courts the power to grant judicial separations on the grounds of adultery, irreconcilable differences, and other causes. Judges could rule on property matters, maintenance and custody and were to be given further powers relating to pensions and financial provisions in nullity cases.

In such a climate and despite the expected support for the divorce referendum, the government delayed and dithered, and the vote which was originally planned for the summer of 1994 was put off for at least another year. Complicated matters relating to property division had held it up, ministers said. They were also hampered by an unusual High Court challenge to the Judicial Separation Act of 1989, brought by a young Cork man who was challenging the right of his wife to a legal separation.

The main thrust of the challenge, which was to dictate the political agenda on the issue, was that the 1989 Act was a blueprint for divorce – and therefore contrary to the ban on divorce and the spirit of the Constitution. His case came before the High Court in July and the judge's judgement was delivered a few weeks later.

In a decision welcomed by many, Mr Justice Murphy upheld the constitutionality of the Act. He said that marriage was more than just a contract between two people, it was a personal relationship with a variety of essential ingredients. If one of those essential ingredients no longer exists, he said, the law is not prevented by the Constitution from recognizing through legislation the 'tragic' reality that a couple's relationship has broken down.

He upheld the constitutionality of a provision within the Act which allows the courts to determine which spouse should reside in the family home when granting a separation. He also ruled that this provision, under which many court orders had already been made, was not 'an unjust attack' on the rights of the excluded spouse, as claimed by the Cork husband.

The judgement was welcomed by the Minister for Equality and Law Reform, Mr Taylor, who had been forced to postpone the intended divorce referendum because of the challenge. 'The government's determination to hold a referendum and to campaign in favour of the removal of the constitutional ban on divorce, remains firm,' he said.

But the way was not entirely clear for such a referendum because of a possible appeal of the decision to the Supreme Court. Any such appeal was not likely to be heard until at least the end of the year, delaying any referendum until at least spring 1995.

The delay gave welcome extra time to those fighting divorce. In blunt criticism of those pushing for the legislation, the influential Archbishop of Dublin Desmond Connell claimed it would destroy the foundation of Irish family traditions and strengthen the movement towards social disorder.

Speaking at a mass in Knock, Co. Mayo, in May 1994, he said that the family was 'under attack from the increasing influences of permissive propaganda' and Catholics needed to look to their defences 'instead of contemplating surrender'. He said the experiences of other countries showed that divorce increased suffering rather than lessened it, and said that the perceived benefit of any such reform was just 'wishful thinking'.

He added: 'Parents are coming under increasing pressures, not least the influence of media support for a materialistic and permissive vision of life, not to speak of their hostility towards Catholic standards.' He echoed the fears of many Catholics when he said the 'permissive drift of recent legislation' would injure the common good, and that the radically anti-social act of divorce would 'tear apart the roots from which children derive their sense of belonging'.

Cardinal Daly agreed. He said divorce was presented as the compassionate, if not the truly Christian, response to marriage breakdown. 'This is very unfair on those who opposed divorce,' he said. 'They are equally motivated by compassion – compassion for the children who are affected by divorce, compassion for the spouses who are affected by the second union of an unfaithful partner, compassion for the couples who, in face of so many social and cultural pressures, are determined to stay faithful to one another to death. No one should attempt to turn the divorce debate into a compassion contest.'

Those who had fought for change and who had seen their hopes for it dashed, tried not to lose heart. Nuala Fennell, former Women's Affairs Minister, who had left politics at the end of 1992 after deciding that there was little more she could do, reflected back on all that had happened.

Concentrating on writing an autobiography of her life as a leading Irish feminist and politician, she expressed her disappointment that more had not been changed. 'I think the real excitement started when Mary Robinson became the first woman President and we thought that things might at last be moving our way,' she said.

'Then the remarkable 1992 came and went and we all felt that Ireland would now really face up to all those taboo issues. Although the back has been broken to a certain extent, I think people have now taken a very definite step back from that position, and would probably be happy to let the matter rest – at least until the next shocking case comes along.'

She did not believe that the far right – whom she described as 'a mix of fanatical religious groups and a kind of reflection from the Catholic Church' – had laid down their arms in Ireland. 'You only have to look how the matter of abortion has divided America in recent years to see that these people are far from beaten.

'And I think the Irish people are very easily swayed. They may have felt indignation over "X", but now they would really rather not interfere. If some eloquent American speaker arrives in their little village and shows them disgusting pictures and shocks them into believing that abortion is a mortal sin, then they will be just as indignant the other way.'

Tony O'Brien, of the IFPA, accepted that the fight was not over, but said he was still optimistic for the future. 'Ireland is at its heart very progressive,' he added. 'In the aftermath of the "X" case it is implementing a degree of progress unprecedented anywhere other than by countries in the former Eastern bloc.

'The pace of change and the acceptance of liberal ideas has been helped by the fact that matters have always been hotly debated in Ireland, unlike Britain. And the climate for change is enhanced by the relative silence of the Catholic Church, largely due to their shame over the Bishop of Galway, Eamonn Casey, who deserves a vote of thanks. By having a passionate affair with a woman who became the mother of his child, he demonstrated that the Church was not infallible, and that it was no greater an authority on moral values than anyone else. That whole ridiculous farce meant that at a time when the Church would normally have been delivering strong anti-abortion statements, it either felt it was not able to do so, or people just were not listening any longer.'

Cardinal Cahal Daly, Archbishop of Armagh and Primate of All Ireland since 1991, admitted that there was a struggle within Ireland, but claimed that it would eventually make for a better church. Suggested changes already in hand included the relinquishing of the Latin Mass, less formality, more authority for lay people and a more human face on the clergy.

'The Catholic Church in Ireland has been ubiquitous,' he said. 'The Church was everywhere serving people but eventually that was going to be seen as trying to control and trying to interfere, and that is the perception of many young people. It is not intended and it never was. We must change that perception and still be wherever there is a need and wherever there is a service to be given.' He accused the media of 'anti-clericalism', an accusation repeated across Ireland by those who said that those in control of the national press in Dublin had forgotten what groundswell of ardent Catholic feeling there still was in the regions.

Others concurred. Roger Sawyer in his book *We Are But Women: Women in Ireland's History*, wrote:

> In certain aspects of life the Catholic Church may have screwed the lid down too tightly. But when seen in comparison to social disintegration elsewhere, the Irish family can still be regarded as an example of what can be achieved by holding fast to the best in Western religion and culture.
>
> It survives, whilst all around standards are falling. Many of its women freely choose to lead from the hearth and send their husbands out to win the bread.

There were other pressing modern issues knocking at Ireland's door. Technological leaps in embryo research and infertility in Britain and the US sent shock waves down the Irish spine.

The world's geneticists claimed that they were fast approaching the time when they would be able to transfer an unwanted aborted foetus to the womb of a woman who wanted it – thus doing away with the need for terminations and solving the infertility problem for millions of couples in one fell swoop.

Under such a procedure it would, in theory, be possible for the unwanted baby of 'X' to have been carried to full term by one of the ardent anti-abortionists who railed against her decision in O'Connell Street. The ethical and moral questions abounded.

An equally unpalatable prospect was the controversial news that a Scottish geneticist proposed to use the eggs from aborted foetuses to treat infertile women. The procedure would mean that the children then born would have all had aborted foetuses as natural mothers. The proposals and their implications stunned many worldwide, and the Irish were not the only ones who found them distasteful. Critics believed the processes to be interfering with God and nature and called for a slowing down of the pace of advance.

But with private medical care funding much of the research and millions to be made from each breakthrough, it was not an area which was likely to be halted and Ireland was already lagging far behind.

Senator Mary Henry called for a national and international debate on such subjects as genetic engineering and genetic testing. 'We should have the strength of character to take part in the international debate,' she said. 'If the technique becomes available, then the people of Ireland will ask why they should be left out, as had happened with test tube babies.'

Critics said such research would be 'opening a Pandora's box' of possibilities which would be repugnant to the Irish moral code and could promote abortion in the long term. 'Do we want to know that our children, before they are even born, carry a strong risk for cancer, heart disease or schizophrenia?' wrote one Irish journalist. 'Do we want to meddle in our own DNA, turning what was once a sacred mystery into a mass chemical experiment?'

In Ireland, neither amniocentesis nor the use of donor eggs to enable infertile women to have babies was legally allowed, though in 1994 the Medical Council lifted the ban on freezing a woman's embryos as part of in-vitro fertilization treatment, but only for married couples. Advocates of such technological breakthroughs being permitted in the Republic – eventually leading, it was hoped, to preventative medical treatment for anything from heart disease to cancer – feared that the emotional treatment of this field would continue to delay its introduction in Ireland.

An estimated 1,000 babies with genetic disorders were born in the Republic each year, yet there were no properly qualified medical genetics staff in any of the State hospitals. In many cases the families were not even told that their child's disorder was genetic and could have been foreseen, even if it was the second child in the family to have been born with such a condition.

The Republic's first publicly appointed medical geneticist, a doctor from Baltimore, Maryland, was due to start work at a children's hospital in Crumlin in 1995. Even so, it was not known how much information he would be able to tell expectant mothers with problem foetuses, for fear that he could be breaking the law and advocating abortion. Supporters of his appointment said it was a first tentative step into a very difficult area, and one which they hoped would be followed up with further similar appointments.

In the face of such problems, the continuing abortion traffic to Britain showed no signs of slowing down although there was still little understanding of the suffering it caused.

To address that problem, the IFPA (celebrating its twenty-fifth anniversary) announced the setting up of the first weekly forum for women who had been through abortions and who wanted to talk about their experiences. Unthinkable in Ireland a decade before, the post-abortion group, organized by veteran campaigner Ruth Riddick, attracted dozens of young girls and women who felt the need to share their experiences and feelings with others.

It was a long way from the day when Miss Riddick stood up in the assembly hall and became the second known woman in Ireland to admit to having had a termination. But for her, it was still not enough. Three months before the 'X' case trial, she bemoaned in a newspaper article how little progress had been made on the abortion issue in Ireland: 'More than half the women who decided to terminate their crisis pregnancies last year . . . had not had access to, or availed of, professional counselling services in Ireland before the (usually irrevocable) decision that is the journey to London or Liverpool.'

She said the Irish like to think they have come a long way in the past ten years – 'that the election of Mary Robinson represented a healing of Irish society'. But instead, she said, there were actually fewer non-directive pregnancy counselling services in 1994 than in 1984, and women's magazines listing reputable abortion providers were plastered with a 'Publisher's Notice' advising readers that the Censorship Board would not permit such information to enter Ireland.

The effects of such censorship also had a ripple effect in the medium of television. In May 1994 a landmark documentary programme on the abortion tourism between Ireland and England, commissioned by the Irish national television station RTE, was due to be screened. Called *50,000 Secret Journeys* to represent the number of Irish women thought to have travelled to England for abortions in the previous ten years, the IR £10,000-production talked to three women about their experiences in a way that had never been seen on television before.

A week before its mid-week broadcast RTE decided to stop it from going out on its 'Tuesday File' slot and replaced it instead with an innocuous programme. Schedulers said later that they felt the programme suffered from 'a possible lack of balance' and might be re-scheduled for later in the year.

RTE had not wished to offend its more traditional viewers. It was, after all, the television station which still screened the 'Angelus', the thrice-daily Catholic devotional exercise. Just before the noon and 6 o'clock news bulletins, the nation's television screens featured an icon of a saint to the accompaniment of the solemn tolling of nine bells calling viewers to prayer.

Little seemed to have changed elsewhere for Ireland's teenage mothers. In the final months of 1993 and in early 1994, the bodies of three dead babies were variously discovered in canals, parks and beaches in Kerry, Dublin and Kildare.

The first body was discovered wrapped in newspaper and plastic in a ruck-sack in Phoenix Park, Dublin. Alongside it in the bag was a partially completed questionnaire on sex and society aimed at schoolchildren. The identity of the baby and its mother was never discovered.

A month later a dead baby girl was found on the banks of the River Feale, near Listowel, Co. Kerry. It had been delivered by the teenage mother on her own and without medical attention, weighed six pounds, and is thought to have been alive when it entered the water. The young mother was later traced and given psychological help.

In February a stillborn baby girl was taken from the Royal Canal near Maynooth, Co. Kildare. It had been in the water six to nine weeks and police were unable to identify it or its mother, although she was also believed likely to have been a local teenager.

The discoveries rekindled calls for better sex education in schools, and for the extension of pregnancy counselling services throughout the Republic. The 23,000-member Irish Country Women's Association condemned the pressures on young mothers 'which lead to the abandoning of a baby without name or ritual' and called on Church and State to take on a more supportive and caring role towards pregnant women and girls.

The Church countered that it was society as a whole which

had to take a more caring attitude. It said that its counselling service, Cura, dealt with 9,000 calls from pregnant women in 1993 and offered free accommodation, medical and nursery care to women who chose to have their babies.

Once again, blame for the dilemma of Ireland's young mothers was continually being placed at the other camp's door. With little or nothing being done to give them practical advice and assistance, dead babies would continue to be found.

TWENTY

Abortion and the law continued to dominate the news. Harry Whelehan, still Attorney General, had rarely had a breathing space from wrestling with the problem which had dominated his first few months in office.

It was he who had supervised the enacting of the new Criminal Justice (Public Order) Act, which was primarily designed to counter general brawls, riots, drunkenness and controversial demonstrations. Billed as a measure to 'protect the public from the irresponsible and anti-social behaviour of those who have no regard for the rights of others', it became law on 3 April 1994. Less than three weeks later one of the first arrests under its new rules was of an anti-abortion campaigner who had been distributing photographs of an aborted foetus in Henry Street in central Dublin. His arrest marked the first of its kind under Section 7 of the new Act which prohibited the distribution or display in a public place of 'threatening, abusive, insulting or obscene' literature. Any such offender was liable to a maximum IR £500 fine and/or three months' imprisonment.

The arrested man, who was unemployed, was taken to Store Street Garda station and released when a pro-life organization came to his defence with a solicitor. A file on his case was sent to the DPP and the police were awaiting the State's instructions on whether or not to proceed against him.

It was an historic official move towards preventing the regular weekly demonstrations of the more extremist anti-abortion campaigners who publicly railed against 'baby slaughter' every Saturday afternoon in Dublin. But, others argued, it was also an infringement of civil rights and the right to free speech, and they criticized its wide discretionary powers which they feared could be used not only against the moral majority but against ordinary, heartfelt expressions of protest such as those against the initial State decisions in the 'X' case.

A few weeks later Mr Whelehan found himself once again under pressure for addressing the abortion issue. He had advised the government that it should not support a proposed United Nations declaration on world population because of its references to abortion. The matter once again set Ireland at odds with its European Union partners, who wished to show unanimous support to the UN declaration in preparation for an important world conference on population and development to be held in Cairo later in the year.

Tom Kitt, the Irish Development Aid Minister, faced stiff opposition when he told the EU that Ireland could not support the draft declaration, which contained several references to abortion, including one that 'all individuals have the basic right to choose when and if they have children'. The proposed wording added: 'The aim of family planning programmes must be to establish the widest possible freedom of choice in matters of procreation. Coercion in family planning programmes, whether physical, economical or psychological, is a breach of human rights and can never be accepted.'

Reluctantly pushed towards a compromise wording to accommodate their problem member, the EU partners were once again forced to accept the fact that Ireland was a country apart and one that had to be handled with care.

The 'X' case trial was due to begin on the morning of Monday, 9 May 1994, in the imposing granite Green Street courthouse of Dublin's Circuit Criminal Court, normally used for IRA and high security cases.

As the accused man neared the moment when he would stand in the dock before a judge and jury, he told his wife for the first time that a DNA test done on the girl's 'boyfriend', the boy 'A', had proved negative with that from the foetus.

Steadfastly supported and buffered by her during the previous two years, he now saw the suspicion in her eyes and broke down and confessed everything to her. The woman to whom he had been married for more than twenty years, the mother of his three children who for so long had loyally stood by him in the most dire of circumstances, was shattered by his confession. 'She was utterly destroyed by it,' said a family friend. 'She realized for the first time just how much he had lied to her and everyone else and she was appalled. It was as terrible a tragedy and betrayal of trust for her as much as it had been for the girl and her family. Everyone felt very, very sorry for her.'

Packing her belongings and taking her children with her, she moved out of the family home and went to stay with her sister in north Dublin. Her relatives rallied round her as much as they could, but she could not be comforted. The defendant was left on his own for the first time.

The next morning, at an unscheduled court appearance at the Circuit Criminal Court, one of the junior defence counsel tried to seek a last-minute adjournment of the case from Judge Michael Moriarty. The court was told that the defendant wanted to appeal to the European Court of Human Rights over the High and Supreme Court decisions not to abandon his trial. The long-suffering judge, who had presided over several previous adjournments in this case, threw out the application.

Later that afternoon, during a final police case conference at the south Dublin police station, a telephone call was received from the defendant's legal advisers. There had been a change of situation, the officers were informed. The accused man would consider pleading guilty to three sample charges – one of indecent assault and two of unlawful carnal knowledge – if the remaining charges were kept on the file and not officially proceeded with.

He would confess to the first indecent assault in the Dublin mountains, to the assault in his home while the girl's parents were in Lourdes and to the final charge of having sex with her in the alleyway behind the swimming pool in Rathmines.

After more than two years of twisting and conniving, and of trying to blacken the girl's good name and that of her family and friends, the defendant was finally ready to admit his role in her abuse.

Anxious not to let him off the hook in any way, the police said they would carefully consider the offer. They had to balance the desirability of not having to go through a full trial and forcing the girl to give evidence with the need to bring the guilty man to justice and see him jailed for an appropriate period of time.

On the three charges as they stood, they discussed, the defendant could face a maximum of life imprisonment. They thought the likely sentence would be more like five to seven years, which is what they could have expected upon his conviction after a trial anyway. After considered discussions with their legal advisers, they decided to agree to a deal.

'Nobody was getting too worried about him not pleading to the other charges,' said one of those connected with the case. 'Nobody was going to deduce from that that he was not admitting to the others.'

Detective Inspector Sourke, recently promoted to Detective Superintendent and about to be transferred from his Garda station, personally telephoned the girl's family to tell them the good news. The relief for everyone was enormous.

Three days later, just after 11 o'clock on the morning of Monday, 9 May, standing in the oak-panelled dock of the Green Street courthouse, the defendant clasped his hands in front of him and pleaded guilty to three charges of unlawful carnal knowledge and indecent sexual assault.

Wearing a grey cashmere blazer, purple shirt, brightly

coloured tie and black trousers, he looked for all the world like the presentable family man he had tried so hard to pretend to be. He spoke only three times, swallowing hard and glancing at his solicitor before answering 'Guilty' to each of the charges – cited as counts three, seven and nine – read out to him by the bespectacled court clerk.

Less than ten feet in front of him, lower down in the well of the tiered court, the girl and her mother sat with their backs to him, gripping hands and utterly motionless as he solemnly entered his pleas. Wearing a dark green tartan jacket and skirt, the girl, who wore her glossy dark hair loose, had entered the courtroom a few minutes earlier holding the hand of silver-haired Detective Garda Aubrey Steadman. She was followed on to the wooden bench seat by her mother, then a counsellor from the Rape Crisis Centre and Detective Ann Vaughan, the police officer who had taken down her initial evidence against the man two years before.

The public gallery was filled with her family members and well-wishers, thirteen of them in all, who smiled and sighed as the guilty pleas were taken. Two elderly female relatives of the defendant sat alone lower down, the only representatives from his side to attend the brief hearing.

The girl's father sat apart with a solicitor at the back of the court to witness the defendant pleading guilty. Friends of the family said there were now irreconcilable differences between him and his family.

Five black-robed and bewigged barristers sat on the front bench beneath the judge and shuffled their papers waiting for their chance to speak. In the end, only two of them did.

Edward Comyn, SC for the prosecution, rose to his feet and told Judge Gerard Buchanan about the High Court and Supreme Court decisions preceding the trial that had allowed it to come before him. Mr Comyn asked for the judge to prohibit the publication of any information, including the identity of the defendant, which would lead 'in any way' to the identification of the girl. He also asked that all those not directly connected with the case be asked to leave the court. Kevin Haugh, SC for the defence, rose to his feet briefly to tell the judge: 'I share this view.'

Judge Buchanan told the twenty-plus reporters in the lofty public gallery: 'The press are expected to act in their usual responsible manner. There is to be no identification of the accused or the victim.' He decided against enacting the public exclusion order until the later full hearing.

Mr Comyn told the court that it would be inappropriate to give full details of the evidence until the judge had been able to read the necessary reports on the impact of the crime on the victim and the probation reports on the accused. The judge agreed. The prosecutor asked for the defendant to be remanded in custody, and Mr Haugh raised no objection.

Judge Buchanan told the defendant that he would be remanded so that pre-sentencing reports on his background and circumstances could be prepared and the man nodded his head of thick greying hair to indicate that he understood. Two uniformed officers sitting with him in the dock then stood ready to usher him down the steep stairs to the courtroom cells.

The girl looked round at the defendant only once, to meet his gaze directly for a moment before he was taken down below. The man did not respond.

The throng of people in the public gallery rose to their feet in unison and broke into spontaneous cheering and applause which lasted several minutes. The man bowed his head as he was led away.

The girl and her mother left the courtroom quickly and were ushered into an ante-chamber where those with them embraced her emotionally. It was the last time she would have to be in court to face him, they told her.

The girl's father, sitting almost unnoticed at the back of the public gallery behind the press benches, was close to tears as he made his way down the central stairs. A solicitor with him squeezed his arm and helped him find his footing on the twisting steps.

The entire hearing, for so long anticipated and so repeatedly sabotaged, had lasted just over ten minutes. But its significance was incalculable. 'The most important thing was that he had stood in the dock and said "Guilty" to the charges,' said one of those involved with the case. 'I don't have any doubt that a jury would have convicted him if the case had gone to trial. But there would always have been a little group of people in this country insisting that he was innocent, a decent Catholic family man who was being wronged, and that the entire case was trumped up by people who wanted to bring abortion into this country.'

After what was effectively his conviction, the defendant was driven from the car park at the side of the courthouse, crouched on the floor in the back of a police van to avoid the lenses of the waiting cameramen.

He was *en route* to Dublin's Mountjoy Prison, a gloomy Victorian jail. Officers in the case said he would be likely to remain in the secure wing of Mountjoy until sentencing and then be moved to Arbour Hill prison where sexual offenders were kept in isolation for their own safety.

The morning after his conviction, the Irish papers featured the case as a major news story. The *Irish Independent* ran a graphic three-page special on the case, with headlines such as: 'Ordeal in the Courtroom', 'Shattering News for Wife Who Stood by Him' and 'The Death of Innocence on the Road to Womanhood'.

Many reporters who covered this penultimate episode of the saga felt afterwards 'almost disappointed' that there had not been a trial. One commented: 'It felt like such an anti-climax, to have him plead guilty in the end, after all those years.'

Another said: 'Although nobody wanted to put the girl through the ordeal of a trial I think many of us felt, as she must have done, that at least it would have fully exposed his manipulation of her. Instead, he had succeeded in letting the matter drag on and on, until right at the very end, when he would admit to only three of the nine charges. It was a despicable move on his part.'

Others connected with the case agreed. One legal adviser described the man's conduct throughout as 'sinister' and wished that he had pleaded guilty from the outset. 'If he had put his hands up then and said OK to one charge, then the girl and her family would not have had to go through two years of hell and he would probably have been out of prison by now.

'Instead, he only compounded the misery further for her family and for his. Judge Costello's initial description of him [as being an evil and depraved man] wasn't far wrong.'

The probation and social services swung into action to prepare their various reports, but immediately ran into difficulties. The Irish system of victim impact reports – assessing how well the victim had coped since the crime was discovered and the defendant convicted – was considered by many as an irrelevance to the sentencing of a defendant. But the judge, in an attempt to be seen to be fair to all sides, had ordered one, and the girl's co-operation was sought by social services. Counselled and questioned and examined continually for over two years, she objected now to undergoing the necessary interviews and initially refused to assist.

'I think she had simply had enough,' said one family friend. 'She had hoped it would all be over with his appearance in court, and she didn't want to have to start being grilled all over again.' Coaxed and coddled over the following weekend, she eventually agreed and the reports were prepared.

The very week of the trial, another unusual abortion case came before the courts and was reported as a small news item in *The Irish Times*.

In a case which was believed to have been the first of its kind brought in Ireland, a 21-year-old woman from north Co. Dublin took the extraordinary step of suing an English abortion clinic for IR £30,000 for personal injuries.

She claimed in the Dublin High Court that despite having gone to the Rosslyn Clinic in East Twickenham, west London, in March 1993 for an abortion, she was not aborted of the foetus and suffered a miscarriage three weeks after returning home.

Her brief statement of claim read in court said: 'As a result . . . of the clinic's negligence and breach of duty . . . she suffered severe personal injury, loss, damage and inconvenience.'

The clinic, which denied liability, sought to have the woman's action struck out on the grounds of jurisdiction, and the case was adjourned until later in the year.

Lawyers and journalists at the High Court were surprised that the woman had brought the case. Although unnamed, she must have risked a great deal of exposure to at least her family and friends by the action, in a situation where secrecy and shame were the norm.

Five days after the 'X' case defendant had appeared in court and pleaded guilty to three of the charges against him, the teenage girl and her mother were once again the subject of an injunction hearing before Mr Justice Declan Costello in the High Court. Bringing actions against five Irish newspapers for their reports which appeared the day after the trial, the girl and her mother sought interim injunctions restraining the publication of any further material about their family life.

John Rogers, SC for the plaintiffs, said that the family were particularly upset by the actions of a reporter from the *Sunday World* newspaper for allegedly 'watching, besetting and importuning' the girl. He told the court of the occasion when the Gardai had to be called to remove the reporter from the family's front garden.

It was feared that the newspaper was planning on running a substantial feature on the case on the following Sunday, so the interim injunctions were sought initially until the Monday afterwards.

Mr Rogers also sought and was granted an order restraining the newspaper from publishing or communicating to any other person any matter concerned with and connected with criminal proceedings at that time before the Circuit Criminal Court, save any matter which could be lawfully disclosed. A similar order was also sought against the *Evening Herald*, the *Irish Independent*, the *Evening Press*, and the [Irish] *Star*.

Mr Justice Costello said that publication of the transcript of questions and answers given in evidence at a preliminary examination at Rathfarnham District Court in November 1992 seemed to have been 'a clear contempt of court' and was 'outrageous'.

Mr Rogers told him that he had alerted the DPP to the publication of the transcript and pointed out that it was in breach of Section 17 of the Criminal Procedures Act 1967, advising that steps should be taken against the newspapers concerned. He said it was 'imperative' that his client's privacy and any proceedings to date should be protected. He was looking for an order restraining the publishing or communication of any fact, matter or information arising from the evidence given by 'X' at Rathfarnham.

He added that the *Evening Press* had run the transcript purporting it to be 'X's story. Mr Justice Costello said that if it was suggested that the article was taken from evidence at the District Court it could be contempt, and if it was suggested that the story was from her then it was 'a complete lie'.

A week later, on Thursday, 19 May, a full hearing for the injunction applications was carried out. Lawyers for all the newspapers involved attended and contested the injunctions. Afterwards one of them described the judge's rulings as 'an absolute crucifixion'. He added: 'For whatever reason, and maybe because he felt he had to do right by the girl this time around, Mr Justice Costello seemed to effectively invent a constitutional right to privacy when its parameters have never been defined in Irish law.

'When we asked for clarification of what he meant by his orders, all he said was that the newspapers' editors should get together and decide what would be an invasion of the girl's privacy and would cause her anguish.'

Mr Justice Costello upheld the family's application for injunctions against the newspapers and claimed that she had a constitutional right to privacy which it was the court's duty to protect. He said the newspapers named could not refer to the family circumstances surrounding the girl, nor any of the evidence which was given at Rathfarnham District Court about the details of the abuse.

Section 17 of the Criminal Procedures Act of 1967 stated that 'no person shall publish or cause to be published any information as to any preliminary examination other than a statement of fact that such examination . . . had been held and of the decision thereof'. But lawyers for the newspapers claimed that this section did not mean that no publication could be made in perpetuity, just until the accused had been convicted. One of them said: 'The intention of the legislature was to protect the accused person in respect of the publication of potentially prejudicial material in advance of his trial.'

He said this argument was supported by an explanatory memorandum to the Bill and debates in the Dáil and the Senate on the subject. Its interpretation was also supported by the wording of the British Magistrates Court Act 1980 (the UK equivalent of the Irish law) which explicitly allowed publication of material from a preliminary examination after the conclusion of the accused's trial. The Court of Appeal later upheld this interpretation and said (in *R* vs *Horsham Justices*): 'This prohibition was solely in the interests of justice to the defendant. It had nothing whatever to do with the possible effect of publication on third parties who might be referred to in the proceedings in sinister or discreditable contexts.'

The lawyers further argued that if Mr Justice Costello was saying that this information could never be published, it was 'an arbitrary and unnecessary restriction upon the constitutional rights of freedom of expression . . . and of the importance of justice being administered in public'.

Mr Justice Costello said he was not deciding that there had been a breach of Section 17 or that the girl's constitutional rights had been infringed. He was merely satisfied that her claim of a breach of statutory duty and a breach of her constitutional right were serious issues to be tried. The judge agreed that the action before him was 'very special' and said the young girl was claiming she had been 'greatly distressed, emotionally disturbed and hurt' by the wrongs done to her by the newspapers.

He was not saying that she would succeed in pursuing any civil actions against the newspapers involved, but that the court had a clear duty to protect her until this issue had been tried. The protection of the girl's constitutional rights to privacy would override the constitutional rights of the journalists concerned to communicate, the judge said.

Asked by Patrick MacEntee, SC for Independent Newspapers, if the newspapers were then prevented from publishing matters that were already in the public domain relating to this case, Mr Justice Costello said he suggested a test was that editors should consider whether what they were going to publish was going to cause anguish, hurt and emotional upset to the plaintiff. That having been done, he said, let them look to the order and see if what they were going to do was prohibited.

The newspapers were shocked and appalled by the wide-ranging scope of the injunctions against them and the implications for any future cases. Once again, they said, the 'X' case was making Irish legal history in a way that nobody could have foreseen.

Counsel for the defendants lodged an appeal in the Supreme Court against the decision, but realized that it was not likely to be heard before 1996. 'If we went to the Supreme Court immediately afterwards, in that climate, we would probably have lost,' one of the lawyers said afterwards. 'Our thinking was that we should put in our appeal to test the water on this vital principle of law at a more appropriate time. This could not be adequately and appropriately discussed if the facts of the case could not even come into the public domain. But if a future Irish government did actually grasp the nettle on abortion legislation, then that would be a better time to discuss this.'

If the Supreme Court were to reject their appeal, the newspapers said they were prepared to go to Strasbourg for a European ruling on the principles of the case. 'This is such an important matter and one that has to be fought to the bitter end,' said one insider. 'It is not that we had anything more to say about the "X" case or about the people involved, but if this ruling stands it would mean that any future case of similar importance to the people of Ireland would never be allowed to be fully discussed and analysed, and that would be the most appalling curbing of press freedom.'

TWENTY-ONE

On Thursday, 2 June, a month before the girl's seventeenth birthday – and one week before the European elections – the defendant was to appear again before the judge at Green Street court.

The girl and her mother did not attend this time, but her father sat at the back of the public gallery once again, his raincoat folded neatly on his arm as he waited for the man who had abused his daughter to enter the dock.

First, a man caught in possession of IR £500,000-worth of cocaine had to be dealt with. Perplexed as to why so many members of the press and legal representatives should be in court for his case, he was sentenced to fourteen years' imprisonment for his crimes by Judge Buchanan.

At precisely 12.28 p.m. the defendant was brought up from the cells. In exactly the same clothes as for his last court appearance, he looked none the less shabbier after his two weeks in custody and bore the expression of a man who had slept badly and who consequently had been unable to shave so thoroughly the following morning.

Flanked by two prison officers on the wooden dock bench, in his left hand he clutched a crumpled tissue, which he squeezed ever tighter as he sat rigidly erect during the first part of the hearing. His right hand twitched constantly as he tapped his forefinger and thumb together rhythmically.

Judge Buchanan excluded members of the public from the court and a woman Garda asked all those remaining in the public gallery to show their press passes. The girl's father and his companion, a solicitor, were asked for theirs and had to quietly explain who they were.

Clement Loscher, the dismissed teacher and author of the controversial pro-life book about the case, sat in front of them and showed the officer his press pass.

Edward Comyn, SC, opened the case and reminded the judge that the defendant had previously pleaded guilty to three charges of an original nine. He said the girl had made it clear that she did not wish to give oral evidence at the hearing, but would be available to see the judge privately if he wished to hear from her. He told the judge that a victim impact report by Dr Paul McCarthy, a child psychiatrist, had been prepared, along with a probation report on the accused.

Inspector Sourke took the oak-panelled witness stand and gave evidence of the police involvement with the case. He told the court how the matter first came to light when the girl's pregnancy was discovered in February 1992 and how blood samples were later taken from the man and the pregnant girl. 'The prosecution evidence on this point would have been that the pregnancy was the responsibility of the accused?' asked Mr Comyn, and Detective Inspector Sourke replied: 'On the balance of probability, yes.'

He said he was present when the girl attended St Mary's Hospital in Manchester on 3 March and was told by Dr Lieberman, the consultant gynaecologist and obstetrician, that the girl had miscarried. 'She underwent monitoring for a foetal heartbeat and there was no foetal heartbeat,' said the Detective Inspector. He agreed with counsel for the defendant that the miscarriage had been 'spontaneous and natural'. He added: 'Dr Lieberman gave me to understand that the pregnancy would not have lasted full term.'

He then told how he personally took the samples he received from Dr Lieberman to Cellmark Diagnostics for testing, the results of which were given to the police in April of that year. Asked to describe the relationship between the accused man and the girl's family, he said it was 'very close': 'The injured party was a close school friend of the daughter of the accused. She would say that there was never a time when she did not know the accused in this case.'

He gave details of where the three sexual assaults took place and what they were, from the first molestation in the north Dublin hills to the full sexual intercourse in an 'unlit lane' in Rathmines in December 1991.

Mr Comyn asked: 'Would it be correct to say that . . . because of the close relationship with the family the defendant would have had plenty of opportunities and have been in a position to have seen the girl?'

Detective Inspector Sourke replied: 'He would have had numerous opportunities of seeing her without raising the suspicions of the parents. The contrary would be true. He was implicitly trusted by the parents of the injured party to such a degree that he was virtually called in to deal with any family problems that arose.'

He was then asked to outline the effects of the case on the girl and her family and replied: 'The overall matter has caused devastation in both families. The injured party and her family have moved from the address they resided in. The injured party has moved schools and indeed so has her younger brother. The overall thing has had an enormous effect on the schooling of the young girl.

'The distress which the whole matter has caused has had a knock-on effect on the family at large, including the parents and the younger brother.'

Asked to give details of the defendant's background, he said he was born in 1949 in a working class inner city area of Dublin and lived in similar areas around the city throughout his childhood until he got married at the age of twenty-two. He said his son was born soon after the defendant married, his eldest daughter – by then fifteen – was at secondary school, and his youngest daughter was five years old.

The man had been a self-employed businessman but was on the dole and legally aided at the time of his conviction. 'It would appear that his wife and family are now estranged and living apart from the family home,' Detective Inspector Sourke added. 'The family, it is fair to say, has suffered an awful lot of distress because of this.' He said the man had no previous criminal convictions.

Cross-examined by Kevin Haugh, SC for the defence, Detective Inspector Sourke agreed that the defendant had been 'a hard-working man, devoted to his family, a respectable businessman and held in the very highest regard in the community'.

Turning to the question of his sentencing, Mr Haugh told Judge Buchanan that it was well recognized that 'considerable discount' could be given to a defendant who pleaded guilty and spared the State the cost of a trial or saved the witnesses the ordeal of giving evidence, adding, however: 'I appreciate that this has been a plea which came very late in the day.'

Judge Buchanan immediately agreed. He said: 'That, of course, immediately occurs to me. That the accused strenuously denied the matters in question and also sought to blame somebody else.'

Mr Haugh continued undaunted with his plea for leniency. He said the case had attracted 'a tidal wave of publicity' which had overwhelmed all those involved. 'I would ask you to view the defendant's actions in these unique circumstances,' he said. 'He found himself in a situation that an accused person in this country has never found himself in before.'

Mr Haugh said his client suffered 'most peculiar' circumstances, in which he was observed by reporters, approached by 'special interest groups' and attracted the attentions of all sorts of persons in the media. He said this attention affected his client's capacity to consider a change of mind on his plea or make an overall re-consideration of his view. 'One is, of course, responsible for the natural bodily functions, but who could have foreseen the consequences or that he could ever have found himself in the situation he was in, under the magnifying glass of such an extraordinary kind of attention. The capacity to change his mind was very much diminished by all of this.'

Mr Haugh added that a substantial part of the delay was caused by the lengthy civil proceedings which had attempted to have the trial abandoned. 'He really ought not to be blamed for that delay,' he added. 'In view of the extraordinary circumstances it would have been wrong for him not to have sought prohibition. It was a specious action, not a delaying tactic.'

Mr Haugh said the consequences of the case had also been 'horrendous' for his client. 'His family has been devastated, his business has been devastated, and long after any prison sentence imposed by this court has been served, his efforts to gain control of his life and build it up again will be severely hampered.'

He said that although he could not legally be named in the press, the defendant was known to his family, to his wife's family and to their friends and neighbours. 'He has destroyed his own life and his own existence.'

He was, he said, a man from very humble beginnings who ultimately ended up where he was through his own personal diligence. 'He had a nice house and a nice family. The censorious price that he will have to pay, and the guilt and remorse he suffers for the destruction to his family is extremely high. To pick up the pieces now will be much harder for him than it will be for an ordinary person. He has asked me to say he is terribly sorry for what he has done.' Mr Haugh pointed out that, in relation to the sexual offences, 'there was no suggestion of threat or force or anything like that'.

The judge rose to consider his verdict for just under forty minutes before returning and passing sentence.

The judge's clerk instructed 'All rise' and all those in court stood for the reappearance of the judge. The defendant rose shakily to his feet and was the only person remaining standing when

Judge Buchanan spoke his name. A church bell tolled solemnly somewhere outside in the damp June afternoon.

The judge cleared his throat and then began. He told the defendant: 'The girl was twelve years and eleven months old on 22 June 1990 when she was indecently assaulted by you. This assault was committed, according to her account, by you feeling her legs and breasts outside her clothing.

'On 17 August 1990 or thereabouts, the girl was then thirteen years of age and had been left by her parents with you and your wife when they went to Lourdes. When other members of the household were in bed, you had full sexual intercourse with her in the sitting room of the house.

'On 7 December 1991 in an alleyway in Rathmines, in your motorcar, you again had full sexual intercourse with her, when she was then fourteen years of age. You have pleaded guilty in relation to these events.

'The law prohibits the defilement of girls under the age of fifteen and prescribes a maximum penalty of life imprisonment.'

The judge said he had read the probation and psychiatric reports which outlined the devastating effect on the family. 'It takes no imagination to fathom the upset and tragedy visited on the family, their friends and neighbours,' he said. 'Detective Inspector Sourke tells me that you have no previous criminal record and that your family too has been devastated by the events. I note from the probation report that you came from humble beginnings but you have made, or had made, a good life for yourself and your family. Your tragedy is obvious.

'Mr Haugh has told me that you have expressed to him and others the remorse you feel at the events that have happened. In considering sentence I have taken into account these facts and also a number of special items.

'The first is that you pleaded guilty to these charges, thereby saving the public trial and further embarrassment and distress to the girl and her family. But I also note that it was only at the late stage that you so pleaded or intimated your intent to plead and thereby occasioned continuing distress to the girl and her family over the intervening period.

'Secondly, I note that you have known of the findings of doctors at the Cellmark Institute in Oxford that you were undoubtedly the father of the girl's pregnancy.

'Thirdly, I note that you deliberately violated the trust placed in you by your friends and neighbours, the girl's family, when they left her in the care of you and your wife when they went on holiday.

'Fourthly, I note that you tried in your interviews with the Garda to blame a neighbouring youth in such a way that, had it not been for the DNA profile, it might have been difficult for the youth to disprove the allegations that you were making.

'Accordingly, having considered all these matters, on count three you will serve seven years in prison, on count seven you will serve seven years consecutively with the sentence on count three and on count nine, you will serve twelve months concurrently with the other sentences.'

The defendant, white of face and wide-eyed, rocked back on his heels at the sentence as if a blast of burning hot air had just hit him in the face. He gripped his hands together in front of him as if in prayer, knuckles white, his thick gold wedding band still on the third finger of his left hand.

Touched at the elbow by a prison guard to indicate that he could now sit down, he descended heavily as he began to contemplate serving the next fourteen years in prison. His face pinched with shock, he ran his hands through his perfectly groomed greying hair and stared hard at the scraped lino floor beneath his polished black shoes.

Mr Haugh rose to his feet and asked the judge for clarification. 'Did you say the second seven year sentence should be served *consecutively*?' he asked.

'That is right,' Judge Buchanan confirmed. Mr Haugh glanced round at his colleagues.

Proceeding with the formalities for the lodging of an appeal against sentence, Mr Haugh then objected to the judge's comments that the defendant had wrongly accused another. He told him that there had been 'some evidence' to support the allegation, from the girl. The judge was not moved. He told the senior counsel: 'I take the gravest view of the suggestion made by the accused in relation to another person at a time when he obviously knew he was the perpetrator of the crimes.'

Mr Haugh persisted. 'This is not an invented, unbased allegation,' he said, and asked for a certificate for leave to appeal. The bespectacled judge refused and retired to his chambers, his black gown flapping indignantly as he swept from the court.

The defendant, supported by a prison officer as he swayed to his feet, was taken down to the cells, ashen-faced.

The public gallery cleared slowly, but for the girl's father who paced out of court ahead of the members of the press and refused to answer any questions.

Twenty minutes later the defendant left the courthouse lying on the floor of a red police van with a coat over his head. There were no jeering onlookers or crowds outside, just a handful of press photographers who caught up with the van as it queued in traffic further up Green Street and took several photographs of the man cowering from view.

Everyone agreed that the sentence had been harsher than expected. The defendant's solicitors told reporters as they left the court that they were planning to appeal against the severity of the sentence, regardless of the judge's initial refusal to give leave, which could be circumvented.

A sweepstake by court reporters – a traditional pastime for those accustomed to long hours awaiting verdicts – had failed to predict anything like the fourteen-year term. The money collected was given to the reporter who had estimated the longest term – eight years – and the majority who had voted for between four and seven years could only watch glumly as the prized pound coins were counted out.

One of the last to leave the courthouse was James O'Higgins, the genial family solicitor who had undertaken to follow the case through to its bitter end. Scurrying from the precincts, he wanted to be one of the first to congratulate the girl and her mother and tell them of the judge's long-awaited sentence.

The following day the Irish newspapers once again featured the case prominently. The *Irish Independent* ran a front-page article headlined: 'X Case Liar Goes to Jail for 14-Year Term.' Its opening paragraph said: 'The sex offender at the centre of the 'X' case last night began a 14-year prison term. His attempt to blame a teenage boy for the crime earned him one of the toughest sentences for sexual assault imposed here in recent times.' The report accused the man of 'a catalogue of lies and deceit' and of withholding the truth for nearly two years.

The *Irish Press* confirmed that the two consecutive terms had not been expected. Donagh Diamond wrote that the first seven-year sentence was 'the sort of figure that those engaged in the futile exercise of trying to see into the judge's mind had come up with'. As the sentence for the second count of unlawful carnal knowledge was announced, he said, 'We waited for the word "concurrent" but instead – with no change of tone to signal it, no special stress – came the word "consecutive". And seven became fourteen.'

The newspaper reported that the length of the man's sentence had been widely welcomed by women's rights groups and others. Rosin McDermott, chairwoman of the Women's Aid organization, was quoted as saying she was pleased the judge 'had rejected any mitigating circumstances and had condemned the man's actions at all levels'.

Grace O'Malley, the respected head of the Dublin Rape Crisis Centre, who counselled Miss 'X' and who was in court to see the defendant jailed, said she thought the sentence highlighted the severity of the crime, and hoped it would 'help to end the ordeal of the young victim'.

The Pro-Life Campaign issued a short statement on the

sentence. It said: 'There is a striking contrast between the lengthy legal process during which the accused was afforded every opportunity to defend his position, and the speed with which the Supreme Court decreed an even heavier sentence on one of the two innocent parties in this tragedy.'

An *Irish Times* editorial said:

With the sentencing of the man at the centre of the 'X' case, a chapter of extraordinary significance in the social history of Ireland comes to a close. The chain of events which was set in train more than two years ago . . . challenged some uncomfortable convictions, redefined Irish law and forced this society to an overdue reappraisal of some of its declared values.

It has been a maturing experience for this society. Perhaps more than any other event of modern times, it has alerted middle-ground thinking to the dangers of allowing moral crusaders of any kind to set the legislative agenda according to their own sectional convictions. It is no truism to say that in the aftermath of this case, Irish society cannot ever be the same again.

The commentator and author Sam Smyth wrote in the *Irish Sunday Independent*:

The harsh sentence shocked the most hard-bitten lawyers and court observers – he will serve longer in prison than many murderers. He is forty-four now, will spend the turn of the millennium in jail and will be in his mid-fifties when released.

The fashionable cashmere jacket, mauve shirt and tastefully gaudy tie he wore in court will be wrapped in a parcel with his name on it and stored in the prison. When he wears them again, he will look as quaint as a granddad in a kaftan.

A few days later it emerged that the defendant sincerely hoped not to spend that length of time behind bars. His decision to apply for leave to appeal against the severity of his sentence in the Court of Criminal Appeal in Dublin was announced.

It was also reported that he was planning to pursue his appeal to the European Court of Human Rights in Strasbourg on the grounds that the Irish judiciary had tried and convicted him in his absence in the civil case (referring to Mr Justice Costello's description of him early on as 'an evil and depraved man').

It was not only the girl's life and that of his family that had been harmed by the defendant and his actions. Ten days after the man's conviction, Paddy Cullen, the popular former Gaelic football goalkeeper and team manager, instigated a number of articles in the Irish Sunday newspapers making it clear that he was not the man in the 'X' case.

Mr Cullen, forty-eight, had, it seemed, been mistaken for the convicted man by a number of people as the 'X' case rumour factory ran rife. This apparently started in 1992 when he sold his high-profile pub in south Dublin and disappeared off the social scene at about the same time as the 'X' case man was arrested.

In an article headlined: 'Paddy Cullen is NOT the "X" Case Man', the retired sportsman, who wanted to nail the lie that had been dogging him once and for all, told the *Sunday Independent*: 'I wasn't around for a while and there was this mystery man involved in a very public court case and people put two and two together and came up with the wrong answer.'

He said that he had received abusive telephone calls and had been forced to change his phone number. His wife Anne said the strain on her family had been enormous. Mr Cullen added that he had decided to confront the rumour publicly when it was rekindled after the 'X' case man's conviction. He was inspired to do so after someone saw him buying a new car and suggested that it was an unusual thing for a man facing a fourteen-year jail term to do.

'It is a very sensitive area because you are defending yourself against something that is mythical,' he added from his new pub in Swords. 'But we need to have this thing stopped. We need it smashed now.' The couple said they hoped to get on with their lives now that it was clear that Mr Cullen was not in prison.

Few believed the government of the day would ever willingly grasp the nettle on the substantive issue of abortion legislation, despite the need for the Supreme Court judgement to be regulated.

The Abortion Information Bill had still not been published, despite the passing of the European elections (in which the coalition government fared badly), by the summer recess. Neither had any legislation on the main issue even been drafted at that stage and the stinging criticism of Mr Justice McCarthy, that all previous governments had cowardly avoided the issue for so long, echoed hollowly in the corridors of the Dáil.

Many believed that it would take another 'X' case or something equally distasteful to force the hand of the State. Once again it seemed, like so many other areas of Irish life, the decisions on such a vital issue would be court-led and not State-led.

Despite all the convulsions and contortions after 'X', the politicians and those who elected them seemed only likely to be forced to examine their consciences on the central argument once again when the private torment of some unhappy Irish citizen burst its way into the open.

Just such a case came sooner than expected in the first week of July 1994, exactly one month after the 'X' case man had been sentenced. Dubbed 'the second "X" case', it involved a 15-year-old pregnant schoolgirl, a victim of incest, who sought leave to have an abortion.

Mr Justice Declan Costello – who had played such a pivotal role in every aspect of the 'X' case – heard the application in camera and granted an injunction preventing the girl from travelling to Britain for an abortion.

The girl had allegedly been sexually abused by her father and was taken into care. After leaving care she became pregnant and said that she did not want to have her baby.

Mr Justice Costello warned against publication of any details of her case, as she was a ward of court, and few details were made public, despite the best efforts of various opposition politicians in the Dáil who urged the government to make a statement on the matter.

What did emerge eventually was that the girl had apparently changed her mind about the abortion and had decided to have her baby. Reporters in Dublin were privately told that she had been happily shopping for baby clothes with her social worker.

Politicians were described as 'hugely relieved' at the news that the controversial matter had been defused before it exploded in their faces. But pro-choice campaigners were horrified that the case had even come before the courts, and they organized rallies and demonstrations in protest.

The Dublin Abortion Information Campaign picketed the Dáil and held a rally in O'Connell Street. Its statement said:

> After the horror and anger generated by the 'X' case . . . we were assured by the government that no woman would ever have to endure such a court ordeal again. It would appear that nothing has changed and that the life and health of Irish women rest on the opinion of the judge, rather than on the constitutional rights which apply to all other citizens.

The Council for the Status of Women declared that it had 'lost patience' with the government's inaction and demanded a meeting with the Taoiseach. Mr Reynolds said only that the Abortion Information Bill was still being prepared and was nearing completion.

An editorial in the Irish Press said: 'What we need from (politicians) is the courage to act, not excuses for inaction. This so-called "X" case should serve as a warning of the dangers in such political procrastination. Next time the government may not be so fortunate.'

It was, perhaps, the most pitiful outcome to what could and should have been the greatest opportunity for the people of Ireland to decide conclusively where they stood on the question of abortion, whether that be for or against.

The 'X' case and all the sadness and controversy that had accompanied it had, after all, it seemed, achieved little more than rhetoric.

The girl's abuse and her subsequent personal misfortunes could not have caused more public anguish and upset. Yet the Republic's legislators had persisted in telling its people to be satisfied with the unsatisfactory system they already had. It was an Irish solution to an Irish problem in every sense of the word.

The girl, one year behind in school and only just taking her Junior Certificate exams at the time of the defendant's imprisonment, was satisfied with the sentence which, she felt, had finally and fully vindicated her name.

Although more cheerful than she had been for some time, she was still confused and hurt by all that had happened and was expected to require further long-term psychological counselling for her five-year ordeal. Occasionally rebellious towards her mother and prone to swings of mood, she was described as 'moderate to poor' by a family friend, who said she was still only really able to take one day at a time.

Denied the enjoyment of her early teenage years, and the later excitement of sexual discovery, she had lost her best friend, her home, the unity of her parents and at least a year of her education. Few children would have had the strength of character to ever fully recover.

Already petite and very slender, she lost even more weight and caused mounting concern when she started to constantly wash her hands, a recognized symptom of obsessive behaviour disorder common in victims of trauma or stress.

Caroline Ainscough, an expert on victims of child abuse and a consultant psychologist at the Stanley Royd Hospital in Wakefield, Yorkshire, said: 'This is a very symbolic reaction to feelings of contamination in child abuse. The victims feel dirty and are trying to cleanse themselves.

'In some extreme cases, they even bathe themselves in bleach. As women they often become fastidious housekeepers or obsessively scrub their own children clean. It is the Lady Macbeth syndrome – cleaning away the stains of their past.

'Anorexia and bulimia are also common reactions to child abuse. People who feel they were trapped in a situation over which they had no control as a child, take control back when they regulate their food intake or the size of their bodies.

'But all these symptoms are normal expressions of emotions felt by such victims and are far better out than in. This girl may yet ride the storm and emerge intact.'

As one family friend said: 'It has taken five years out of that girl's childhood and destroyed her parents' marriage. Why on earth should she behave normally after that?

'Everyone is just hoping that, with her attacker locked up and her name finally vindicated, she can now look to the future without further fear and start to relive what is left of her life.'

Another friend of the family was much more optimistic. He said: 'I think what a great many people fail to realize is that this young girl is amazingly tough – she has had to be with all that has happened in her life.

'She is bright and resilient and fiery. I genuinely believe that she is strong enough to overcome this dreadful episode in her life and turn it to her long-term advantage.

'I even think that when she is older and is able to reflect back on all that happened, she may well speak out one day and tell the world "I was 'X' and I'm all right" – which would be a wonderful thing to hear.'

Chronology

Early 1800s: Abortion first made illegal during the Victorian era of the United Kingdom.

1861: Offences Against the Person Act make it an offence punishable by life imprisonment to 'procure a miscarriage', in an effort to stop the rising number of back-street abortionists and their incumbent deaths. Those who assist in abortions face three years' imprisonment.

1929: The Censorship of Publications Act (still applicable in Ireland) prohibits the publication, display, distribution or sale of written material 'which might reasonably be supposed to advocate the procurement of abortion or miscarriage'. Updated in 1946, it prohibited all literature which advocated the 'unnatural prevention of conception'.

1935: The Criminal Law Amendment Act makes the sale, advertising and importation of all recognized contraceptives illegal.

1936: The Abortion Law Reform Association (ALRA) is formed to campaign against legal restrictions on doctors so that they can perform abortions when medical circumstances prevail.

1937: Irish Constitution is adopted, reflecting the teaching of the Roman Catholic Church. British legislation is inherited into the southern Free State for convenience.

1938: Dr Aleck Bourne is acquitted of carrying out an abortion on a 14-year-old girl, breaking legal ground as the first time in Britain that the health of the woman is accepted as grounds for the operation.

1939: A government-appointed committee, chaired by Norman Birkett, recommends that the abortion law should be amended in mainland Britain. The outbreak of World War II prevents any further debate.

1960s: The drug Thalidomide, given to pregnant women to stop morning sickness, leads to the birth of thousands of deformed babies, bringing the abortion debate back into sharp focus.

1966: An Abortion Reform Law Bill in Britain, sponsored by David Steel MP, later the Liberal leader, causes an uproar from religious groups, doctors and politicians.

1967: The Abortion (NHS Family Planning) Act is passed in Britain, legalizing abortion under certain circumstances in England, Wales and Scotland. Northern Ireland, the Channel Islands and the Isle of Man are excluded.

1968: The Act comes into effect in the UK on 27 April.

1969: The first Fertility Guidance Clinic is opened in Ireland, opposite government buildings.

1972: Ireland votes to join the European Community as a member state. In a referendum the population votes five to one in favour.

1973: *Roe* vs *Wade* case in US Supreme Court effectively allows for abortion on demand.

1977: The Lane Committee report into the Abortion Act unanimously supports its working. The Parliamentary committee says: 'By facilitating a great number of abortions, the Act has relieved a vast amount of suffering.
'It has also helped to focus attention on the paramount need for preventative action, for more education in sex-life and . . . for the widespread provision of contraceptive advice and facilities.'

1979: The Family Planning (Health) Act becomes law in Ireland, authorizing contraceptives to be sold on prescription at chemists and only for those with bona fide family planning reasons.

1979: Women's Right to Choose group set up in Ireland to decriminalize abortion.

1980: Irish Pregnancy Counselling Centre opens for the first time in Ireland.

1983: The Irish people vote overwhelmingly against abortion in a referendum (850,000 votes against 400,000), which brings about the Eighth Amendment (Article 40.3.3) to the Irish Constitution, acknowledging the right to life of the unborn, with due regard to the equal right of the mother.

1985: After a few successful prosecutions of people selling contraceptives, the (Health) Family Planning Amendment Act is narrowly passed, making contraceptives available to over-eighteens without a prescription.

1986: The Society for the Protection of the Unborn Child in Ireland wins a High Court action against Open Door pregnancy counselling service, banning it from providing information on abortion in other countries to Irish women.

1988: The Irish Supreme Court upholds the decision and orders Open Door Counselling and the Well Woman Centre to 'perpetually restrain from assisting pregnant women within the jurisdiction to travel abroad to obtain abortions by referral to a clinic, by the making for them of travel arrangements, or by informing them of the identity and location of and the method of communication with a specified clinic or clinics'.

1990

APRIL: Abortion is legalized in Belgium, allowing the operation in the first twelve weeks of pregnancy or later in special cases. King Baudouin I, a devout Catholic and king for forty years, abdicates temporarily in protest at the new law. The ruling leaves Ireland the only EC member state still to deem abortion unlawful.

JUNE: The Human Fertilization and Embryology Act is passed in Britain, reducing the upper time limit for an abortion from twenty-eight to twenty-four weeks.

JULY: The 'X' case girl's sexual abuse begins.

1991: European Court of Justice rules in *SPUC* vs *Grogan and Others* that Irish women have an explicit right to travel freely within the EC to avail themselves of abortion services.

FEBRUARY: Virgin Megastore is prosecuted for selling condoms at special Condom Counter in Dublin. On appeal, the prosecution is upheld and the fine increased to IR £500. The Dublin-based rock group U2 pay the fine.

DECEMBER: 'X' case foetus is conceived.

1992

JANUARY: Charles Haughey resigns as Taoiseach of the Fianna Fail/Progressive Democratic coalition. Albert Reynolds replaces him.

FEBRUARY: Maastricht Treaty signed. The High Court prevents 'X' from leaving Ireland for abortion.

MARCH: Supreme Court overturn decision. 'X' has miscarriage.

MAY: Bishop Eamonn Casey exposed as the father of a teenage son.

JUNE: Irish voters say 'Yes' to the pro-European Maastricht Treaty.

JULY: The 'X' case defendant is charged.

AUGUST: High Court rules on *SPUC* vs *USI*.

OCTOBER: European Court of Human Rights overturns 1988 injunctions against Open Door Counselling and Well Woman Centre.

NOVEMBER: 'X' gives first evidence at pre-trial deposition. A national referendum on abortion is held with inconclusive results. The right to travel and information is voted in. A new government is voted in and promises legislation.

1993

JUNE: The sale of condoms is made legal to everyone in Ireland. Medical Council rules abortions unethical.

JULY: Homosexuality made legal in Ireland.

NOVEMBER: High Court judicial review of case rejects application to have trial dismissed.

1994

MARCH: Supreme Court judgement of appeal against High Court decision rejects plea for trial prohibition. Trial date is set.

MAY: The 'X' case defendant, charged with nine offences, pleads guilty to three charges at Dublin's Green Street Criminal Court and is remanded for a month for sentencing. 'X's family are granted rights of privacy injunctions against five newspapers and leave to pursue civil action.

JUNE – Judge Gerard Buchanan sentences 'X' case defendant to fourteen years' imprisonment. Defendant's lawyers announce intention to appeal against the sentence and to the European Court of Human Rights on the grounds that members of the judiciary were allegedly biased against him.

Glossary of Irish Terms Used

GARDA SIOCHANA (gorda shickorna): The Irish police force –
literally 'guard of peace'

GARDAI (gordee): Plural term used for police officers

OIREACHTAS (er-ahtas): The National Parliament of the Republic
of Ireland

SEANAD (shan-ed): The Senate or Upper House of the legislature

DÁIL (doil): The House of Representatives or Lower House of
Parliament

TAOISEACH: (tee-shoc) Prime Minister of the Republic

TANAISTE (ton-aster): Deputy Prime Minister of the Republic

SC (SENIOR COUNSEL): Senior barrister, Irish equivalent of QC or
Queen's Counsel.

TD (TEACHTA DAILE): literally, someone who goes to the Dáil, Irish
equivalent of MP or Member of Parliament.

FIANNA FAIL (feeana foil): Irish political party

FINE GAEL (feena gale): Irish political party

Bibliography

The Attorney General vs *X and Others*, 1992, Incorporated Council of Law Reporting for Ireland, Judgements of the High Court and Supreme Court, edited by Sunniva McDonagh.

The Abortion Papers, edited by Ailbhe Smyth, Attic Press, 1992.

'Cellmark Diagnostics: DNA Fingerprinting/DNA Profiling', ICI/Zeneca publicity literature, provided by Dr Paul Debenham, Cellmark, Abingdon, Oxon.

'Abortion & the Law in the Republic of Ireland: An Overview 1861–1993', Ruth Riddick, Open Line Counselling, March 1993.

'The Attorney General vs X and Rex vs Dudley & Stephens Reconsidered', Justice Roderick J. O'Hanlon, *Irish Law Times*, April 1992.

'Right to Life; Right to Travel; Right to Information', Second Stage Speech by the Minister for Justice Padraig Flynn, 20 October 1992.

Rex vs Bourne, The All England Law Reports 1938, Vol. 3.

The King vs *Bourne, The Law Reports 1939*, Vol. 1, King's Bench Division, Court of Appeal.

Pro Life? The Irish Question, Michael Solomons, Lilliput Press, 1993.

'A Guide to Ethical Conduct and Behaviour and to Fitness to Practice', Medical Council, 1989.

The Society for the Protection of the Unborn Child Ireland Ltd vs *Stephen Grogan and Others*, 'Judgement of the Court of Justice of the European Communities, October 4 1991'.

'Bunreacht na hEireann: Constitution of Ireland, 1937', Government Publications.

'Health Statistics: 1991/1992', Department of Health, Government Publications.

All in a Life: Garret FitzGerald, An Autobiography, Gill & MacMillan, 1991.

The Second Partitioning of Ireland: The Abortion Referendum 1983, Tom Hesketh, Brandsma Books, Dublin, 1990.

The Crozier and the Dáil: Church State Relations in Ireland, John Cooney, Mercier Press, 1986.

A Doctor's Creed: The Memoirs of a Gynaecologist, Aleck Bourne, Victor Gollancz Ltd, 1962 (Courtesy of the British Medical Association).

Murder Will Out: A Book of Irish Murder Cases, Tom Reddy, Gill & Macmillan, 1990.

Politics et Al, Martyn Turner (cartoon used courtesy of Martyn Turner, *The Irish Times* and the Cartoonists and Writers' Syndicate), Irish Times Books, Dublin, 1992.

The Irish Penitentials, Vol. V, L. Bieler, Dublin, 1963.

'An Outline of Fertility Control Focusing on the Element of Abortion in the Republic of Ireland', R. S. Rose, 1976.

Irish Law Times, extracts, 1992–3.

Breaking Free: Help for Survivors of Sexual Abuse, Caroline Ainscough and Kay Toon, Sheldon Press, 1993.

'Abortion Law in Northern Ireland: The Twilight Zone', Paper for the Standing Advisory Commission on Human Rights, Professor Simon Lee, May 1993.

'An A to K to Z of Abortion Law in Northern Ireland: Abortion on Remand', Paper for the Standing Advisory Commission on Human Rights, Professor Simon Lee, February 1994.

Life's Dominion, Ronald Dworkin, HarperCollins, 1993.

A Dictionary of Irish Law, Henry Murdoch, Topaz Publications, 1993.

'We are but Women': Women in Ireland's History, Roger Sawyer, Routledge, 1993.

Additional invaluable sources were *The Irish Times*, *Irish Independent*, *Sunday Tribune* and *Irish Press* newspapers.

Index

☐	GAVIN MAXWELL: A LIFE Douglas Botting	0-586-07109-1	£8.99
☐	THE KENNETH WILLIAMS DIARIES Russell Davies	0-00-638090-5	£9.99
☐	MAY THE LORD IN HIS MERCY BE KIND TO BELFAST Tony Parker	0-00-638254-1	£6.99
☐	SURVIVOR'S SONG Mark and Delia Owens	0-00-638096-4	£7.99

All these books are available from your local bookseller or can be ordered direct from the publishers.

To order direct just tick the titles you want and fill in the form below:

Name: _____

Address: _____

_____

_____

Postcode: _____

Send to: HarperCollins Mail Order, Dept 8, HarperCollins*Publishers*, Westerhill Road, Bishopbriggs, Glasgow G64.2QT.

Please enclose a cheque or postal order or your authority to debit your Visa/Access account –

Credit card no: _____

Expiry date: _____

Signature: _____

– to the value of the cover price plus:

UK & BFPO: Add £1.00 for the first and 25p for each additional book ordered.

Overseas orders including Eire, please add £2.95 service charge.

Books will be sent by surface mail but quotes for airmail despatches will be given on request.

24 HOUR TELEPHONE ORDERING SERVICE FOR ACCESS/VISA CARDHOLDERS –

TEL: GLASGOW 041-772 2281 or LONDON 081-307 4052